ELLET J. WAGGONER

The *Everlasting* Covenant

Redeeming Grace

The
Everlasting Covenant

Redeeming Grace

by

Ellet J. Waggoner

This book is a compilation of articles on the subject of the everlasting covenant which Ellet J. Waggoner published in the *Present Truth* (UK edition) from May 7, 1896 to May 13, 1897.

© 2020

ISBN: 978-0-9945585-8-9

Contents

1. The Gospel Message - The Everlasting Gospel 7
2. The Purchased Possession - The First Dominion 15
3. The Promise to Abraham - The Call to Abraham 22
4. The Call of Abraham - Building an Altar 26
5. The Call of Abraham - Making a Covenant 32
6. The Call of Abraham - Flesh Against the Spirit 37
7. The Call of Abraham - The Covenant Sealed (Part 1 of 2) 40
8. The Call of Abraham - The Covenant Sealed (Part 2 of 2) 46
9. The Call of Abraham - The Test of Faith 49
10. The Call of Abraham - The Promise and the Oath 55
11. The Call of Abraham - The promise of Victory 59
12. The Promises to Israel - A General View 62
13. The Promises to Israel - Israel, A Prince of God 69
14. The Promises to Israel - Israel in Egypt 77
15. The Promises to Israel - The Time of the Promise 84
16. The Promises to Israel - The Reproach of Christ 86
17. The Promises to Israel - Giving the Commission 91
18. The Promises to Israel - Preaching the Gospel in Egypt 94
19. The Promises to Israel - How Pharaoh's Heart Was Hardened 98
20. The Promises to Israel - Saved by the Life 102
21. The Promises to Israel - The Final Deliverance 106
22. The Promises to Israel - The Song of Deliverance 111
23. The Promises to Israel - Bread from Heaven 115
24. The Promises to Israel - Life from God 120
25. The Promises to Israel - Life from the Word 124
26. The Promises to Israel - Living Water from the Rock 128
27. The Promises to Israel - Object Teaching 134

(more chapters over page)

28. The Promises to Israel - The Entering of the Law (Part 1 of 2) 139
29. The Promises to Israel - The Entering of the Law (Part 2 of 2) 144
30. The Promises to Israel - Sinai and Calvary 151
31. The Promises to Israel - Mount Sinai and Mount Zion 155
32. The Promises to Israel - The Covenants of Promise 160
33. The Promises to Israel - The Veil and the Shadow 168
34. The Promises to Israel - Two Laws 173
35. The Promises to Israel - Entering the Promised Land 179
36. The Promises to Israel - Vainglory and Defeat 184
37. Israel: A Missionary People 189
38. The Promises to Israel - The Promised Rest (Part 1 of 2) 199
39. The Promises to Israel - The Promised Rest (Part 2 of 2) 205
40. The Promises to Israel - Another Day (Part 1 of 2) 212
41. The Promises to Israel - Another Day (Part 2 of 2) 218
42. The Promises to Israel - Again in Captivity (Part 1 of 3) 224
43. The Promises to Israel - Again in Captivity (Part 2 of 3) 230
44. The Promises to Israel - Again in Captivity (Part 3 of 3) 236
45. The Promises to Israel - The Time of the Promise at Hand 243
46. The Promises to Israel - The Lost Tribes of Israel 249
47. The Promises to Israel - The Lost Everlasting Covenant Complete 254

Chapter 1

The Gospel Message - The Everlasting Gospel

The Present Truth, May 7, 1896

WHEN the humble shepherds on the plains of Bethlehem were astonished by the shining of the glory of the Lord round about them, as they watched their flocks by night, their fears were quieted by the voice of the angel of the Lord, who said, "Fear not; for, behold, I bring you good tidings of great joy, which shall be to all people. For unto you is born this day in the city of David a Saviour, which is Christ the Lord." Luke 2:10, 11.

The words, "good tidings," are from the one Greek word which elsewhere is rendered "Gospel;" so that we might properly read the message of the angel thus: "Behold, I bring you the Gospel of great joy, which shall be to all people." In that announcement to the shepherds we learn several important things.

1. That the Gospel is a message that brings joy. "The kingdom of God is... righteousness, and peace, and joy in the Holy Ghost." Christ is anointed "with the oil of gladness," and He gives "the oil of joy for mourning."
2. It is a message of salvation from sin. For before this time the same angels had foretold to Joseph the birth of this infant, and had said, "Thou shall call His name Jesus; for He shall save His people from their sins." Matthew 1:21.
3. It is something which concerns everybody, – "which shall be to all people." "For God so loved the world, that He gave His only begotten Son, that whosoever believeth in Him should not perish, but have everlasting life." John 3:16.

This is assurance enough for everybody; but as if to emphasize the fact that the poor have equal rights in the Gospel with the rich, the first announcement of the birth of Christ was to men in the humblest walks of life. It was not to the chief priests and scribes, nor to the nobles, but to shepherds, that the joyful news was first told. So the Gospel is not beyond the understanding of the uneducated. Christ Himself was born and brought up in deep poverty; He preached the Gospel to the poor, and "the common people heard Him gladly." Mark 12:37. Since it is thus presented to the common people, who form the bulk of the whole world, there is no doubt about it's being a world message.

The Desire of all Nations

But although the Gospel is first of all to the poor, it is not something mean and ignoble. Christ became poor that we might become rich. The great apostle who was chosen to give the message to kings, and to the great men of the earth, said in view of His hoped-for visit to the capital of the world, "I am not ashamed of the Gospel of Christ; for it is the power of God unto salvation to every one that believeth." Romans 1:16. The one thing that the entire world is seeking after is power. Some seek it by means of wealth, others through politics, others through learning, and still others in various other ways; but in whatever enterprise men engage, the object is the same, – power of some kind. There is unrest in the heart of every man, an unsatisfied longing, placed there by God Himself. The mad ambition that drives some to trample on scores of their fellow-creatures, the unceasing struggle for wealth, and the reckless round of pleasures into which many plunge, are all vain endeavors to satisfy this longing.

God has not placed in the human heart a longing for any of these things; but the quest for them is a perversion of that desire which He has implanted in the human breast. He desires that man should have His power; but none of the things, which men ordinarily seek, give the power of God. Consequently, none of these things satisfy. Men set a limit to the amount of wealth which they will amass, because they think that when that limit is reached they will be satisfied; but when the fixed amount has been gained, they are as unsatisfied as ever; and so they go on seeking for satisfaction by piling up wealth, not realizing that the desire of the heart cannot be met in that manner. He who implanted that desire is the only one who can satisfy it. God is manifested in Christ, and Christ is indeed "the desire of all nations" (Haggai 2:7), although there are so few who will believe that in Him alone is their perfect rest and satisfaction. To every unsatisfied mortal the invitation is given, "O taste and see that the Lord is good; blessed is the man that trusteth in Him. O fear the Lord, ye His saints; for there is no want to them that fear Him." Psalms 34:8, 9. "How precious is Thy loving-kindness, O God! And the children of men take refuge under the shadow of Thy wings. They shall be abundantly satisfied with the fatness of Thy house; and Thou shalt make them drink of the river of Thy pleasures." Psalms 36:7, 8, R.V.

Power is what men desire in this world, and power is what the Lord wants them to have. But the power, which they are seeking, would ruin them, and the power, which He desires them to have, is power that will save them. The Gospel brings to all men this power, and it is nothing less than the power of God. It is for everybody, if they will accept it. Let us study the nature of this power, for when we have discovered it; we shall have before us the whole Gospel.

The Power of the Gospel

In the vision which the beloved disciple had of the time just preceding the coming of the Lord, the Gospel message which prepares men for that event is thus described: –

"And I saw another angel fly in the midst of heaven, having the everlasting Gospel to preach to them that dwell on the earth, and to every nation, and kindred, and tongue, and people, saying with a loud voice, Fear God, and give glory to Him; for the hour of His judgment is come; and worship Him that made heaven and earth, and the sea, and the fountains of waters." Revelation 14:6, 7.

Here we have plainly set before us the fact that the preaching of the Gospel consists in preaching God as the Creator of all things, and calling on men to worship Him as such. This corresponds to what we have read in the Epistle to the Romans, that the Gospel "is the power of God unto salvation." What the power of God is we learn a little farther on, where the apostle, speaking of the heathen, says: –

"That which may be known of God is manifest in them; for God hath showed it unto them. For the invisible things of Him from the creation of the world are clearly seen, being understood by the things that are made, even His eternal power and Godhead." Romans 1:19, 20. That is to say, ever since the creation of the world, men have been able to see the power of God, if they would use their senses, for it is clearly to be discerned in the things, which He has made. Creation shows the power of God. So the power of God is creative power. And since the Gospel is the power of God unto salvation, it follows that the Gospel is the manifestation of creative power to save men from sin.

But we have learned that the Gospel is the good news of salvation through Christ. The Gospel consists in the preaching of Christ and Him crucified. The apostle says: "For Christ sent me not to baptize, but to preach the Gospel; not with wisdom of words, lest the preaching of the cross of Christ should be made of none effect. For the preaching of the cross is to them that perish foolishness; but unto us which are saved it is the power of God." 1 Corinthians 1:17, 18.

And still further: "We preach Christ crucified, unto the Jews a stumbling-block, and unto the Greeks foolishness; but unto them which are called, both Jews and Greeks, Christ the power of God, and the wisdom of God." 1 Corinthians 1:23, 24. And this is why the apostle said, "And I brethren, when I came to you, came not with excellency of speech or of wisdom, declaring unto you the testimony of God. For I determined not to know anything among you, save Jesus Christ, and Him crucified." 1 Corinthians 2:1, 2.

The preaching of Christ and Him crucified is the preaching of the power of God, and therefore it is the preaching of the Gospel, for the Gospel is the power of God. And this is exactly in harmony with the thought that the preaching of the Gospel is the setting forth of God as the Creator; for the power of God is creative power, and Christ is the one by whom all things were created. No one can preach Christ without preaching Him as the Creator. All are to honor the Son even as they honor the Father. Whatever preaching fails to make prominent the fact that Jesus Christ is the Creator of all things, is not the preaching of the Gospel.

Creation and Redemption

"In the beginning was the Word, and the Word was with God, and the Word was God. . . All things were made by Him; and without Him was not any thing made that was made. . . And the Word was made flesh, and dwelt among us full of grace and truth." John 1:1-14. "By Him were all things created, that are in heaven, and that are in earth, visible and invisible, whether they be thrones, or dominions, or principalities, or powers; all things were created by Him, and for Him; and He is before all things, and by Him all things consist." Colossians 1:16, 17.

Let us give more careful attention to the last text, and see how creation and redemption meet in Christ. In verses 13 and 14 we read that God "hath delivered us from the power of darkness, and hath translated us into the kingdom of His dear Son, in whom we have redemption through His blood, even the forgiveness of sins." And then, after a parenthetical remark as to who Christ is, the apostle tells us how it is that we have redemption through His blood. This is the reason: "For by Him were all things created," etc. The Revised Version gives the more literal rendering, "For in Him were all things created, . . . and He is before all things, and in Him all things consist."

So the preaching of the everlasting Gospel is the preaching of Christ the creative power of God, through whom alone salvation can come. And the power by which Christ saves men from sin is the power by which He created the worlds. We have redemption through His blood; the preaching of the cross is the preaching of the power of God; and the power of God is the power that creates; therefore the cross of Christ has in it creative power. Surely that is power enough for anybody. No wonder that the apostle exclaimed, "God forbid that I should glory, save in the cross of our Lord Jesus Christ." Galatians 6:14.

The Mystery of God

To some it may be a new thought that creation and redemption are the same power; to all it is and must ever be a mystery. The Gospel itself is a mystery. The Apostle Paul desired the prayers of the brethren, that utterance might be given him, "to make known the mystery of the Gospel." Ephesians 6:19. Elsewhere he says that he was made a minister of the Gospel, according to the gift of the grace of God, given unto him by the effectual working of His power, that he "should preach among the Gentiles the unsearchable riches of Christ; and to make all see what is the fellowship of the mystery, which from the beginning of the world have been hid in God, who created all things by Jesus Christ." Ephesians 3:8, 9. Here again we see the mystery of the Gospel to be the mystery of creation.

This mystery was made known to the apostle by revelation. How the revelation was made known to him we learn in his Epistle to the Galatians, where he says, "But I certify you, brethren, that the Gospel which was preached of me is not after man.

For I neither received it, neither was I taught it, but by the revelation of Jesus Christ." And then he makes the matter still more definite, by saying, "But when it pleased God, who separated me from my mother's womb, and called me by His grace, to reveal His Son in me, that I might preach Him among the heathen, immediately I conferred not with flesh and blood." Galatians 1:11, 12, 15, 16.

Let us sum up the last few points.

1. The Gospel is a mystery.
2. It is a mystery that is made known by revelation of Jesus Christ.
3. It was not merely that Jesus Christ revealed it to him, but that he was made to know the mystery by the revelation of Jesus Christ in him. Paul had to know the Gospel first, before he could preach it to others; and the only way in which he could be made to know it was to have Christ revealed in him. The conclusion therefore is that the Gospel is the revelation of Jesus Christ in men.

This conclusion is plainly stated by the apostle in another place, where he says that he was made a minister "according to the dispensation of God which is given to me for you, to fulfill the word of God; even the mystery which hath been hid from ages and from generations, but now is made manifest to His saints; to whom God would make known what is the riches of the glory of this mystery among the Gentiles, which is Christ in you the hope of glory." Colossians 1:25-27. So we are fully assured that the Gospel is the making known of Christ in men. Or rather, the Gospel is Christ in men, and the preaching of it is the making known to men of the possibility of Christ dwelling in them. And this agrees with the statement of the angel, that they should call the name of Jesus Emmanuel, "which, being interpreted, is God with us" (Matthew 1:23); and also with the statement by the apostle that the mystery of God is God manifest in the flesh. When the angels made known to the shepherds the birth of Jesus, it was the announcement that God had come to men in the flesh; and when it was said that this good news should be to all people, it was revealed that the mystery of God dwelling in human flesh was to be declared to all men, and repeated in all who should believe Him.

And now let us briefly sum up all that we have thus far learned.

1. The Gospel is the power of God unto salvation. Salvation is only by the power of God, and wherever the power of God is, there is salvation.
2. Christ is the power of God.
3. But Christ's salvation comes through the cross; therefore the cross of Christ is the power of God.
4. So the preaching of Christ and Him crucified is the preaching of the Gospel.

5. The power of God is the power that creates all things. Therefore the preaching of Christ and Him crucified, as the power of God, is the preaching of the creative power of God put forth for the salvation of men.

6. This is so, because Christ is the Creator of all things.

7. Not only so, but also in Him all things were created. He is the first-born of all creation; when He was begotten, "in the days of eternity," all things were virtually created, because all creation is in Him. The substance of all creation, and the power by which all things should be made to appear, were in Christ. This is simply a statement of the mystery that only the mind of God can comprehend.

8. The mystery of the Gospel is God manifest in human flesh. Christ on earth is "God with us." So Christ dwelling in the hearts of men by faith is all the fullness of God in them.

9. And this means nothing less than the creative energy in God working in men through Jesus Christ, for their salvation. "If any man be in Christ, he is a new creature." 2 Corinthians 5:17. "We are His workmanship, created in Christ Jesus unto good works." Ephesians 2:10

The apostle indicates all this when he says that to preach the unsearchable riches of Christ is to make all see "what is the fellowship of the mystery, which from the beginning of the world have been hid in God, who created all things by Jesus Christ."

A Summary

In the following portion of Scripture, we have the details of this mystery well summarized: –

"Blessed be the God and Father of our Lord Jesus Christ, who hath blessed us with all spiritual blessings in heavenly places in Christ; according as He hath chosen us in Him before the foundation of the world, that we should be holy and without blame before Him in love; having predestinated us unto the adoption of children by Jesus Christ to Himself, according to the good pleasure of His will, to the praise of the glory of His grace, wherein He hath made us accepted in the Beloved. In whom we have redemption through His blood, the forgiveness of sins, according to the riches of His grace; wherein He hath abounded toward us in all wisdom and prudence; having made known unto us the mystery of His will, according to His good pleasure which He hath purposed in Himself; that in the dispensation of the fullness of times He might gather together in one all things in Christ, both which are in heaven, and which are on earth; even in Him; in whom also we have obtained an inheritance, being predestinated according to the purpose of Him who worketh all things after the counsel of His own will; that we should be to the praise of His glory, who first trusted in Christ. In whom ye also trusted, after that ye heard the word of truth, the Gospel of your salvation; in whom also after that ye believed, ye were sealed with that Holy Spirit of promise, which is the earnest of our inheritance until the redemption of the purchased possession, unto the praise of His glory. Wherefore I . . . cease not to give thanks for you, making mention of you in my prayers; that the God of our Lord Jesus Christ, the Father of glory, may give unto you the Spirit of wisdom and revelation in the knowledge of Him; the eyes of your understanding being enlightened; that ye may know what is the hope of His calling, and what the riches of the glory of His inheritance in the saints, and what is the exceeding greatness of His power to us-ward who believe, according to the working of His mighty power, which He wrought in Christ, when He raised Him from the dead, and set Him at His own right hand in the heavenly places." Ephesians 1:3-20.

Now we will note the different points of this statement:

1. All blessings are given to us in Christ. "He that spared not His own Son, but delivered Him up for us all, how shall He not with Him also freely give us all things." Romans 8:32.
2. This gift of all things in Christ is in accordance with the fact that He has chosen us in Him before the foundation of the world, that in Him we might obtain holiness. "For God hath not appointed us unto wrath, but to obtain salvation by our Lord Jesus Christ." 1 Thessalonians 5:9.
3. In that choice the destiny determined for us is that we should be sons.
4. Accordingly He accepts us in the Beloved.
5. In the Beloved we have redemption through His blood.
6. All this is the making known to us of the mystery, namely, that in the fullness of times He will gather together in one household all things in Jesus Christ, both things in the heaven and things on the earth.
7. This being the fixed purpose of God, it follows that in Christ we have already obtained an inheritance; for God makes all things work out the purpose of His own will.
8. All who believe in Christ are sealed with the Holy Spirit, which is called the Holy Spirit of promise, because it is the surety of the promised inheritance.
9. This seal of the Holy Spirit is the pledge of our inheritance until the redemption of the purchased possession. "Grieve not the Holy Spirit of God, whereby ye are sealed unto the day of redemption." Ephesians 4:30.
10. Those who have the Spirit as the seal, know what is the riches of the glory of the inheritance; that is, the glory of the future inheritance becomes theirs now, through the Spirit.

In this we see that the Gospel involves an inheritance; in fact, the mystery of the Gospel is really the possession of the inheritance, because in Him we have obtained an inheritance. Now let us see how the matter is stated in the eighth of Romans. We shall not quote the Scripture entire, but simply summarize it.

Those who have the Holy Spirit of promise are the sons of God; "for as many as are led by the Spirit of God, they are the sons of God." If we are children, we are necessarily heirs, heirs of God because sons of God. And if heirs of God, we are joint heirs with Jesus Christ. The one thing above all others that Christ is desirous that we should know is that the Father has loved us even as He loved Him.

But of what are we heirs together with Christ? – Why, of all creation, because the Father has constituted Him "heir of all things" (Hebrews 1:2), and has said, "He that overcomes shall inherit all things." Revelation 21:7. And this is shown by what follows in Romans 8. We are now sons of God, but the glory of the sons of God doth not yet appear. Christ was the Son of God, yet He was not recognized as such by the world; "therefore the world knoweth us not, because it knew Him not." 1 John 3:1. In possessing the Spirit, we are in possession of "the riches of the glory of the inheritance;" and that glory will in due time be revealed in us, in a measure far exceeding all present sufferings.

"For the earnest expectation of the creation waiteth for the revealing of the sons of God. For the creation was subjected to vanity, not of its own will, but by reason of Him who subjected it in hope that the creation itself shall be delivered from the bondage of corruption into the liberty of the glory of the children of God. For we know that the whole creation groans and travaileth in pain together until now. And not only so, but ourselves also, which have the first fruits of the Spirit, even we ourselves groan within ourselves, waiting for our adoption, to wit, the redemption of our body." Romans 8:19-23.

Man by creation was a son of God; but through sin he became a child of wrath, even a child of Satan, to whom he rendered obedience, instead of to God. But through the grace of God in Christ those who believe are made sons of God, and receive the Holy Spirit. Thus, they are sealed as heirs until the redemption of the purchased possession, that is, of the whole creation, which is waiting for its redemption when the glory shall be revealed in the sons of God.

Chapter 2

The Purchased Possession - The First Dominion

The Present Truth, May 14, 1896

Redemption means to buy back. And what is to be bought back? Evidently that which was lost; for that is what the Lord came to save. And what was lost? Man, for one thing; "for thus saith the Lord, ye have sold yourselves for naught; and ye shall be redeemed without money." Isaiah 52:3. What else was lost? Necessarily all that man had. And what was that?

"And God said, Let us make man in our image, after our likeness; and let them have dominion over the fish of the sea, and over the fowl of the air, and over the cattle, and over all the earth, and over every creeping thing that creepeth upon the earth. So God created man in His own image, in the image of God created He him; male and female created He them. And God blessed them, and God said unto them, Be fruitful, and multiply, and replenish the earth, and subdue it: and have dominion over the fish of the sea, and over the fowl of the air, and over every living thing that moves upon the earth." Genesis 1:26-28.

The Psalmist says of men: "Thou hast made him a little lower than the angels, and hast crowned him with glory and honor. Thou madest him to have dominion over the works of Thy hands; Thou hast put all things under his feet; all sheep and oxen, yea, and the beasts of the field; the fowl of the air, and the fish of the sea, and whatsoever passeth through the paths of the seas." Psalms 8:5-8.

This was man's original dominion, but it was not retained. In the Epistle to the Hebrews we have these words of the Psalmist: –

"For not unto angels did He [God] subject the world to come, whereof we speak. But one hath somewhere testified, saying, what is man, that Thou art mindful of him? Or the son of man, that Thou visitest him? Thou madest him a little lower [or, "for a little while lower"] than the angels; thou crowned him with glory and honor, and didst set him over the works of Thy hands. Thou put all things in subjection under his feet. For in that He subjected all things unto him, He left nothing that is not subject to him. But now we see not yet all things subjected to him. But we see Jesus, who was made a little lower ["for a little while lower"] than the angels, because of the suffering of death crowned with glory and honor; that by the grace of God, He should taste death for every man." Hebrews 2:5-9, R.V.

A wonderful picture is in these words opened to our view. God has put the earth, and all that pertains to it, under the rule of man. But that is not the case now. "We see not yet all things put under him." Why? Because man lost everything by the fall. But we see that Jesus, who was made "lower than the angels," that is, was made man, so that all who will believe may be restored to the lost inheritance. So that just as surely as Jesus died and rose again, and just as surely as by His death and resurrection those who believe in Him shall be saved, so surely will the lost inheritance be restored to those who are redeemed.

This is indicated in the first words of the passage quoted from the Book of Hebrews: "Unto the angels had He not put in subjection the world to come, whereof we speak." Well, has He put the world to come in subjection to man? Yes; for when the earth was created He put it in subjection to man, and Christ has taken man's fallen state in order to redeem both him and his lost possession, for He came to save that which is lost; and since in Him we have obtained an inheritance it is clear that in Christ we have in subjection the world to come, which is nothing less than the earth renewed as it was before the fall.

This is shown also by the words of Isaiah: "They shall go to confusion together that are makers of idols. But Israel shall be saved in the Lord with an everlasting salvation; ye shall not be ashamed nor confounded world without end. For thus saith the Lord that created the heavens; God Himself that formed the earth and made it; He hath established it, He created it not in vain, He formed it to be inhabited; I am the Lord; and there is none else. I have not spoken in secret, in a dark place of the earth; I said not unto the seed of Jacob, Seek ye Me in vain; I the Lord speak righteousness, I declare things that are right." Isaiah 45:16-19.

The Lord formed the earth to be inhabited, and since He works all things after the counsel of His own will, it is certain that His design will be carried out. But when He had made the earth, the sea, and all things that are in them, and man upon the earth, He "saw everything that He had made, and, behold, it was very good." Genesis 1:31. Then since God's plan is to be carried out, it is evident that the earth is yet to be inhabited by people who are very good, and that it is to be at that time in a perfect condition.

When God made man, He "crowned him with glory and honor," and gave him "dominion over the works of His hands." He was therefore king, and as his crown indicates, his kingdom was one of glory. By sin he lost the kingdom and the glory, "For all have sinned, and come short of the glory of God." Romans 3:23. Then Jesus stepped into his place, and through death, which He tasted for every man; He became "crowned with glory and honour."

It is the man Christ Jesus, (1 Timothy 2:5) who has thus won back the dominion that the first man Adam lost. He did this in order that He might bring many sons to glory. In Him we have obtained an inheritance; and since it is "the man Christ Jesus" who is now "in the presence of God for us," it is plain that the world to come, of which is the new earth, – "the first dominion," – is still man's portion.

The following text also makes this clear: "Christ was once offered to bear the sins of many; and unto them that look for Him shall He appear the second time without sin unto salvation." Hebrews 9:28. When He was offered, He bore the curse, in order that the curse might be removed. "Christ hath redeemed us from the curse of the law, being made a curse for us; for it is written, Cursed is every one that hangeth on a tree." Galatians 3:13. But when the curse of sin came upon man, it came also upon the earth; for the Lord said to Adam: "Because thou hast hearkened unto the voice of thy wife, and hast eaten of the tree, whereof I commanded thee, saying, Thou shalt not eat of it; cursed is the ground for thy sake; in sorrow shalt thou eat of it all the days of thy life; thorns also and thistles shall it bring forth unto thee." Genesis 3:17, 18. When Christ had been betrayed into the hands of sinful men, "when they had platted a crown of thorns, they put upon His head, and a reed in His right hand; and they bowed the knee before Him, and mocked Him, saying, Hail, King of the Jews! And they spit upon Him, and took the reed, and smote Him on the head." Thus when Christ bore the curse that came on man; He at the same time bore the curse of the earth. So when He comes to save those who have accepted His sacrifice, He comes to renew the earth as well.

The Time of Restitution

Therefore it is that the Apostle Peter said: "And He shall send Jesus Christ which before was preached unto you; whom the heaven must receive until the times of restitution of all things, which God hath spoken by the mouth of all His holy prophets since the world began." Acts 3:21. And so we have the words of Christ: "When the Son of man shall come in His glory, and all the holy angels with Him, then shall He sit upon the throne of His glory; and before Him shall be gathered all nations; and He shall separate them one from another, as a shepherd divides His sheep from the goats; and He shall set the sheep on His right hand, but the goats on the left. Then shall the King say unto them on his right hand, Come, ye blessed of My Father, inherit the kingdom prepared for you from the foundation of the world." Matthew 25:31-34. This will be the consummation of the work of the Gospel.

Now let us return to the words of the apostle in Ephesians 1. There we learned that in Christ we are predestinated to the adoption of sons; and as we learned in another place, if we are sons we are heirs of God, and joint-heirs with Jesus Christ. Therefore it is that in Christ we have obtained an inheritance, for He has gained the victory, and is set down at the right hand of the Father, awaiting the time when His foes shall be made

His footstool, and all things be put in subjection under Him. This is as sure as that He overcame. As the pledge of this inheritance, which we have in Him, He has given the Holy Spirit. It is of the nature of the inheritance, and therefore makes known what is the riches of His glory of the inheritance. In other words, the fellowship of the Spirit makes known the fellowship of the mystery.

The Spirit is the representative of Christ. Therefore, the Spirit dwelling in men is Christ in men the hope of glory. And Christ in men is creative power in men, creating them new creatures. The Spirit is given "according to the riches of His glory," and that is the measure of the power by which we are to be strengthened. So the riches of the glory of the inheritance, made known through the Spirit, is nothing less than the power by which God will create all things new by Jesus Christ, as in the beginning, and by which He will create man anew, so that he may be fitted for that glorious inheritance. Thus, it is that when the Spirit is given in the fullest measure, those to whom it is given taste "the good word of God, and the powers of the world to come." Hebrews 6:5.

So the Gospel does not deal exclusively in the future. It is present and personal. It is the power of God unto salvation to everyone that believeth, or that is believing. While we believe we have the power, and that power is the power by which the world to come is to be made ready for us, even as it was made in the beginning. Therefore, in studying the promise of the inheritance we are simply studying the power of the Gospel to save us in this present evil world.

Who are Heirs?

"And if ye are Christ's, then are ye Abraham's seed, and heirs according to the promise." Galatians 3:29.

Of what are we heirs if we are Abraham's seed? Why, evidently of the promise to Abraham. If we are Christ's, then we are heirs with Him, for they are Christ's who have the Spirit, and they who have the Spirit are heirs of God and joint-heirs with Jesus Christ. So to be a joint-heir with Christ is to be an heir of Abraham."

Heirs according to the promise. "What promise? The promise made to Abraham. And what was that promise? Read Romans 4:13, for an answer: "For the promise, that he should be the heir of the world, was not to Abraham or to his seed, through the law, but through the righteousness of faith." So then, they who are Christ's are heirs of the world. We have already learned this from many texts, but now we see it connected definitely with the promise to Abraham.

We have also learned that the inheritance is to be bestowed at the coming of the Lord, for it is when the Lord comes in His glory that He says to the righteous, "Come, ye blessed of My Father, inherit the kingdom prepared for you from the foundation of the world." When the world was created it was designed for the habitation of man and was given to him. But that dominion was lost. True, men now live on the earth, but they do not enjoy the inheritance that God originally gave to men. That was the possession of a perfect creation by perfect beings. Nay, they do not even possess it; for "one generation passeth away, and another generation cometh; but the earth abideth for ever." Ecclesiastes 1:4. While the earth abideth for ever, "Our days on the earth are as a shadow, and there is none abiding." 1 Chronicles 29:15. No one really possesses anything of this world. Men labor and fight to amass wealth, and then they "perish, and leave their wealth to others." Psalms 49:10. But God works all things after the counsel of His own will; not one of His purposes will fail; and so as soon as man had sinned and lost his inheritance, a restoration was promised through Christ, in these words: "And I will put enmity between thee and the woman, and between by seed and her seed; it shall bruise thy head, and thou shalt bruise his heel." Genesis 3:15. In these words the destruction of Satan and all his work was foretold. The "great salvation" "at the first began to be spoken by the Lord." Thus "the first dominion" (Micah 4:8), even "the kingdom and dominion, and the greatness of the kingdom under the whole heaven, shall be given to the people of the saints of the Most High, whose kingdom is an everlasting kingdom." Daniel 7:27. That will be real possession, for it will be everlasting.

The Promise of His Coming

But all this is to be consummated at the coming of the Lord in glory, "Whom the heaven must receive until the times of restitution of all things, which God hath spoken by the mouth of all His holy prophets since the world began." Acts 3:21.

Therefore, the coming of the Lord to restore all things has been the grand hope set before the church ever since the fall of man. The faithful have always looked forward to that event, and although the time has seemed long, and the majority of people doubt the promise, it is as sure as the word of the Lord. The promise, the doubts of the unbelieving, and the certainties of the fulfillment of the promise are vividly set forth in the following portion of Scripture: –

"This second epistle, beloved, I now write unto you; in both which I stir up your pure minds by way of remembrance; that ye may be mindful of the words which were spoken before by the holy prophets, and of the commandment of us the apostles of the Lord and Saviour; knowing this first, that there shall come in the last days scoffers, walking after their own lusts, and saying, Where is the promise of his coming? For since the fathers fell asleep, all things continue as they were from the beginning of the creation. For this they willingly are ignorant of, that by the word of God the heavens were of old, and the earth standing out of the water and in the water [compacted out of water and amidst water, R.V.]; whereby the world that then was, being overflowed with water, perished; but the heavens and the earth, which are now, by the same word are kept in store, reserved unto fire against the day of judgment and perdition of ungodly men.

But, beloved, be not ignorant of this one thing, that one day is with the Lord as a thousand years, and a thousand years as one day. The Lord is not slack concerning His promise, as some men count slackness; but is longsuffering to us-ward, not willing that any should perish, but that all should come to repentance. But the day of the Lord will come as a thief in the night; in the which the heavens shall pass away with a great noise, and the elements shall melt with fervent heat, the earth also and the works that are therein shall be burned up. Seeing then that all these things shall be dissolved, what manner of persons ought ye to be in all holy conversation and godliness, looking for and hasting unto the coming of the day of God, wherein the heavens being on fire shall be dissolved, and the elements shall melt with fervent heat? Nevertheless we, according to His promise, look for new heavens and a new earth, wherein dwelleth righteousness." 2 Peter 3:1-13.

Now read the passage again and note the following points: Those who scoff at the promise of the coming of the Lord are willingly ignorant of some of the plainest and most important events recorded in the Bible, namely the creation and the flood. The word of the Lord created the heavens and the earth in the beginning. "By the word of the Lord were the heavens made, and all the host of them by the breath of His mouth." Psalms 33:6. By the same word the earth was covered with water, the water with which the earth was stored being made to contribute to its destruction. By the flood the earth "perished;" the earth in its present condition bears scarcely any resemblance to that which existed before the flood. By the same word by which the earth was created and destroyed, the earth, which is now, is kept until the time of the perdition of ungodly men, when a lake of fire instead of a flood of water will overwhelm it. "Nevertheless we, according to His promise, look for new heavens and a new earth, wherein dwelleth righteousness." The same word accomplishes it all.

The Grand Climax

To us it appears that the coming of the Lord has been the one grand event toward which everything has been tending ever since the fall. The "promise of His coming" is the same as the promise of a new heavens and a new earth. This was the promise to the "fathers." Those who scoff at it cannot deny that the Bible contains the promise, but as no change has appeared since the fathers fell asleep, they think that there is no probability of its fulfillment. They ignore the fact that things have changed much since the beginning of creation; and they have forgot that the word of the Lord endureth forever. "The Lord is not slack concerning His promise." Notice that it is the singular, not the plural form of the word. It is not promises, but promise. It is a fact that the Lord does not forget any of His promises, but the apostle Peter is here speaking of a definite promise, namely, the promise of the coming of the Lord, and the restoration of the earth. It will be a "new earth" in very fact, because it will be restored to the condition in which it was when it was first made.

Now although it has been a long time, as man counts, since the promise was made, "the Lord is not slack concerning His promise," because He has all time for His own. A thousand years are with Him as one day. So then it has been scarcely a week since the promise was first made, at the time of the fall. Only about half a week has elapsed since the "fathers fell asleep." The passage of a few thousand years does not abate one jot of the promise of God. It is as sure as when it was first made. He has not forgotten. The only reason why He has delayed thus long, is that "He is long-suffering to usward; not willing that any should perish, but that all should come to repentance." So we should "account that the long-suffering of the Lord is salvation," and should gratefully accept the kindness thus graciously offered, instead of taking His merciful delay as an evidence of lack of good faith on His part.

It should not be forgotten that while a thousand years is with Lord as one day, one day is with Him also as a thousand years. What does that mean? Simply that while the Lord may wait a long time as man counts, before carrying out His plans, that should not be taken as evidence at any stage that to do a given amount of work will necessarily take as great a length of time as has been taken for the same amount of work in the past. One day is just as good as a thousand years with the Lord, whenever He chooses to have the work of a thousand years done in a single day. And this will yet be seen. "For He will finish the work, and cut it short in righteousness; because a short work will the Lord make in the earth." One day will suffice for the work of a thousand years. The day of Pentecost was but a sample of the power with which the work of the Gospel is yet to go.

And now that we have had this summary of what the Gospel of the kingdom really is, and have been referred to the promise to the fathers as the foundation for our faith, we may next take up the study of that promise, beginning with Abraham, whose children we must be if we are to be heirs with Christ.

Chapter 3

The Promise to Abraham - The Call to Abraham

The Present Truth, May 21, 1896

In studying this promise, two portions of Scripture must ever be kept in mind. The first is in the words of Jesus: "Ye search the Scriptures, because ye think that in them ye have eternal life; and these are they which bear witness of Me." "If ye believed Moses, ye would believe Me; for He wrote of Me. But if ye believe not his writings, how shall ye believe My words?" John 5:39, 46, 47, R.V

The only Scriptures in the days of Christ were the books now known as the Old Testament; these testify of Him. They were given for no other purpose. The Apostle Paul wrote that they are able to make men wise unto salvation, through faith, which is in Christ Jesus (2 Timothy 3:15); and among those writings the books of Moses are especially pointed out by the Lord as revealing Jesus. He who reads the writings of Moses, and the entire Old Testament, with any other expectation than to find Christ, and the way of life through Him, will utterly fail of understanding them. His reading will be in vain.

The other text is 2 Corinthians 1:19, 20: "For the Son of God, Jesus Christ, who was preached among you by us, even by me and Sylvanus and Timothy, was not yea and nay, but in Him is yea. For how many soever be the promises of God, in Him is the yea; wherefore also through Him is the Amen, unto the glory of God through us." No promise of God has ever been given to man except through Christ. Personal faith in Christ is the one thing necessary in order to receive whatever God has promised, God is no respecter of persons: He offers His riches freely to everybody; but no one can have any part in them except as he receives Christ. This is perfectly fair, since Christ is given to all if they will but have Him.

With these principles in mind, we read the first account of the promise of God to Abraham. "Now the Lord said unto Abram, Get thee out of thy country, and from thy kindred, and from thy father's house, unto the land that I will show thee; and I will make of thee a great nation, and I will bless thee, and make thy name great; and be thou a blessing; and I will bless them that bless thee, and him that curseth thee will I curse; and in thee shall all the families of the earth be blessed." Genesis 12:1-3 R.V.

At the very outset we may see that this promise to Abraham was a promise in Christ. The Apostle Paul writes: "The scripture, foreseeing that God would justify the Gentiles by faith, preached beforehand the Gospel unto Abraham, saying, In thee shall all the nations be blessed. So then they which be of faith are blessed with the faithful Abraham." Galatians 3:8, 9 R.V. From this we learn that when God said that in Abraham all the families of the earth should be blessed, He was preaching the Gospel to him. The blessing that was to come upon the people of the earth through him could be enjoyed only through faith.

Abraham and the Cross

The preaching of the Gospel is the cross of Christ. Thus the Apostle Paul says that he was sent to preach the Gospel, but not with wisdom of words, lest the cross of Christ should be made of none effect. And then he adds that the preaching of the cross is the power of God to them that are saved. 1 Corinthians 1:17, 18. And this is but another way of saying that it is the Gospel, for the Gospel is the power of God unto salvation. Therefore since the preaching of the Gospel is the preaching of the cross of Christ (and there is no salvation by any other means), and God preached the Gospel to Abraham when He said, "In thee shall all the families of the earth be blessed," it is very clear that in that promise the cross of Christ was made known to Abraham, and that the promise thus made was one that could be gained only through the cross.

This fact is made very clear in Galatians 3. Following the statement that the promise of blessing is to all the nations of the earth through Abraham, and that they which be of faith are blessed with faithful Abraham, are the words, "Christ hath redeemed us from the curse of the law, being made a curse for us; for it is written, Cursed is every one that hangeth on a tree; that the blessing of Abraham might come on the Gentiles through Jesus Christ; that we might receive the promise of the Spirit through faith." Galatians 3:13, 14. Here we have it stated in the most explicit terms that the blessing of Abraham, which was to come on all the families of the earth, was to come only through the cross of Christ.

This is a point that needs to be well fixed in the mind at the very beginning. All the misunderstandings of the promises of God to Abraham and his seed have arisen through a failure to see the Gospel of the cross of Christ in them. If it be continually remembered that all the promises of God are in Christ, to be enjoyed only through His cross, and that consequently they are spiritual and eternal in their nature, there will be no difficulty, and the study of the promise to the fathers will be a delight and a blessing.

We read that Abraham, in obedience to the call of the Lord, went forth from his father's house, and from his native land. "And Abram took Sarai his wife, and Lot his brother's son, and all their substance that they had gathered, and the souls that they had gotten in Haran[1]; and they went forth to go into the land of Canaan; and into the land of Canaan they came. And Abram passed through the land unto the place of Sichem, unto the plain of Moreh. And the Canaanite was then in the land. And the Lord appeared unto Abram, and said, Unto thy seed will I give this land; and there builded he an altar unto the Lord, who appeared unto him. And he removed from thence unto a mountain on the east of Bethel, and pitched his tent, having Bethel on the west, and Hai on the east; and there he builded an altar unto the Lord, and called on the name of the Lord." Genesis 7:5-8.

It is best for us to perceive the real meaning of God's promises and dealings with Abraham from the very start, and then our subsequent study will be easy, since it will be but the application of these principles. In this last scripture there are a few subjects introduced, which occupy a very prominent place in this study, and so we will note them here. First,

The Seed

The Lord said to Abraham, after he had reached the land of Canaan, "Unto thy seed will I give this land." If we but hold to the Scriptures we shall not have a moment's difficulty in ascertaining who the seed is. "Now to Abraham and his seed were the promises made. He saith not, And to seeds, as of many; but as of one, And to thy seed, which is Christ." Galatians 3:16. This ought forever to settle the matter, so that there could be no dispute about it. The seed of Abraham, to whom the promise was made, is Christ. He is the heir.

But we also may be joint-heirs with Christ. "For as many of you as have been baptized into Christ have put on Christ. There is neither Jew nor Greek, there is neither bond nor free, there is neither male nor female; for ye are all one in Christ Jesus. And if ye be Christ's, then are ye Abraham's seed, and heirs according to the promise." Galatians 3:27-29.

Those who have been baptized into Christ have put on Christ, and are therefore one in Him. So when it is said that Christ is the seed of Abraham, to whom the promises were made, all who are in Christ are included. But nothing outside of Christ is included in the promise. To say that the inheritance promised to the seed of Abraham could be possessed by any except those who were Christ's through faith in Him is to ignore the Gospel, and to deny the word of God. "If any man be in Christ he is a new creature." 2 Corinthians 5:17. Therefore since the promise of the land was to Abraham and His seed, which is Christ and those who have put Him on by baptism, and who are therefore new creatures, it follows that the promise of the land was only to those who were new creatures in Christ – children of God through faith in Christ Jesus. This again is additional evidence that all the promises of God are in Christ, and that the promises to Abraham can be shared only through the cross of Christ.

---

[1] (On page 23) *Haran*. The Hebrew letter beginning this name is a guttural, difficult to represent by Roman letters, and difficult for English people to pronounce. It is much like the German ch. In the English Bible it is sometimes represented by the letter "H" and sometimes by "Ch." Compare the proper name "Rachel" in Jeremiah 31:15 and Matthew 2:18.

Let this principle, therefore, never for a moment be forgotten in reading about Abraham and the promise to him and his seed, – that the seed is Christ and those who are in Him. This and nothing else.

The Land

Abraham was in the land of Canaan when God said to him, "Unto thy seed will I give this land." Turn now to the words which the martyr Stephen, full of the Holy Ghost, his face shining like that of an angel, said to his persecutors: "The God of glory appeared unto our father Abraham, when he dwelt in Mesopotamia, before he dwelt in Charran, and said unto him, Get thee out of thy country, and from thy kindred, and come into the land which I shall show thee. Then came he out of the land of the Chaldeans, and dwelt in Charran; and from thence, when his father was dead, he removed him into this land wherein ye now dwell." Acts 7:2-4.

This is but a repetition of what we have already read in Genesis 12. Now read the next verse: "And He gave him none inheritance in it, no, not so much as to set his foot on; yet He promised that He would give it to him for a possession, and to his seed after him, when as yet he had no child."

We learn here that although it is sometimes merely stated, "Unto thy seed will I give this land," Abraham himself was always included in the promise. This is made very evident in the repetitions of the promise that follow in the book of Genesis.

But we learn more, and that is that Abraham actually received no inheritance of land. He had not so much of the land as to set his foot on; yet God had promised it to him and to his seed after him. What shall we say to this? –That the promise of God failed? –Not by any means. God "cannot lie." "He abideth faithful." Abraham died without having received the promised inheritance, yet he died in faith. We must therefore learn from this the lesson that the Holy Spirit wished the Jews to learn, namely, that the promised inheritance could be received only through Jesus and the resurrection. This also is made very clear by the words of the Apostle Peter: –

"Ye are the children of the prophets, and of the covenant which God made with our fathers, saying unto Abraham, "And in thy seed shall all the kindreds of the earth be blessed." Unto you first God, having raised up His Son Jesus, sent Him to bless you, in turning away every one of you from his iniquities." Acts 3:25, 26.

The blessing of Abraham, as we have learned, comes on the Gentiles, or all the families of the earth, through Jesus Christ and His cross; but the blessing of Abraham is connected with the promise of the land of Canaan. That also was to be possessed only through Christ and the resurrection. If it had been otherwise, Abraham would have been disappointed, instead of dying in full faith of the promise. But this also will appear more plainly as we proceed.

Chapter 4

The Call of Abraham - Building an Altar

The Present Truth, May 28, 1896

Everywhere Abraham went he built an altar to the Lord. As you read this, remember that the promise that all nations should be blessed in Abraham, specified families. The religion of Abraham was a family religion. The "family altar" was never neglected in his household. This is not an empty figure of speech, but comes from the practice of the fathers to whom the promise was made, and of which we are partakers if we are of their faith and practice.

An Example for Parents

God said of Abraham, "I know him, that he will command his children and his household after him, and they shall keep the way of the Lord, to do justice and judgment; that the Lord may bring upon Abraham that which He hath spoken of him." Genesis 28:19.

Note the words, "He will command his children and his household after him, and they shall keep the way of the Lord, to do justice and judgment." He would not simply command them to do it, and there let the matter rest; but He would command them, and the result would be that they would keep the way of the Lord. His teaching would be effective.

We may be sure that the commands of Abraham to his children and his household were not harsh and arbitrary. We shall understand them better if we consider the nature of the commandments of God. They "are not grievous." "His commandment is life everlasting." He who thinks to follow the example of Abraham in commanding his family, by harsh, arbitrary rules, and by acting the part of a stern judge, or a tyrant, making threats of what he will do if his commands are not obeyed, and enforcing his commands, not in the spirit of love, because they are right, but because he is stronger than his children, and has them in his power, has much need to learn of the God of Abraham. "And, ye fathers, provoke not your children to wrath; but bring them up in the nature and admonition of the Lord." Ephesians 6:4.

At the same time we may be sure that the commands of Abraham were not like Eli's, weak and querulous reproofs to his wicked and worthless sons: "Why do ye such things? For I hear of your evil dealings by all this people. Nay, my sons; for it is no good report that I hear." 1 Samuel 2:23, 24.

On the other hand, Abraham transmitted a blessing to all eternity, because the commands, which he gave to his children, had restraining power.

Abraham was to be a blessing to all people. Wherever he went he was a blessing. But this blessing began in his family. This was the centre. From the family circle the heavenly influence went out to the neighbors. And now we may well notice more closely the statement that when Abraham built an altar, he "called upon the name of the Lord." Genesis 12:8; 13:4. In Dr. Young's translation this is rendered, "He preached in the name of Jehovah." Without calling attention to the various places where the same expression is found, it is worthwhile to note that the Hebrew words are identical with those used in Exodus 34:5, where we read that the Lord descended in the cloud, and stood by Moses, "and proclaimed the name of the Lord."

We may therefore understand that when Abraham erected the family altar he not only taught his immediate family but he "proclaimed the name of the Lord" to all around him. Like Noah, Abraham was a preacher of righteousness. As God preached the Gospel to Abraham, so Abraham preached the Gospel to others.

Abraham and Lot

"And Abram was very rich in cattle, in silver, and in gold." "And Lot also, which went with Abram, had flocks, and herds, and tents. And the land was not able to bear them that they might dwell together; for their substance was great, so that they could not dwell together. And there was strife between the herdsmen of Abram's cattle and the herdsmen of Lot's cattle; and the Canaanite and the Perizzite dwelled then in the land. And Abram said unto Lot, Let there be no strife, I pray thee, between thee, and me and between my herdsmen and thy herdsmen; for we be brethren. Is not the whole land before thee? Separate thyself, I pray thee, from me; if thou wilt take the left hand, then I will go to the right; or if thou depart to the right hand, then I will go to the left." Genesis 8:5-8.

When we understand the nature of the promise of God to Abraham, we can understand the secret of his generosity. Suppose Lot should choose the best part of the country; that could make no difference with Abraham's inheritance. Having Christ, he had all things. He did not look for his possessions in this present life, but in the life to come. He would accept with thankfulness whatever prosperity the Lord might send him; but if his riches in this life should be small, that would not diminish the inheritance that was promised him.

There is nothing like the presence and blessing of Christ to settle all disputes, or to prevent them. In the course taken by Abraham, we have a true Christian example. As the eldest he might have stood upon his dignity, and have claimed his "rights." But he could not have done so as a Christian. Love "seeketh not its own." Abraham manifested the true Spirit of Christ. When professed Christians are eager to grasp the things of this world, and are troubled lest they shall be deprived of some of their rights, they show that they are unmindful of the enduring inheritance, which Christ offers.

The Promise Repeated

Abraham's Christian courtesy, which was the result of his faith in the promise through Christ, as not unrecognized by the Lord. We read: –

"And the Lord said unto Abram, after that Lot was separated from him, Lift up now thine eyes, and look from the place where thou art northward, and southward, and eastward, and westward; for all the land which thou seest, to thee will I give it, and to thy seed for ever. And I will make thy seed as the dust of the earth; so that if a man can number the dust of the earth, then shall thy seed also be numbered. Arise, walk through the land in the length of it and in the breadth of it; for I will give it unto thee." Genesis 8:14-17.

We will not forget that "to Abraham and his seed were the promises made; He saith not, and to seeds, as of many; but as of one, and to thy Seed, which is Christ." There is no other seed of Abraham except Christ and those who are His. Therefore this innumerable posterity, which was promised to Abraham, is identical with that spoken of in the following scripture: –

"After this I beheld, and, lo, a great multitude, which no man could number, of all nations, and kindreds, and people, and tongues, stood before the throne, and before the Lamb, clothed with white robes, and palms in their hands; and cried with a loud voice, saying, Salvation to our God which sitteth upon the throne, and unto the Lamb." "And one of the elders answered, saying unto me, what are these which are arrayed in white robes? And whence came they? And I said unto him, Sir, thou knowest. And he said unto me, these are they which came out of great tribulation, and have washed their robes, and made them white in the blood of the Lamb." Revelation 7:9, 10, 13, 14.

We have already learned that the blessing of Abraham comes on all nations through the cross of Christ, so that in the statement that this innumerable company have washed their robes, and made them white in the blood of the Lamb, we see the fulfillment of the promise to Abraham, of an innumerable seed.

"If ye be Christ's, then are ye Abraham's seed, and heirs according to the promise." Galatians 3:29.

The reader should not fail to notice in the repetition of the promise in Genesis 13, that the land figures very prominently. We found it in the preceding chapters, and shall find it as the central feature of the promise wherever it occurs.

Abraham and Melchizedek

The brief story of Melchizedek forms a link which unites us and our times most closely with Abraham and his times, and shows that the "Christian dispensation," so called, existed in the days of Abraham as well as now.

The fourteenth chapter of Genesis tells us all that we know of Melchizedek. The seventh chapter of Hebrews repeats the story and makes some comments upon it. Besides this we have references to Melchizedek in the sixth chapter, and in Psalms 110:4.

The story is this: Abraham was returning from an expedition against the enemies that had carried away Lot, when Melchizedek met him, bringing bread and wine. Melchizedek was king of Salem, and priest of the Most High God. In this capacity he blessed Abraham, and to him Abraham gave a tenth part of the spoil, which he had recovered. That is the story, but from it there are some very important lessons drawn.

In the first place we learn that Melchizedek was a greater man than Abraham, because, "without all contradiction the less is blessed of the better," (Hebrews 7:7), and because Abraham gave him the tenth part of all.

He was a type of Christ and was like Him: "Made like unto the Son of God." He was a type of Christ in that he was both king and priest. His name signifies, "king of righteousness;" and Salem, of which he was king, means "peace;" so that he was not only priest, but king of righteousness and king of peace. So of Christ it is said: "The Lord said unto My Lord, Sit Thou at My right hand, until I make Thine enemies Thy footstool." "The Lord hath sworn, and will not repent, Thou art a priest for ever, after the order of Melchizedek." Psalms 110:1, 4. And the name whereby He shall be called is "The Lord our Righteousness." Jeremiah 23:6.

Christ's kingly priesthood is thus set forth in the Scriptures: "Thus speaketh the Lord of hosts, saying, Behold the man whose name is The BRANCH; and He shall grow up out of His place, and He shall build the temple of the Lord; even He shall build the temple of the Lord; and He shall bear the glory, and shall sit and rule upon His throne; and He shall be a priest upon His throne; and the counsel of peace shall be between them both." Zechariah 6:12, 13. The power, by which Christ as priest makes reconciliation for the sins of the people, is the power of the throne of God, upon which He sits.

But the main thing with reference to Melchizedek is that Abraham lived under the same "dispensation" that we do. The priesthood was the same then as now. Not only are we the children of Abraham, if we are of faith, but our great High Priest, who is passed into the heavens, is by the oath of God made a High Priest forever, "after the order of Melchizedek." Thus, in a double sense it is shown that "if ye be Christ's, then are ye Abraham's seed, and heirs according to the promise." "Your father Abraham rejoiced to see My day; and he saw it, and was glad." John 8:56.

Abraham therefore was a Christian as much as any one who has ever lived since the crucifixion of Christ. "The disciples were called Christians first in Antioch." But the disciples were no different after they were called Christians from what they were before. When they were known only as Jews, they were Christians just as much as they were after they were called such. The name is of but little account. The name "Christians" was given them because they were followers of Christ; but they were followers of Christ before they were called Christians, just as much as they were afterwards, Abraham, hundreds of years before the days of Jesus of Nazareth, was just what the disciples were who in Antioch were called Christians; he was a follower of Christ. Therefore he was in the fullest sense of the word a Christian. All Christians, and none others, are children of Abraham.

The reader will notice that in Hebrews 7 we are referred to the case of Abraham and Melchizedek for proof that the paying of tithes is not a Levitical ordinance. Long before Levi was born, Abraham paid tithes. And he paid them, too, to Melchizedek, whose priesthood is the Christian priesthood. Therefore, those who are Christ's and thus children of Abraham will also give tithes of all.

It will be noticed that the tithe was a well-known thing in the days of Abraham. He gave tithes to God's priest as a matter of course. He recognized the fact that the tithe is the Lord's. That record in Leviticus is not the origin of the tithing system, but is simply a statement of a fact. Even the Levitical order "paid tithes in Abraham." We are not told when it was first made known to men, but we see that it was well known in the days of Abraham. In the book of Malachi, which is specially addressed to those living just before "the great and terrible day of the Lord," we are told that those who withhold the tithe are robbing God.[2]

The argument is very simple: Abraham gave tithes to Melchizedek; the Melchizedek priesthood is a priesthood by which righteousness and peace come; it is the priesthood by which we are saved. Abraham gave tithes to Melchizedek, because Melchizedek was the representative of the Most High God, and the tithe is the Lord's. If we are Christ's then we are children of Abraham; and therefore if we are not children of Abraham, then we are not Christ's. But if we are Abraham's children, we shall do the works of Abraham.

---

[2] It should be understood that no man, nor any human power, neither the Church nor the State, has anything to do with requiring people to pay tithe. "The tithe is the Lord's" and with Him alone people have to do in the matter of tithes. Tithes do not belong to the State, nor is the State empowered to collect them for the Lord. Whether or not a person will pay the Lord's tithe to the Lord is a matter for himself alone to decide, just the same, as whether or not he will worship God at all, whether he will keep the Sabbath or not, etc.

Whose are we?

One other item should not be overlooked in passing. It is the fact that Melchizedek who was king of righteousness and peace, and priest of the Most High God, brought out to Abraham bread and wine, of which Christ said, "This is my body," and "this is my blood." It may be said that the bread and wine were for the refreshment of Abraham and his followers. Very true; but that does not in the least detract from the significance of the fact, for we are continually to eat the flesh and drink the blood of Christ. Melchizedek came out in his capacity of king and priest, and Abraham recognized him as such. Note the connection in Genesis xiv. 18, 19: "And Melchizedek king of Salem brought forth bread and wine; and he was the priest of the Most High God. And he blessed him and said, Blessed be Abram, of the Most High God, possessor of heaven and earth." It is quite evident that the bread and wine, which Melchizedek brought forth, acquired special significance from the fact that he was the priest of the Most High God. The Jews in the days of Christ scoffed at the statement that Abraham rejoiced to see His day. They could see no evidence of the fact. May we not see in this transaction one evidence that Abraham saw Christ's day, which is the day of salvation?

Chapter 5

The Call of Abraham - Making a Covenant

The Present Truth, June 28, 1896

THE fifteenth chapter of Genesis contains the first account of the covenant made with Abraham. "The word of the Lord came unto Abram in a vision, saying, Fear not Abram; I am thy shield, and thy exceeding great reward."

Notice the statement that God said that He Himself was Abraham's reward. If we are Christ's, then we are Abraham's seed, and heirs according to the promise. Heirs of what? – "Heirs of God, and joint-heirs with Christ." Romans 8:17. The same inheritance is mentioned by the Psalmist: "The Lord is the portion of mine inheritance." So here again we have a link to connect all God's people with Abraham. Their hope is nothing else but the promise of God to him.

The promise, which God had made to Abraham, was not to him only, but to his seed as well. Therefore, Abraham said to the Lord, "What wilt Thou give me, seeing I go childless, and the steward of my house (or, "he that shall be possessor of mine house") is this Eliezer of Damascus? And Abraham said, Behold, to me Thou hast given no seed; and, lo, one born in my house is mine heir." Abraham did not know the plan of the Lord. He knew the promise, and believed it but as he was old, and had no child, he supposed that the seed promised to him must come through his trusted servant. But that was not God's plan. Abraham was not to be the progenitor of a race of servants, but of free men.

"And, behold, the word of the Lord came unto him, saying, This shall not be thine heir; but he that shall come forth out of thine own bowels shall be thine heir. And he brought him forth abroad, and said, Look now toward heaven, and tell the stars, if thou be able to number them; and He said unto him, So shall thy seed be. And he believed in the Lord; and He counted it to him for righteousness." Genesis 15:4-6.

"And he believed in the Lord." The root of the verb rendered believed, is the word "Amen." Its idea is that of firmness, a foundation. When God spoke the promise, Abraham said "Amen," or, in other words, he built upon God, taking His word as a sure foundation. Compare this with Matthew 7:24, 25.

God promised a great household to Abraham. But this house was to be built upon the Word of God, the Lord, and Abraham so understood it, and began at once to build. Jesus Christ is the foundation, for "other foundation can no man lay than that is laid, which is Jesus Christ." 1 Corinthians 3:11. The house of Abraham is the house of God, which is "built upon the foundation of the apostles and prophets, Jesus Christ Himself being the chief corner stone." Ephesians 2:20. "To whom coming, as unto a living stone, disallowed indeed of men, but chosen of God, and precious, ye also, as lively stones, are built up a spiritual house, an holy priesthood, to offer up spiritual sacrifices, acceptable to God by Jesus Christ. Wherefore also it is contained in the Scripture, Behold, I lay in Sion a chief corner stone, elect, precious; and he that believeth [buildeth] on Him shall not be confounded." 1 Peter 2:4-6.

"Abraham believed God, and it was counted to him for righteousness." Why? –Because faith means building upon God and His word, and that means the receiving of the life of God in His word. Note in the verses last quoted, from Peter that the foundation upon which the house is built is a living stone. The foundation is a living foundation, which gives life to those who come to it, so that the house, which is built upon it, is a living house. It grows by the life of the foundation. "Believe in the Lord your God, so shall ye be established." In this text the words "believe" and "be established," are both from the one root, "Amen," and we might read it thus: "Build upon the Lord your God, so shall ye be built up." But the foundation upon which we build is righteous: "The Lord is upright; He is my Rock, and there is no unrighteousness in Him." Therefore since faith means to build upon God and His holy word, it is self-evident that faith is righteousness to the one who possesses and exercises it.

Jesus Christ is the source of all faith. Faith has its beginning and end in Him. There can be no real faith that does not center in Christ. Therefore, when Abraham believed in the Lord, he believed in the Lord Jesus Christ. God has never been revealed to man except through Christ. The fact that Abraham's belief was personal faith in the Lord Jesus Christ is further shown by the fact that it was counted unto him for righteousness. But there is no righteousness except through the faith of Jesus Christ. He "is made unto us wisdom, and righteousness, and sanctification, and redemption." 1 Corinthians 1:30. No righteousness will be of any worth at the appearing of the Lord except "that which is through the faith of Christ, the righteousness which is of God by faith." Philippians 3:9. But since God himself counted Abraham's faith for righteousness, it is plain that his faith was centered in Christ alone, in whom he was made righteous.

And this demonstrates that the promise of God to Abraham was through Christ alone. The seed was that only which is through the faith of Christ, for Christ Himself is the seed. Abraham's posterity, that was to be as the stars for number, will be the innumerable host who wash their robes in the blood of the Lamb. The nations that were to come from him will be "the nations of them which are saved." Compare Matthew 8:11.

"For how many so ever be the promises of God, in Him is the yea; wherefore also through Him is the Amen." 2 Corinthians 1:20, R.V.

"In the same day the Lord made a covenant with Abram, saying, Unto thy seed have I given this land," etc. Genesis 15:18. The making of this covenant is recorded in the preceding verses. First, we have the promise of an innumerable posterity, and of land. God said, "I am the Lord, that brought thee out of Ur of the Chaldees, to give thee this land to inherit it." Verse 7. This verse must be kept in mind while reading verse 18, lest we get the wrong impression that there was something promised to Abraham's seed, which did not include him. "Now to Abraham and his seed were the promises made." Nothing was promised to the seed that was not also promised to Abraham.

Abraham believed the Lord, yet he said, "Lord God, whereby shall I know that I shall inherit it?" Then follows the record of the dividing of the heifer and the she goat and the ram. This is referred to in Jeremiah 34:18-20, when God reproved the people for transgressing the covenant.

"And when the sun was going down, a deep sleep fell upon Abram; and, lo, an horror of great darkness fell upon him. And He said unto Abram, Know of a surety that thy seed shall be a stranger in a land that is not theirs, and shall serve them; and they shall afflict them four hundred years; and also that nation, whom they shall serve, will I judge, and afterward they shall come out with great substance. And thou shalt go to thy fathers in peace; thou shalt be buried in a good old age. But in the fourth generation they shall come hither again; for the iniquity of the Amorites is not yet full." Genesis 15:12-16.

We have seen that this covenant was one of righteousness by faith. For the promised seed and the land were to be Abraham's through faith in God's word, which was counted to him for righteousness. Now let us see what more we can learn from the verses just quoted.

For one thing, we learn that Abraham was to die before the possession was bestowed. He was to die in a good old age, and his seed was to be a stranger in a foreign land for four hundred years.

Not only Abraham himself, but his immediate descendants also, would be dead before the seed should come into the land that was promised them. As a matter of fact, we know that Isaac died before the children of Israel went down into Egypt, and that Jacob and all his sons died in the land of Egypt.

"Now to Abraham and his seed were the promises made." The chapter before us tells the same thing. It is evident that a promise made to the seed of Abraham cannot be fulfilled by bestowing the thing promised upon only a part of the seed; and that which was promised to Abraham and his seed cannot be fulfilled unless Abraham shares it as well as his seed.

What does this demonstrate? –Simply this, that the promise in the fifteenth chapter of Genesis, that Abraham and his seed should possess the land, had reference to the resurrection of the dead, and to nothing short of that. This is true, even though it should be claimed that the eighteenth verse excludes Abraham from the covenant there spoken of; for as we have seen, it is clear that many of the immediate descendants of Abraham would be dead before the time of the promise; and we know that Isaac and Jacob and the twelve patriarchs were dead long before that time.

Even if Abraham be left out of the question, yet the fact remains that the promise to the seed must include all of the seed, and not a part merely. But Abraham cannot be left out of the promise. Therefore we have positive evidence that in this chapter we have the record of the preaching of "Jesus and the resurrection" to Abraham.

To Be Fulfilled After the Resurrection

This enables us to understand why Stephen, when he was on his trial for preaching Jesus, began his talk with a reference to these very words. Speaking of Abraham's coming into the land of Canaan, he said that God "gave him none inheritance in it, no, not so much as to set his foot on; yet He promised that He would give it to him for a possession, and to his seed after him, when as yet he had no child." Acts 7:5. In thus referring to this promise, which was well known to all the Jews, Stephen showed them most plainly that it could be fulfilled only by the resurrection of the dead through Jesus.

"And thou shalt go to thy fathers in peace; thou shalt be buried in a good old age. But in the fourth generation they shall come hither again; for the iniquity of the Amorites is not yet full."

From this we learn how it was that Abraham died in faith, although he had not received the promise. If he had expected to receive it in this present life, he would have been disappointed when death came before the fulfillment of the promise. But God plainly told him that he must die before it was fulfilled. Therefore, since Abraham believed God, it is very clear that he understood about the resurrection, and looked for it. Yea, he triumphed in it. The resurrection of the dead, we shall see, was ever the central hope of the true children of Abraham.

But we learn something more. In the fourth generation, or after the lapse of four hundred years, his seed was to come out of bondage, into the Promised Land. Why could they not possess the land at once? –Because the iniquity of the Amorites was not then full. That shows that God would give the Amorites time to repent, or, failing that, to fill up the measure of their iniquity, and thus demonstrate their unfitness to possess the land.

And that teaches us further that the land, which God promised, to Abraham and his seed could be possessed only by righteous people. God would not cast out of the land those of whom there was any seeming prospect that they might become righteous. But the fact that the people who were to be destroyed from before the children of Abraham were to be cast out because of their wickedness shows that the possessors of the land were expected to be righteous. And thus we learn that the seed of Abraham, to whom the land was promised, were to be righteous people. This has already been shown by the fact that the seed was promised to Abraham only through the righteousness of faith.

Chapter 6

The Call of Abraham - Flesh Against the Spirit

The Present Truth, June 11, 1896

"Now Sarai Abram's wife bare him no children; and she had an handmaid, an Egyptian, whose name was Hagar. And Sarai said unto Abram, behold now, the Lord hath restrained me from bearing; I pray thee go in unto my maid; it may be that I may obtain children by her. And Abram hearkened unto the voice of Sarai."

This was the great mistake of Abraham's life; but he learned a lesson from his mistake, and it was recorded for the purpose of teaching that lesson to all. We will presume that the reader is acquainted with the sequel – how the Lord told Abraham that Ishmael, the son of Hagar was not the heir that He had promised, but that Sarah his wife should bear him a son, and how Hagar and Ishmael were sent away, after Isaac was born. So we may proceed at once to some of the important lessons that are suggested by this transaction.

In the first place, we should learn the folly of man's trying to fulfill the promises of God. God had promised to Abraham an innumerable seed. When the promise was made, it was beyond all human possibility that Abraham should have a son by his wife, but he accepted the word of the Lord, and his faith was counted to him for righteousness. This in itself was evidence that the seed was not to be an ordinary seed, but that it was to be a seed of faith.

But his wife had not the faith that he had. Yet she thought that she had faith, and even Abraham doubtless thought that in carrying out her advice he was working in harmony with the word of the Lord. The mistake was in harkening to the voice of his wife, instead of to the Lord. They reasoned that God had promised them a large family, but that since it was impossible for her to have children, it was very evident that He intended that they should devise some other means of bringing it about. Thus it is that human reason deals with the promises of God.

Yet how shortsighted the whole thing was. God had made the promise; therefore He alone could fulfill it. If a man makes a promise, the thing promised may be performed by another, but in that case the one who made the promise fails to carry out his word. So even though that which the Lord had promised could have been gained by the device, which was adopted, the result would have been to shut the Lord out from fulfilling His word. They were therefore working against God. But His promises cannot be performed by man. In Christ alone can they be performed. It is easy enough for us all to see this in the case before us; yet how often, in our own experience, instead of waiting for the Lord to do what He has promised, we become tired of waiting, and try to do it for Him, and thus make failures.

Spiritual and Literal

Years afterwards the promise was fulfilled in God's own way, but it was not until both Abraham and his wife fully believed the Lord. "Through faith also Sara herself received strength to conceive seed, and was delivered of a child when she was past age, because she judged Him faithful who had promised." Hebrews 11:11. Isaac was the fruit of faith. "For it is written, that Abraham had two sons, the one by a bondmaid, the other by a freewoman. But he who was of the bondwoman was born after flesh; but he of the freewoman was by promise."

Many people overlook this fact. They forget that Abraham had two sons, one by a bondwoman, and the other by a freewoman; one born after the flesh, and the other born after the Spirit. Hence the confusion with respect to the "literal" and the "spiritual" seed of Abraham. People talk as though the word "spiritual" were opposed to "literal." But this is not the case. "Spiritual" is opposed only to "fleshly," or carnal.

Isaac was born after the Spirit, yet he was as real and literal a child as Ishmael was. So the true seed of Abraham are only those who are spiritual, but that does not make them any the less real. God is Spirit, yet He is a real God. Christ had a spiritual body after His resurrection, yet He was a real, literal being, and could be handled the same as other bodies. So the bodies of the saints after the resurrection will be spiritual, yet they will be real. Spiritual things are not imaginary things. Indeed, that which is spiritual is more real than that which is fleshly, because only that which is spiritual will endure forever.

From this case, therefore, we learn most conclusively that the seed, which God promised to Abraham, which should be as the sand of the sea and the stars of heaven for number, and which should inherit the land, is a spiritual seed. That is, it is a seed, which comes through the agency of the Spirit of God. The birth of Isaac, like that of the Lord Jesus, was miraculous. It was supernatural. Both were brought about through the agency of the Spirit. In both we have an illustration of the power by which we are to become sons of God, and thus heirs of the promise.

The seed of Abraham after the flesh are Ishmaelites. He was a wild man, or, as the Revised Version has it, "A wild ass among men." Genesis 16:12. Moreover, he was the son of a bondwoman, and therefore not a freeborn son. Now the Lord had already signified, when speaking of Eliezer, Abraham's servant, that the seed of Abraham were to be free. Therefore, if Abraham had only remembered the words of the Lord, instead of harkening to the voice of his wife, he would have been saved much trouble.

It is worthwhile to dwell at length upon this phase of the subject, for it will save much confusion as to the true seed of Abraham, and the true Israel. Let the points be stated once more.

Ishmael was born after the flesh and could not be the seed. Therefore those who are only of the flesh cannot be the children of Abraham, and heirs according to the promise.

Isaac was born after the Spirit, and was the true seed. "In Isaac shall thy seed be called." Therefore all the children of Abraham are they alone who are born of the Spirit. "We, brethren, as Isaac was, are the children of promise." Galatians 4:28.

Isaac was freeborn; and none but those who are free are the children of Abraham, "So, then, brethren, we are not children of the bondwoman, but of the free." Galatians 4:31. What this freedom is, the Lord showed in His talk to the Jews, recorded in the eighth of John. "If ye abide in My word, then are ye truly My disciples; and ye shall know the truth, and the truth shall make you free. They answered unto Him, We are Abraham's seed, and have never yet been in bondage to any man; how sayest Thou, Ye shall be made free? Jesus answered them, Verily, verily; I say unto you, every one that committeth sin is the bondservant of sin. And the bondservant abideth not in the house forever; but the Son abideth forever. If therefore the Son shall make you free, ye shall be free indeed." Verses 31-36, R.V. And later He declared to them that if they were really the children of Abraham, they would do the works of Abraham. Verse 39.

Here again we see that which we learned from the promise in the fifteenth chapter of Genesis that the promise seed was to be a righteous seed, since it was promised only through Christ, and was sure to Abraham only through his faith.

The sum of the whole matter is that in the promise to Abraham there is the Gospel, and only the Gospel; and any attempt to make the promises apply to any other than those who are Christ's through the Spirit, is an attempt to nullify the promises of the Gospel of God. "If ye are Christ's then are ye Abraham's seed, and heirs according to the promise." Galatians 3:29. "Now if any man have not the Spirit of Christ, he is none of His." Romans 8:9. So if any man has not the Spirit of Christ, the Spirit by which Isaac was born, he is not a child of Abraham, and has no claim to any part of the promise.

Chapter 7

The Call of Abraham - The Covenant Sealed (Part 1 of 2)

July 17, 2010

NOW we come to a record which opens up the promise in a most wonderful manner. More than twenty-five years had passed since God first made the promise to Abraham.[3] Doubtless the time had been prolonged by the false step that Abraham took through listening to the reasoning of his wife. More than thirteen years had elapsed since that time. But Abraham had learned the lesson, and so God could lead him again.

"And when Abram was ninety years old and nine, the Lord appeared to Abram, and said unto him, I am the Almighty God; walk before Me, and be thou perfect." Genesis 17:1. The margin has it, "upright, or sincere." As in I Chronicles 12:33, 38, the meaning is, single-hearted. God told Abraham to be sincere before Him, and not double-hearted. When we recall the story recorded in the preceding chapter, we see the force of this injunction. We see also the force of the statement, "I am the Almighty God." God would let him know that He was fully able to perform His promise, and that therefore he should trust Him with a perfect or an undivided heart.

A New Name

"And Abram fell on his face; and God talked with him, saying, As for Me, behold, My covenant is with thee, and thou shalt be a father of many nations. Neither shall thy name any more be called Abram but thy name shall be Abraham; for a father of many nations have I made thee." Genesis 17:3-5.

The name Abram signifies "Father of height." Abram's father was a heathen, and the name may have had some reference to heathen worship in high places. But now his name becomes Abraham, "Father of many peoples." In the change of name in the cases of Abraham and Jacob, we have a hint of the new name, which the Lord gives to all who are His. See Revelation 2:17; 3:12. "And thou shalt be called by a new name, which the mouth of the Lord shall name."

---

[3] Abraham was seventy-five years old when he left Haran (Genesis 12:4), and the promise was first made known to him before he left Mesopotamia. Acts 7:2.

This giving to Abraham a new name did not indicate any change in the promise, but was simply a token to Abraham that God meant what He said. His name should ever afterward be a reminder to him of the promise. Some have thought that the giving of this new name marked a change in the nature of the promise to him; but a careful consideration of the promise as previously recorded will show that this cannot be. Abraham was just the same after his new name that he was before. It was while his name was still Abram that he believed God, and his faith in the promise was counted for righteousness. It was while His name was Abram that God preached the Gospel to him, saying, "In thee shall all families of the earth be blessed."

We may not make any distinction in the promises of God to Abraham, saying that some of them were temporal, and only for the fleshly seed, and that others were spiritual and eternal. "For the Son of God, Jesus Christ, who was preached among you by us, . . . was not yea and nay, but in Him is yea. For how many soever be the promises of God, in Him is the yea; wherefore also through Him is the Amen, unto the glory of God through us." 2 Corinthians 1:19, 20, R.V. "Now to Abraham and his seed were the promises made. He saith not, And to seeds, as of many; but as of one, And to thy seed, which is Christ." Note that the promises, no matter how many they are, all come through Christ. Note also that the apostle speaks of Abraham and not of Abram. He does not say that some were made to Abram, and some to Abraham. And this point is still more emphatic when we read the words of Stephen, "The God of glory appeared unto our father Abraham, when he was in Mesopotamia, before he dwelt in Charran." Acts 7:2. Although he was then known as Abram, the promise was the same as when he was known as Abraham. Every subsequent reference to him in the Bible, even to the first promises, uses the name Abraham. This is why we have referred to him only as Abraham.

The Lord continued, after telling Abraham of the change in his name, "And I will establish My covenant between Me and thee and thy seed after thee in their generations for an everlasting covenant, to be a God unto thee and to thy seed after thee. And I will give unto thee, and to thy seed after thee, the land wherein thou art a stranger, all the land of Canaan, for an everlasting possession; and I will be their God." Genesis 17:7, 8.

Let us take up the different parts of this covenant in detail. The central part of it is the Promised Land, the land of Canaan. It is the same as in the fifteenth chapter. The promise is to give it to Abraham and his seed. The covenant is the same that was made there; but here we have it sealed.

Notice that it is

An "Everlasting Covenant"

that the Lord made with him. It is the one everlasting covenant, which is so often spoken of in the Bible. It is "through the blood of the everlasting covenant" that men are made perfect in every good work to do the will of God. Hebrews 13:20. Moreover, the land promised in this everlasting covenant, was to be

"An Everlasting Possession,"

for both Abraham and his seed. Mark well that Abraham himself, as well as his seed, was promised the land for an everlasting possession. It is not an inheritance that is simply to be the possession of his family forever, but both Abraham and his seed together were to have it for an everlasting possession.

But a land can be held for an everlasting possession only by those who have

Everlasting Life

Therefore in this covenant we find the promise of everlasting life. It could not be otherwise, because when the covenant was first made, as recorded in the fifteenth chapter, Abraham was told that he should die before the land should be given for a possession; and Stephen said that God did not give him so much as to set his foot on. Therefore it could be his only through the resurrection; and when the resurrection takes place, then there will be no more death. For "we shall all be changed, in a moment, in the twinkling of an eye, at the last trump; for the trumpet shall sound, and the dead shall be raised incorruptible, and we shall be changed. For this corruptible must put on incorruption, and this mortal must put on immortality." 1 Corinthians 15:51-53.

So we see that the making of this everlasting covenant with Abraham was simply the preaching of the everlasting Gospel of the kingdom, and the assuring to him of a part in its blessings. The promise to Abraham was a Gospel promise, and nothing else, and the covenant was the everlasting covenant, of which Christ is Mediator. Its scope is identical with that of the new covenant, in which God says, "I will put my law in their inward parts, and write it in their hearts; and will be their God, and they shall be My people." Hebrews 8:10. But this will appear more plainly as we proceed.

A Covenant of Righteousness

The Lord said to Abraham after this restatement of the covenant with him and his seed, "And ye shall circumcise the flesh of your foreskin; and it shall be a token of the covenant betwixt Me and thee." Genesis 17:11. Now if we turn to the Epistle to the Romans we shall learn much more of the meaning of this transaction. We must have the Scripture before us in order that we may consider it understandingly, and so we will quote it at length.

"What shall we say then that Abraham our father, as pertaining to the flesh, hath found? For if Abraham were justified by works, he hath whereof to glory; but not before God. For what saith the Scripture? Abraham believed God, and it was counted unto him for righteousness. Now to him that worketh is the reward not reckoned of grace, but of debt. But to him that worketh not, but believeth on Him that justifieth the ungodly, his faith is counted for righteousness. Even as David also described the blessedness of the man unto whom God imputeth righteousness without works, saying, Blessed are they whose iniquities are forgiven, and whose sins are covered. Blessed is the man to whom the Lord will not impute sin. Cometh this blessedness then upon the circumcision only, or upon the uncircumcision also? for we say that faith was reckoned to Abraham for righteousness. How then was it reckoned? when he was in circumcision, or in uncircumcision? Not in circumcision, but in uncircumcision, and he received the sign of circumcision, a seal of the righteousness of the faith which he had yet being uncircumcised; that he might be the father of all them that believe, though they be not circumcised; that righteousness might be imputed unto them also; and the father of circumcision to them who are not of the circumcision only, but who also walk in the steps of that faith of our father Abraham, which he had being yet uncircumcised. For the promise, that he should be the heir of the world, was not to Abraham, or to his seed, through the law, but through the righteousness of faith." Romans 4:1-13.

The subject of the entire chapter is Abraham and justification by faith. The apostle takes the case of Abraham as an illustration of the truth presented in the preceding chapter, namely, that a man is made righteous by faith. The blessing that Abraham received is the blessing of sins forgiven, through the righteousness of Jesus Christ. See verses 6-9. Therefore when we read in Genesis 7:2, 3, that in Abraham all the families of the earth should be blessed, we know that the blessing referred to is the forgiveness of sins. This is positively proved by Acts 3:25, 26: "Ye are the children of the prophets, and of the covenant which God made with our fathers, saying unto Abraham, And in thy seed shall all the kindreds of the earth be blessed. Unto you first God, having raised up His Son Jesus, sent Him to bless you, in turning away every one of you from his iniquities."

This blessing came to Abraham through Jesus Christ and His cross, even as it comes to us. For "Christ hath redeemed us from the curse of the law, being made a curse for us; . . . that the blessing of Abraham might come on the Gentiles through Jesus Christ; that we might receive the promise of the Spirit through faith." Galatians 3:13, 14. So we find that the blessings of the covenant with Abraham are simply the blessings of the Gospel, and they are brought to us through the cross of Christ. Nothing was promised in that covenant except that which comes through the Gospel; and everything that the Gospel contains was in it.

Circumcision was given as the seal of this covenant. But the promise, the covenant, the blessing, and everything, came to Abraham before he was circumcised. Hence he is the father of the uncircumcised as well as of the circumcised. Jews and Gentiles are alike sharers in the covenant and its blessings, provided they have the faith that Abraham had.

In Genesis 17:11 we are told that circumcision was given as the sign of the covenant that God made with Abraham. But in Romans 4:11 we are told that it was given him as a seal of the righteousness which he had by faith. In other words, it was the assurance and seal of the forgiveness of sins through the righteousness of Christ. Therefore we know that the covenant, of which circumcision was the seal, was a covenant of righteousness by faith; that all the blessings promised in it are on the basis of righteousness through Jesus Christ. This again shows us that the covenant made with Abraham was the Gospel and that only.

A Grant of Land

But in this covenant the central promise was concerning land. All the land of Canaan was promised to Abraham and his seed for an everlasting possession. And then the seal of the covenant – circumcision – was given – a seal of the righteousness, which he had by faith. This shows that the land of Canaan was to be possessed only by faith. And here we have a practical lesson as to the possession of things by faith. Many people think that a thing that is possessed by faith is only possessed in imagination. But the land of Canaan was a real country, and was to be actually possessed. Possession of it was to be gained however, only through faith. That is, faith was to give them the possession of it. This was indeed the case. By faith the people crossed the river Jordan, and "by faith the walls of Jericho fell down, after they were compassed about seven days." But of this we shall have more hereafter.

The land of Canaan, which was promised in the covenant, was to be had through the righteousness of faith, which was sealed by circumcision, the seal of the covenant.

Read now Romans 4:13 once more, and we shall see how much was involved in this promise. "For the promise, that he should be the heir of the world, was not to Abraham, or to his seed, through the law, but through the righteousness of faith." This righteousness of faith we are told in verse eleven was sealed by circumcision; and circumcision was the seal of the covenant which we have recorded in Genesis 17.

Therefore, we know that the promise of land, which the covenant with Abraham contained, was nothing less than the promise of the whole earth. As we come to the fulfillment of the promise, we shall see more plainly how it can be that the promise of the land of Canaan included the possession of the whole earth; but the fact may be briefly indicated here.

The covenant in which that land was promised, was, as we have seen, a covenant of righteousness. Its basis was the righteousness of faith. It was an everlasting covenant, promising an everlasting inheritance to both Abraham and his seed, which meant for them everlasting life. But grace reigns through righteousness unto eternal life only through Jesus Christ our Lord. Eternal life can be had only in righteousness.

Moreover, since the promise was to Abraham, as well as to his seed, and Abraham was assured that he should die long before the inheritance was bestowed, it is evident that it could be gained only through the resurrection, which takes place at the coming of the Lord, when immortality is bestowed. But the coming of Christ is at "the times of restitution of all things, which God hath spoken by the mouth of all His holy prophets since the world began." Acts 3:21. Therefore we are shut up to the fact that the inheritance of righteousness, which was promised to Abraham for an everlasting possession, to be had through the resurrection, at the coming of the Lord, was the "new earth, wherein dwelleth righteousness," for which we look according to the promise of God.

Chapter 8

The Call of Abraham - The Covenant Sealed (Part 2 of 2)

The Present Truth, June 25, 1896

"The Sign of Circumcision"

AND now we must carry a little further the study of the seal of the covenant, namely, circumcision. What does it signify, and what is it in reality? We have learned that it signifies righteousness by faith. It was given to Abraham as a token of the possession of such righteousness, or, as an assurance that he was "accepted in the Beloved, in whom we have redemption through His blood, the forgiveness of sins, according to the riches of His grace." Ephesians 1:6, 7. What circumcision really is may be learned from the following scripture: –

"For circumcision verily profiteth, if thou keep the law; but if thou be a breaker of the law, thy circumcision is made uncircumcision. Therefore if the uncircumcision keep the righteousness of the law, shall not his uncircumcision be counted for circumcision? And shall not uncircumcision, which is by nature, if it fulfill the law, judge thee, who by the letter and circumcision dost transgress the law? For he is not a Jew, which is one outwardly; neither is that circumcision, which is outward in the flesh. But he is a Jew, which is one inwardly; and circumcision is that of the heart, in the Spirit, and not in the letter; whose praise is not of men, but of God." Romans 2:25-29.

Circumcision was the sign of righteousness by faith. But that righteousness is the righteousness required by the law of God. Circumcision never amounted to anything unless the law was kept. In fact, the keeping of the law is real circumcision. The Lord requires truth in the inward parts. An outward show, with no righteousness within, is an abomination to Him. The law must be in the heart, or else there is no real circumcision. But the law can be in the heart only by the power of the Lord through the Spirit. "The law is spiritual," (Romans 7:14), that is it is of the nature of the Holy Spirit, and the law can be in the heart only as the Spirit of God dwells there. Circumcision is therefore nothing less than the sealing of righteousness in the heart by the Holy Spirit. This is what Abraham received. His circumcision was the scale of the righteousness of faith, which he had. But the righteousness of faith was that by which he was to inherit the promised possession. Therefore circumcision was the pledge of his inheritance. Now read the following text: –

"It whom we have redemption through His blood, the forgiveness of sins, according to the riches of His grace. . . in whom also we have obtained an inheritance being predestinated according to the purpose of Him that worketh all things after the counsel of His own will; that we should be to the praise of His glory, who first trusted in Christ. In whom ye also trusted, after that ye heard the word of truth, the Gospel of your salvation; in whom also after that ye believed, ye were scaled with that Holy Spirit of promise, which is the earnest of our inheritance until the redemption of the purchased possession." Ephesians 1:7-14.

The word of truth is the Gospel of salvation. When we believe the Gospel, we are sealed by the Holy Spirit, and that seal is the pledge or assurance of our inheritance, until it is bestowed at the coming of the Lord. Abraham had, therefore, the Holy Spirit as the pledge of the inheritance that was promised him. The possession of the Spirit shows that we have a right to the inheritance, because the Spirit brings righteousness, and the inheritance is one of righteousness. Righteousness, and that only, will dwell in the new earth.

In harmony with the above text, we have also the following:

"And ye are complete in Him [Christ], which is the head of all principality and power; in whom also ye are circumcised with the circumcision made without hands, in putting off the body of the sins of the flesh by the circumcision of Christ." Colossians 2:10, 11.

God's promise to Abraham had been made long before the time of which we are writing. The making of the covenant is recorded in the fifteenth chapter of Genesis. But after the covenant was made, Abraham fell into the error recorded in the sixteenth chapter. He saw his mistake, and repented of it, and turned to the Lord again in full faith, and thus received the assurance of forgiveness and acceptance; and circumcision was given as the reminder of it.

The Scriptures, which we have read in the New Testament concerning circumcision, are not the statement of something new. Circumcision was always just what it is there said to be. It always meant righteousness in the heart, and had no significance whatever when that righteousness was absent. This is plainly indicated in Deuteronomy 30:5, 6: "And the Lord thy God will bring thee into the land which thy fathers possessed, and thou shalt possess it; and He will do thee good, and multiply thee above thy fathers. And the Lord thy God will circumcise thine heart, and the heart of thy seed, to love the Lord thy God with all thine heart, and with all thy soul, that thou mayest live."

Why the Outward Sign?

The question very naturally arises, 'Why was the outward sign of circumcision given to Abraham, if he already had everything that it implied?' Since circumcision is of the heart by the Spirit, and is nothing but the possession of righteousness by faith, and Abraham had that before he received the sign of circumcision, why was the sign given?

It is a reasonable question, and happily may easily be answered. The reader will first notice, however, that that which Abraham received is in Romans 4:11 called "the sign of circumcision." The real circumcision he already had. In harmony with this is the statement that that which was in the flesh, made by hands, was only "called circumcision." Ephesians 2:11. It was not circumcision in fact.

Now the reason why this sign was given, which was only a sign, and which brought nothing to its possessor, and which was a false sign unless the righteousness of faith was in the heart, will be seen when we consider what had taken place after the covenant was made with Abraham. He had entered into an arrangement, the object of which was to work out the promise of the Lord. Abraham and Sarah believed that the promise was to be theirs, but they thought that they must work it out. But since the promise was of an inheritance of righteousness, the thought that they could work it out was in reality the very common idea that men can work out the righteousness of God. So when God repeated the covenant, He gave to Abraham a sign, which should always be a reminder of his attempt to work out the promise of God, and his failure. It did not give him anything, but was on the contrary a reminder that he could do nothing of himself, and that everything was to be done in him and for him by the Lord. The cutting off of a portion of flesh showed that the promise was not to be gained by the flesh but by the Spirit. Ishmael was born after the flesh, but Isaac after the Spirit.

The same purpose was also served by it for his descendants. It was to keep continually before them the mistake of their father Abraham, and to warn them against making the like error. It was to show them that "the flesh profiteth nothing." In after times they perverted this sign, and assumed that the possession of it was an assurance of their righteousness, whether they kept the law or not. They trusted that it brought them righteousness and made them the peculiar favorites of the Lord. But the Apostle Paul showed the truth in regard to the matter by saying, "We are the circumcision, which worship God in the Spirit, and rejoice in Christ Jesus, and have no confidence in the flesh." Philippians 3:3. The Jews came to look upon it as bringing to them everything, because they trusted in their own righteousness; whereas its only object was to teach them not to put confidence in themselves.

Chapter 9

The Call of Abraham - The Test of Faith

December 18, 2010

We pass by a period of several years. The number of years we cannot tell, but Isaac, the child of faith and promise had been born, and had grown to be a young man.[4] Abraham's faith had grown stronger and more intelligent, for he had learned that God fulfills His own promises. But God is a faithful teacher, and does not allow His pupils to leave a lesson until it is thoroughly learned. It is not enough for them to see and acknowledge that they have made a mistake in the lesson that He has given them. Such acknowledgement of course ensures forgiveness; but, having seen the error, they must go over the same ground again, and possibly many times, until they have learned it so well that they can go without stumbling. It is solely for their own good. It is no kindness on the part of a parent or teacher to allow his children to pass by lessons that are unlearned, simply because they are difficult.

So "it came to pass after these things, that God did prove Abraham, and said unto him, Abraham; and he said, Here am I. And He said, Take now thy son, thine only son, whom thou lovest, even Isaac, and get thee into the land of Moriah; and offer him there for a burnt offering upon one of the mountains which I will tell thee of." Genesis 22:1, 2.

In order to understand what this proving meant, we must have a clear idea of what was bound up in Isaac – of what was embraced in the promise that had been made to Abraham, which was to be fulfilled through Isaac. We have already studied it, and so have only to recall the fact. God had said to Abraham, "In thy seed shall all the families of the earth be blessed," and, "In Isaac shall thy seed be called." As we have seen, the blessing was the blessing of the Gospel, the blessing which comes through Christ and His cross. But this, since God had so said, was to be fulfilled through Isaac. The promised seed, consisting of Christ and of all who are His, was to come through Isaac. Thus we see that to human sight the requirement of God seemed like cutting off all hope of the promise ever being fulfilled.

---

[4] That he was not a little child, as our ideas of the word "lad," might lead us to suppose, is evident from the fact that he was able to carry the wood for the sacrifice up the mountain. Josephus says that he was twenty-five years old, and that age is indicated by the chronology in the margin of our Bibles.

But the promise was the promise of salvation through Jesus Christ, the seed. The promise had been very explicit, "In Isaac shall thy seed be called," and that seed was first of all Christ. Therefore Christ the Saviour of all men could come only in Isaac's line. But Isaac was yet a young man and unmarried. To cut him off would be, so men would reason, to cut off all prospects of the Messiah, and so to cut off all hope of salvation. To all appearance Abraham was called upon virtually to put the knife to his own throat, and to cut off the hope of his own salvation.

Thus we can see that it was not merely Abraham's fatherly affection that was tried, but his faith in the promise of God. A severer test no man was ever called upon to undergo, for no other man ever could be in the same position. The entire hope of the whole human race was bound up in Isaac, and Abraham was asked apparently to destroy it with a stroke of the knife. Well might the one who could stand such a test be called "the father of the faithful." We may well believe that Abraham was strongly tempted to doubt if this requirement came from the Lord; it seemed to be so directly contrary to God's promise.

Temptations

To be tempted, and sorely tempted, is not a sin. "My brethren, count it all joy when ye fall into divers temptations." James 1:2. The Apostle Peter speaks of the same inheritance which was promised to Abraham, and says that we greatly rejoice in it, "though now for a season, if need be, ye are in heaviness through manifold temptations; that the trial of your faith, being much more precious than of gold that perisheth, though it be tried with fire, might be found unto praise and honor and glory at the appearing of Jesus Christ; whom having not seen, ye love; in whom though now ye see Him not, yet believing, ye rejoice with joy unspeakable and full of glory; receiving the end of your faith, even the salvation of your souls." 1 Peter 1:6-9.

These temptations cause heaviness, says the apostle. They weigh one down. If it were otherwise – if it took no effort to endure them – they would not be temptations. The fact that a thing is a temptation means that it is something, which appeals to all the feelings, and to endure which almost takes the very life. Therefore we may know, without casting the slightest reflection upon Abraham's faith, that it cost him a terrible struggle to obey the command of the Lord.

Doubts were suggested to his mind. Doubts come from the devil, and no man is so good that he is free from the suggestions of Satan. Even the Lord Himself had to bear them. He "was tempted in all points like as we are, yet without sin." Hebrews 4:15. The sin does not consist in the devil's whispering doubts in our ears, but in our acting upon them. This Christ did not do. Neither did Abraham; yet he who thinks that the patriarch started upon his journey without first having a sore struggle, must be unmindful not only of what was involved in the proposed test, but of the feelings of a father.

The tempter would suggest, "This cannot be the requirement of the Lord, because He has promised you an innumerable posterity, and has said that it must come through Isaac." Again and again would this thought come; but it could not stand, because Abraham knew full well the voice of the Lord. He knew that the call to offer up Isaac came from the same source as the promise. The repetition of that suggestion of the tempter would only make more sure the fact that the requirement, was from the Lord.

But that would not end the struggle. A strong temptation to disregard the command would be found in his own affection for his son. The requirement probed that very deeply: "Take now thy son, thine only son whom thou lovest." And there was the fond and proud mother. How could he make her believe that it was the Lord that had spoken to him? Would she not reproach him for following the fancies of a disordered mind? How could he break the matter to her? Or, if he should proceed to make the sacrifice without letting her know of it, how could he meet her on his return? Besides, there were the people. Would they not accuse him of murdering his son? We may be sure that Abraham had a desperate struggle with all these suggestions that would crowd upon his mind and heart.

But faith gained the victory. His time of wavering had long since passed, and now "he staggered not at the promise of God through unbelief; but was strong in faith, giving glory to God." Romans 4:20. "By faith Abraham, when he was tried, offered up Isaac; and he that had received the promises offered up his only begotten son, of whom it was said, That in Isaac shall thy seed be called; accounting that God was able to raise him up even from the dead; from whence also he received him in a figure." Hebrews 11:12-19.

The whole thing, from first to last, involved the resurrection of the dead. The birth of Isaac was really the bringing of life from the dead. It was by the power of the resurrection. Abraham had once, through harkening to his wife, failed to trust God's power to bring him a son from the dead. He had repented of his failure, but must needs be tested upon that point, to ensure that he had thoroughly learned the lesson. The result proved that he had.

The Only Begotten Son

"He that had received the promises offered up his only begotten son, of whom it was said, That in Isaac shall thy seed be called; accounting that God was able to raise him up even from the dead." Note the expression, "his only begotten son." We cannot read it without being reminded that "God so loved the world, that He gave His only begotten Son, that whosoever believeth in Him should not perish, but have everlasting life." John 3:16. In Abraham's offering his only begotten son we have a figure of the offering of the only begotten Son of God. And Abraham so understood it. He had already rejoiced in Christ. He knew that through the promised Seed should come the resurrection of the dead; and it was his faith in the resurrection of the dead, which can come only through Jesus, that enabled him to stand the test.

Abraham offered up his only begotten son, in confidence that he would be raised from the dead because God would offer up His only begotten Son. Nay, more, God had already offered His only begotten Son, "who verily was foreordained before the foundation of the world," but who had yet to be manifested. 1 Peter 1:20. And herein we can see the marvelous faith of Abraham, and how fully it comprehended the purpose and the power of God. For the Messiah, the Seed through whom all the blessings were to come to men, was to be born of Isaac's line. Isaac was to be cut off without an heir. Yet Abraham had such confidence in the life and power of the word of the Lord that he believed that it would fulfill itself. He believed that the Messiah who was to come of Isaac's line, and whose death alone could destroy death and bring the resurrection, and who had not yet come into the world, had power to raise up Isaac from the dead, in order that the promise might be fulfilled, and He be yet born into the world. Greater faith than that of Abraham could not possibly exist.

The Resurrection and the Life

In this we see not only proof of the pre-existence of Christ but also of Abraham's knowledge of it. Jesus said, "I am the resurrection and the life." John 11:25. He was the Word that was in the beginning with God, and that was God. He was the resurrection and the life in the days of Abraham as well as in the time of Lazarus. "In Him was life," even endless life. Abraham believed it, for he had already proved its power, and he was confident that the life of the Word would bring Isaac to life in order that the promise might be fulfilled.

Abraham started forth on his journey. Three days he pursued his weary way, in which there was ample time for the tempter to assail him with all manner of doubts. But doubt was fully mastered when "on the third day Abraham lifted up his eyes, and saw the place afar off." Genesis 22:4. Evidently some sign that the Lord had given him appeared on the mountain, and he knew beyond all doubt that the Lord was leading him. The struggle was over, and he went forward to the completion of his task, fully assured that God would bring Isaac from the dead.

"And Abraham said unto his young men, Abide ye here with the ass; and I and the lad will go yonder and worship, and come again to you." Verse 5. If there were not a single line in the New Testament about this matter, we might know from this verse that Abraham had faith in the resurrection. "I and the lad will go yonder and worship, and come again to you." In the original it is made very clear: We will go, and we will come again to you. The patriarch had such confidence in the Lord's promise that he fully believed that although he should offer up Isaac as a burnt offering, his son would be raised again, so that they would both return together. "Hope maketh not ashamed." Having been justified by faith, he had peace with God through our Lord Jesus Christ. The trial of his faith had been patiently endured, for we must know that the bitterness of the struggle was now over, and a rich experience of the life that is in the Word had come to him, producing an unwavering hope.

The Sacrifice Completed

We all know the outcome. Isaac carried the wood to the appointed place. The altar was built, and he was bound and laid upon it. Here still we have the likeness to the sacrifice of Christ. God gave His only begotten Son, yet the Son went not unwillingly. Christ "gave Himself for us." So Isaac freely yielded himself as a sacrifice. He was young and strong, and could easily have resisted or fled if he had wished. But he did not. The sacrifice was his as well as his father's. As Christ carried His own cross, so Isaac carried the wood for his own sacrifice, and meekly yielded his body to the knife. In Isaac we have a type of Christ, who was "led as a lamb to the slaughter;" Abraham's statement, "God will provide Himself a lamb," was but the expression of his faith in the Lamb of God.

"And Abraham stretched forth his hand, and took the knife to slay his son. And the angel of the Lord called unto him out of heaven, and said, Abraham, Abraham; and he said, Here am I. And he said, Lay not thine hand upon the lad, neither do thou anything unto him; for now I know that thou fearest God, seeing that thou hast not withheld thy son, thine only son, from Me. And Abraham lifted up his eyes, and looked, and behold behind him a ram caught in a thicket by his horns; and Abraham went and took the ram, and offered him up for a burnt offering instead of his son." Genesis 22:10-13. The son's life was spared, yet the sacrifice was as truly and as completely made as though he had been put to death.

The Work of Faith

Let us turn to read what this transaction teaches us as to the relation of faith and works. "Wilt thou know, O vain man, that faith without works is dead? Was not Abraham our father justified by works when he had offered Isaac his son upon the altar? Seest thou how faith wrought with his works, and by works was faith made perfect? And the Scripture was fulfilled, which saith, Abraham believed God, and it was imputed unto him for righteousness; and he was called the friend of God." James 2:20-23.

How is it possible for anyone to suppose that here is any contradiction or modification of the doctrine of justification by faith as set forth in the writings of the Apostle Paul? All the Scriptures teach that faith works. "Faith which worketh by love" (Galatians 5:6) is declared to be the one necessary thing. The Thessalonian brethren were commended for their "work of faith." 1 Thessalonians 1:2, 3.

So the case of Abraham is used as an illustration of the working of faith. God had made a promise to him; he had believed the promise, and his faith had been counted to him for righteousness. His faith was the kind that works righteousness. Now that faith received a practical test, and the works showed that it was perfect. Thus the Scripture was fulfilled which says, "Abraham believed God, and it was imputed to him for righteousness." This work was the demonstration of the fact that faith had justly been imputed to him for righteousness. It was faith that wrought with his works. The work that Abraham did was a work of faith. His works did not produce his faith, but his faith produced his works. He was justified, not by faith and works, but by faith, which works.

The Friend of God

"And he was called the friend of God." Jesus said to His disciples, "Henceforth I call you not servants; for the servant knoweth not what his lord doeth; but I have called you friends; for all things that I have heard of My Father, I have made known unto you." Friendship between two means mutual confidence. In perfect friendship each one reveals himself to the other in a way that he does not to the outside world. There can be no perfect friendship where there is distrust and restraint. Between perfect friends there is a perfect understanding. So God called Abraham his friend, because they perfectly understood each other. This sacrifice fully revealed the character of Abraham. God had said before, "I know him;" and now again He said; "Now I know that thou fearest God." And Abraham on his part understood the Lord. The sacrifice of his only begotten son indicated that he knew the loving character of God, who for man's sake had already given His only begotten Son. They were united in a mutual sacrifice and a mutual sympathy. No one could appreciate the feelings of God so well as Abraham could.

No other person can ever be called upon to undergo the same test that Abraham endured, because the circumstances can never again be the same. Never again can the fate of the world be bound up in a single person, and hang, as it were, in the balance. Yet each child of Abraham will be tested, because only they who have the faith of Abraham are the children of Abraham. Each one may be the friend of God, and must be such if he is a child of Abraham. God will manifest Himself unto His people, as He does not unto the world.

But we must not forget that friendship is based upon mutual confidence. If we wish the Lord to be confidential with us, we must make Him our confidant. If we confess our sins, laying out before Him in secret all our weaknesses and difficulties, then He will show Himself a faithful friend, and will reveal to us His love, and His power to deliver from temptation. He will show us how He has been tempted in the same way, suffering the same infirmities, and will show us how to overcome. Thus in loving interchange of confidences, we shall sit together in heavenly places in Christ Jesus, and may sup together. He will show to us wonderful things; for "the secret of the Lord is with them that fear Him; and He will show them His covenant." Psalms 25:14.

Chapter 10

The Call of Abraham - The Promise and the Oath

The Present Truth, July 9, 1896

THE sacrifice had been made; Abraham's faith had been tested and found perfect; "And the angel of the Lord called unto Abraham out of heaven the second time, and said, By Myself have I sworn, saith the Lord, for because thou hast done this thing, and hast not withheld thy son, thine only son; that in blessing I will bless thee, and in multiplying I will multiply[5] thy seed as the stars of heaven, and as the sand which is upon the sea-shore; and thy seed shall possess the gate of His enemies; and in thy seed shall all the nations of the earth be blessed; because thou hast obeyed My voice." Genesis 22:15-18.

In the Epistle to the Hebrews we learn the significance of the fact that God swore by Himself. The reader will at once see that the following Scripture has direct reference to that which has just been quoted: –

"When God made promise to Abraham, because He could swear by no greater, He swear by Himself, saying, Surely blessing I will bless thee, and multiplying I will multiply thee. And so, after he had patiently endured, he obtained the promise. For men verily swear by the greater; and an oath for confirmation is to them an end of all strife. Wherein God, willing more abundantly to show unto the heirs of promise the immutability of His counsel, confirmed it by an oath; that by two immutable things, in which it was impossible for God to lie, we might have a strong consolation, who have fled for refuge to lay hold upon the hope set before us; which hope we have as an anchor of the soul, both sure and steadfast, and which entereth into that within the veil; whither the forerunner is for us entered, even Jesus, made an high priest for ever after the order of Melchizedek." Hebrews 6:13-20.

---

[5] "Blessing I will bless," and "multiplying I will multiply," is the literal translation of a very common Hebrew idiom. Emphasis in the Hebrew is denoted by repetition. Put into ordinary English, the text would read, "I will surely bless thee, and I will surely multiply thy seed." Similar instances may be seen in the margin of Genesis 2:16, 17, "eating thou mayest eat," and "dying thou shalt die," for "thou mayest freely eat," and "thou shalt surely die." In Exodus 3:7, "I have surely seen," the same idiom occurs, "Seeing I have seen." In Acts 7:34, this emphatic repetition is preserved in "I have seen, I have seen."

The oath was not for Abraham's sake. His belief in God was complete without the oath to back the promise. His faith had been shown to be perfect, before the oath was given. Moreover, if it had been given for his sake, there would have been no necessity of putting it on record, since he was dead long before the record was written. But God was willing more abundantly to show unto the heirs of promise the immutability of His counsel, and so He confirmed the promise by an oath.

In Christ Alone

And who are heirs of the promise? –The next clause tells us. The oath was in order that "we might have a strong consolation." The oath was given for our sakes. This shows that the covenant with Abraham concerns us. Those who are Christ's are Abraham's seed, and heirs according to the promise; and this oath was given to be an encouragement to us when we flee for refuge to Christ.

How plainly this last reference shows us that the whole of the covenant with Abraham, with all of its included promises, is purely Gospel. The oath backs the promise; but the oath gives consolation to us when fleeing for refuge to Christ; therefore the promise has reference to that which is to be gained in Christ. This is also shown in the text, which has so often been repeated, "If ye are Christ's, then are ye Abraham's seed, and heirs according to the promise." The promise had nothing else in view but Christ and the blessings, which are bestowed through His cross.

Thus it was that the Apostle Paul, whose determination was to know nothing but "Jesus Christ and Him crucified," could also say that he stood and was judged "for the hope of the promise made of God unto the fathers." Acts 26:6. The "hope of the promise made of God unto the fathers," is "the hope set before us" in Christ, and which is made "more abundantly" sure by the oath of God to Abraham.

The oath of God confirmed the covenant. The oath by which the promise was confirmed gives us strong consolation when we flee for refuge to the sanctuary where Christ is priest in our behalf, after the order of Melchizedek. Therefore, that oath was the same as the oath that made Christ priest forever after the order of Melchizedek. This is clearly set forth in the statement that Christ was made priest "with an oath by Him that said unto Him, The Lord swore, and will not repent. Thou art a priest for ever after the order of Melchizedek" (Hebrews 7:21), and that He is able therefore to save them to the uttermost that come to God by Him.

Still further, the oath by which Christ was made priest after the order of Melchizedek was the oath by which He is made surety of a "better covenant," (verse 22) even the new covenant. But the oath by which Jesus was made priest after the order of Melchizedek was the same as the oath by which the covenant with Abraham was confirmed. Therefore the covenant with Abraham is identical in its scope with the new covenant.

There is nothing in the new covenant that is not in the covenant with Abraham; and no one will ever be included in the new covenant, who is not a child of Abraham through the covenant made with him.

What wonderful consolation is lost by those who fail to see the Gospel and the Gospel only in the promise of God to Abraham. The "strong consolation" which the oath of God gives us, is in Christ's work as "a merciful and faithful high priest in things pertaining to God, to make reconciliation for the sins of the people." As a priest He presents His blood, through which we have redemption, even the forgiveness of sins. As a priest He not only provides mercy for us, but "grace to help in time of need." This is assured to us "without respect of persons," by the oath of God.

"Strong Consolation"

Here is a poor, timid, trembling soul, cast down and despondent by a sense of sins committed, and of general weakness and unworthiness. He is afraid that God will not accept him. He thinks that he is too insignificant for God to notice, and that it would make no difference to anybody, not even to God, if he were lost. To such the Lord says, "Hearken to Me, ye that follow after righteousness, ye that seek the Lord; look unto the rock whence ye are hewn, and to the hole of the pit whence ye are digged. Look unto Abraham your father, and to Sarah that bare you; for I called him alone [when he was but one, R.V.], and blessed him, and increased him. For the Lord shall comfort Zion; He will comfort all her waste places; He will make her wilderness like Eden, and her desert like the garden of the Lord; joy and gladness shall be found therein, thanksgiving, and the voice of melody." Isaiah 51:1-3.

Look to Abraham, brought up a heathen, and see what God did for him and what He promised to him, confirming it with an oath by Himself, for your sake. You think that it would make no difference with the Lord if you were lost, because you are so obscure and insignificant. Why, your worthiness or unworthiness has nothing whatever to do with the matter. The Lord says, "I, even I, am He that blotteth out thy transgressions for Mine own sake, and will not remember thy sins." Isaiah 43:25. For His own sake? Yes, certainly; because of His great love wherewith He loved us, He has placed Himself under bonds to do it. He swore by Himself to save all that come to Him through Jesus Christ, and "He abideth faithful; He cannot deny Himself." 2 Timothy 2:13.

Think of it; God swore by Himself! That is, He pledged Himself, and His own existence, to our salvation in Jesus Christ. He put Himself in pawn. His life for ours, if we are lost while trusting Him. His honor is at stake. It is not a question of whether or not you are insignificant and of little or no worth. He Himself says that we are "less than nothing." Isaiah 40:17. He says that "we have sold ourselves for naught," (Isaiah 52:3), which shows our true value; but we are redeemed without money, even by the precious blood of Christ. The blood of Christ is the life of Christ; and the life of Christ bestowed upon us makes us partakers of His worth. The only question is, Can God afford to break or forget His oath? And the answer is that we have "two immutable things, in which it was impossible for God to lie."

Think of what would be involved in the breaking of that promise and that oath. The word of God, which brings the promise, is the word which created the heavens and the earth, and which upholds them. "Lift up your eyes on high, and see who hath created these, that bringeth out their host by number; He calleth them all by name; by the greatness of His might, and for that He is strong in power, not one is lacking. Why sayest thou, O Jacob, and speakest, O Israel, my way is hid from the Lord, and my judgment is passed away from my God?" Isaiah 40:25-27. The preceding part of this same chapter speaks of the word of God, which has created all things, and that it shall stand for ever, and the words are quoted by the Apostle Peter, with the additional statement, "And this is the word which by the Gospel is preached unto you." 1 Peter 1:25.

It is the word of God in Christ that upholds the universe, and keeps the innumerable stars in their places. "In Him all things consist." If He should fail, the universe would collapse. But God is no surer than His word, for His word is backed by His oath. He has pledged His own existence to the performance of His word. If His word should be broken to the humblest soul in the world, He Himself would be disgraced, dishonored, and dethroned. The universe would go to chaos and annihilation.

Thus, the entire universe is in the balance to ensure the salvation of every soul that seeks it in Christ. The power manifested in it is the power pledged to the help of the weak. So long as matter exists, so long will the word of God be sure. "Forever, O Lord, Thy word is settled in heaven." Psalm 119:89. It would be a sad loss to you if you should fail of salvation; but it would be a far greater loss to the Lord if you should fail through any fault of His.

Then let the aforetime doubting soul sing: –

> *"His oath, His covenant, His blood,*
> *Support me in the whelming flood;*
> *When all around my soul gives way,*
> *He then is all my hope and stay."*

Chapter 11

The Call of Abraham - The promise of Victory

The Present Truth : July 16, 1896

WE have noted the repetition of the promise, and the oath, which confirmed it. But there is yet one very important feature of the promise, which has not been specially noted. It is this: "And thy seed shall possess the gate of his enemies." Genesis 22:17. This is worth most careful attention, for it presents the consummation of the Gospel.

Let it never be forgotten that "to Abraham and his seed were the promises made. He saith not, and to seeds, as of many; but as of one, and to they seed, which is Christ." Galatians 3:16. There is only one seed, and that is Christ; but "as many as have been baptized into Christ, have put on Christ," so that they are all one in Christ Jesus. And "if ye be Christ's, then are ye Abraham's seed, and heirs according to the promise." Verse 29. The seed is Christ and those who are His, and it is nothing else. The Bible nowhere sets forth any other seed of Abraham. Therefore, the promise to Abraham amounted to this: Christ, and those who are His – thy seed – shall possess the gate of their enemies.

By one man sin came into the world. The temptation came through Satan, the arch-enemy of Christ. Satan and his hosts are the enemies of Christ, and of everything that is like Christ. They are the enemies of all good, and of all men. "The enemy" that sowed the tares is the devil. The name "Satan" means adversary. "Your adversary the devil, as a roaring lion, walketh about, seeking whom he may devour." 1 Peter 5:8. The promise that Abraham's seed should possess the gate of his enemies is the promise of victory over sin and Satan, through Jesus Christ.

This is shown by the words of Zacharias the priest, when he was filled with the Holy Ghost. He prophesied, saying, "Blessed be the Lord God of Israel; for He hath visited and redeemed His people, and hath raised up an horn of salvation for us in the house of His servant David; as He spake by the mouth of His holy prophets, which have been since the world began: that we should be saved from our enemies, and from the hand of all that hate us; to perform the mercy promised to our fathers, and to remember His holy covenant; the oath which He swear unto our father Abraham, that He would grant unto us, that we being delivered out of the hand of our enemies might serve Him without fear, in holiness and righteousness before Him all the days of our life." Luke 1:68-75.

These words were spoken on the occasion of the birth of John the Baptist, the forerunner of Christ. They are a direct reference to the promise and the oath, which we are studying. The Holy Spirit prompted them. Therefore we are simply following the Spirit when we say that the promise of possession of the gate of our enemies means deliverance from the power of the hosts of Satan. When Christ sent out the twelve, He "gave them power and authority over all devils." Luke 9:1. This power is to be with His church till the end of time, for Christ said, "These signs shall follow them that believe; in My name shall they cast out devils," etc. Mark 16:17. And again, "He that believeth on Me, the works that I do shall he do also; and greater works than these shall he do; because I go unto My Father." John 14:12.

But death came by sin, and as Satan is the author of sin, so he has the power of death. A theology derived from heathenism may lead man to say that death is a friend; but every funeral train, and every bitter tear shed for the dead, proclaims that it is an enemy. The Bible so declares it, and tells of its destruction. Speaking of and to the brethren, it says: –

"For as in Adam all die, even so in Christ shall all be made alive. But every man in his own order; Christ the first fruits; afterwards they that are Christ's at His coming. Then cometh the end, when He shall have delivered up the kingdom to God, even the Father; when He shall have put down all rule and all authority and power. For He must reign, till he hath put all enemies under His feet. The last enemy that shall be destroyed is death." 1 Corinthians 15:22-26.

This tells us that the end is at the coming of the Lord, and that when that takes place all Christ's enemies will have been put under His feet, in accordance with the word of the Father to the Son, "Sit Thou at My right hand, until I make Thine enemies Thy footstool." Psalms 110:1. The last enemy that shall be destroyed is death. John in vision saw the dead small and great stand before God to be judged, at the last great day. Those, whose names were not in the Lamb's book of life, were cast into the lake of fire. "And death and hell were cast into the lake of fire. This is the second death." "Blessed and holy is he that hath part in the first resurrection; on such the second death hath no power." Revelation 20:14, 6.

The promise, "Thy seed shall possess the gate of his enemies," cannot be fulfilled except by victory over all enemies by all the seed. Christ has conquered; and we even now may give thanks to God, who "giveth us the victory through our Lord Jesus Christ;" but the battle is not yet over, even with us; there are very many who will be Overcomers at last, who have not yet enrolled themselves under the Lord's banner; and some who are now His may turn from the faith. The promise therefore embraces nothing less than the completion of the work of the Gospel, and the resurrection of all the righteous – the children of Abraham – and the putting on of immortality, at the second coming of Christ.

"If ye are Christ's, then are ye Abraham's seed, and heirs according to the promise." But the possession of the Holy Spirit is the distinguishing characteristic of those who are Christ's. "Now if any man have not the Spirit of Christ, he is none of His." But whoever has the Spirit has the surety of the resurrection, for "if the Spirit of Him that raised up Jesus from the dead dwell in you, He that raised up Christ from the dead shall also quicken your mortal bodies by His Spirit that dwelleth in you." Romans 8:11.

Thus we see that the hope of the promise made to Abraham was the resurrection of the dead, at the coming of the Lord. The hope of Christ's coming is the "blessed hope" that has cheered God's people since the days of Abraham, yea, even from the days of Adam. We often say that all the sacrifices pointed forward to Christ, and we almost as often fail to realize what that statement means. It cannot mean that they pointed forward to the time when forgiveness of sins should be obtained, for all the patriarchs had that as much as anyone has had it since the crucifixion of Christ. Abel and Enoch are especially mentioned, among a multitude of others, as having been justified by faith. The cross of Christ was as real a thing in the days of Abraham as it possibly can be to any who lives to day.

What then is the real significance of the statement that all the sacrifices from Abel down to the time of Christ pointed to Christ? It is this: It is clear that they showed the death of Christ; that needs no second statement. But what is the death of Christ without the resurrection? Paul preached only Christ and Him crucified; yet he most vigorously preached "Jesus and the resurrection." To preach Christ crucified is to preach Christ risen. But the resurrection of Christ has in it the resurrection of all that are His. The well instructed and believing Jew, therefore, showed, by the sacrifices that he offered, his faith in the promise to Abraham, which should be fulfilled at the coming of the Lord. The flesh and blood of the victim represented the body and blood of Christ, just the same as the bread and the wine of the Lord's supper, by which we, even as they did, "show the Lord's death till He come."

Chapter 12

The Promises to Israel - A General View

The Present Truth, July 23, 1896

"By faith Abraham, when he was called to go out into a place which he should after receive for an inheritance, obeyed; and he went out not knowing whither he went. By faith he sojourned in the land of promise as in a strange country, dwelling in tabernacles with Isaac and Jacob, the heirs with him of the same promise; for he looked for a city, which hath foundations, whose builder and maker is God. Through faith also Sara herself received strength to conceive seed and was delivered of a child when she was past age, because she judged Him faithful who had promised. Therefore sprang there even of one, and him as good as dead, so many as the stars of the sky in multitude, and as the sand which is by the sea shore innumerable. These all died in faith, not having received the promises, but having seen them afar off, and were persuaded of them and embraced them and confessed that they were strangers and pilgrims on the earth. For they that say such things declare plainly that they seek a country. And truly, if they had been mindful of that country from whence they came out, they might have had opportunity to return. But now they desire a better country, that is, an heavenly; wherefore God is not ashamed to be called their God; for He hath prepared for them a city." Hebrews 11:8-16.

All Heirs

The first thing that we note in this scripture is that all these were heirs. We have already learned that Abraham himself was to be no more than an heir in his lifetime, because he was to die before His seed returned from captivity. But Isaac and Jacob, his immediate descendants, were likewise heirs. The children were heirs with their father of the same promised inheritance.

Not only this, but there sprang from Abraham "so many as the stars of the sky in multitude, and as the sand which is by the sea-shore innumerable." These were also heirs of the same promise, for these also "all died in faith, not having received the promises, but having seen them afar off, and were persuaded of them, embraced them, and confessed that they were strangers and pilgrims on the earth."

Mark this, the vast host of Abraham's descendants "died in faith, not having received the promises." Note that it says "promises." It was not simply a part that they did not receive, but the whole. All the promises are in Christ only, who is the seed, and they could not be fulfilled to those who are His before they are to Him; and even He yet waits for His foes to be made His footstool.

In harmony with these words, that they died in faith, not having received the promises, but confessed that they were strangers and pilgrims on the earth, we have the words of King David hundreds of years after the deliverance from Egypt, "I am a stranger with Thee, and a sojourner, as all my fathers were." Psalm 39:12. And when at the height of his power he delivered the kingdom to his son Solomon, in the presence of all the people, he said, "For we are strangers before Thee, and sojourners, as were all our fathers; our days on the earth are as a shadow, and there is none abiding." 1 Chronicles 29:15.

The reason why this innumerable company did not receive the promised inheritance is stated in these words: "God having provided some better thing for us, that they without us should not be made perfect." The further particulars will be considered when we come to their times.

A City and Country

Abraham looked for a city, which hath foundations, whose builder, and maker is God.

The city with foundations is thus described in Revelation 21:10-14, 19: – "And he carried me away in the Spirit to a great and high mountain, and showed me that great city, the holy Jerusalem, descending out of heaven from God, having the glory of God; and her light was like unto a stone most precious, even like a jasper stone, clear as crystal; and had a wall great and high, and had twelve gates, and at the gates twelve angels, and names written thereon; which are the names of the twelve tribes of the children of Israel; on the east three gates; on the north three gates; on the south three gates; and on the west three gates. And the wall of the city had twelve foundations, and in them the names of the twelve apostles of the Lamb." "And the foundations of the wall of the city were garnished with all manner of precious stones."

That is a partial description of the city for which Abraham looked. His descendants also looked for the same city, for we read descriptions of it in the ancient prophets. They might have had a home on this earth, if they had desired. The land of the Chaldees was as fertile as the land of Palestine, and it would have sufficed for a temporal home for them as well as any other land. But neither one would satisfy them, for "now they desire a better country, that is an heavenly; wherefore God is not ashamed to be called their God; for He hath prepared for them a city."

This scripture kept in mind will guide us in all our subsequent study of the children of Israel. The true children of Abraham never looked for the fulfillment of the promise on this present earth, but in the earth made new.

Isaac an Illustration

This desire for a heavenly country made the true heirs very easy to get along with in temporal affairs, as is illustrated in the life of Isaac. He went to sojourn in the land of the Philistines, and sowed in that land, "and received in the same year an hundredfold; and the Lord blessed him. And the man waxed great, and went forward, and grew until he became very great; for he had possession of flocks, and possession of herds, and great store of servants; and the Philistines envied him . . . And Abimelech said unto Isaac, Go from us; for thou art much mightier than we. And Isaac departed thence, and pitched his tent in the valley of Gerar, and dwelt there." Genesis 26:12-17.

Although Isaac was mightier than the people in whose land he dwelt, he went from them at their request, even when he was prospering abundantly. He would not strive for the possession of an earthly estate.

The same spirit was manifested after he went to dwell in Gerar. The servants of Isaac dug anew the wells that had belonged to Abraham, and also dug in the valley and found living water. But the herdsmen of Gerar strove with them, saying, "The water is ours." So they went and dug another well; but the herdsmen of Gerar claimed that also. "And he removed from thence, and dug another well; and for that they strove not; and he called the name of it Rehoboth; and he said, For now the Lord hath made room for us, and we shall be fruitful in the land." Genesis 26:18-22.

"And the Lord appeared to him the same night, and said, I am the God of Abraham thy father; fear not for I am with thee, and will bless thee, and multiply thy seed for My servant Abraham's sake. And he builded an altar there, and called upon the name of the Lord, and pitched his tent there." Genesis 26:24, 25.

Isaac had the promise of a better country, that is, a heavenly, and therefore he would not strive for the possession of a few square miles of land on this sin-cursed earth. Why should he? It was not the inheritance that the Lord had promised him; and why should he fight for a part in the land wherein he was only a sojourner? True, he had to live, but he allowed the Lord to manage that for him. When driven from one place, he went to another, until at last he found quiet, and then he said, "The Lord hath made room for us." In this he showed the true spirit of Christ, "who, when He was reviled, reviled not again; when he suffered, He threatened not; but committed Himself (His cause) to Him that judgeth righteously." 1 Peter 2:23.

In this we have an example. If we are Christ's, then are we Abraham's seed, and heirs according to the promise. Therefore we shall follow the precepts of Christ. Here is one: "I say unto you, that ye resist not evil; but whosoever shall smite thee on thy right cheek, turn to him the other also. And if any man will sue thee at the law,[6] and take away thy coat, let him have thy cloak also" (Matthew 5:39, 40), are thought by many professed Christians to be fanciful, and altogether impractical. But they are designed for daily use. Christ practiced them, and we have an example in the case of Isaac.

"But we should lose everything that we have in the world, if we should do as the text says," we hear it said. Well, even then we should be in no worse circumstances than Christ the Lord was here on earth. But we are to remember, "your heavenly Father knoweth that ye have need of all these things." He, who cares for the sparrows, is able to care for those who commit their case to Him. We see that Isaac was prospered even though he did not "fight for his rights." The promise, which was made to the fathers, is also made to us, by very same God. "When they were but a few men in number; yea, very few, and strangers" in the land; "when they went from one nation to another, and from one kingdom to another people, He suffered no man to do them wrong; yea, He reproved kings for their sakes; saying, Touch not Mine anointed and do My prophets no harm." Psalm 105:12-15. That same God still cares for those who put their trust in Him.

The inheritance, which the Lord has promised to His people, the seed of Abraham, is not to be obtained by fighting, except with spiritual weapons – the armor of Christ – against the hosts of Satan. They who seek the country, which God has promised, declare that they are strangers and pilgrims on this earth. They cannot use the sword, even in self-defense, much less for conquest. The Lord is their defender. He says: "Cursed be the man that trusteth in man, and maketh flesh his arm, and whose heart departeth from the Lord. For he shall be like the heath in the desert, and shall not see when good cometh; but shall inhabit the parched places in the wilderness, in a salt land and not inhabited. Blessed is the man that trusteth in the Lord, and whose hope the Lord is. For he shall be as a tree planted by the waters, that spreadeth out her roots by the river, and shall not see when heat cometh, but her leaf shall be green." Jeremiah 27:5-8. He has not promised that all our wrongs shall be righted at once, or even in this life; but He doth not forget the cry of the poor, and He has said, "Vengeance is Mine; I will repay." Romans 7:19. "Therefore let them that suffer according to the will of God commit the keeping of their souls to Him in well-doing, as unto a faithful Creator." 1 Peter 4:19. We may do this in full confidence that "the Lord will maintain the cause of the afflicted, and the right of the poor." Psalm 140:12.

---

[6] (On page 64) The thoughtful reader will see in this an exhortation to avoid lawsuits. If one would sue you for your coat, it is better to settle it by giving him both your coat and your cloak than to go to law. This is practical wisdom. Lawsuits are like lotteries; a great deal of money is spent on them, and very little gained. Of course, it will be said, "If we don't defend our rights people will take away everything we have." And so it would be if God had no care for His people. But defending one's rights does not by any means always preserve them, as many a man has proved to his cost.

Esau's Infidelity

The case of Esau furnishes another incidental proof that the inheritance promised to Abraham and his seed was not a temporal one, to be enjoyed in this life, but eternal, to be shared in the life to come. The story is told in these words: –

"And Jacob sod pottage; and Esau came from the field, and he was faint: and Esau said to Jacob, Feed me, I pray thee, with that same red pottage; for I am faint; therefore was his name called Edom. And Jacob said, Sell me this day thy birthright. And Esau said, Behold I am at the point to die; and what profit shall this birthright do me? And Jacob said, Swear to me this day; and he swear unto him; and he sold his birthright unto Jacob. Then Jacob gave Esau bread and pottage of lentils; and he did eat and drink, and rose up, and went his way; thus Esau despised his birthright." Genesis 25:29-34.

In the Epistle to the Hebrews Esau is called a "profane person," because he sold his birthright. This shows that there was something besides mere foolishness in the transaction. One would say that it was childish to sell a birthright for a meal of victuals; but it was worse than childish; it was wicked. It showed that he was an infidel, feeling nothing but contempt for the promise of God to his father.

Notice these words of Esau's, when Jacob asked him to sell his birthright: "Behold, I am at the point to die; and what profit shall this birthright do me?" He had no hope beyond this present life, and looked no further. He did not feel sure of anything that he did not actually possess in this present time. No doubt he was very hungry. It is probable that he felt as if he were really at the point of death; but even the prospect of death made no difference with Abraham and many others. They died in faith, not having received the promises, but were persuaded of them, and embraced them. Esau, however, had no such faith. He had no belief in an inheritance beyond the grave. Whatever he was to have he wanted now. Thus it was that he sold his birthright.

The course of Jacob is not by any means to be commended. He acted the part of a supplanter, which was his natural disposition. His case is an illustration of a crude unintelligent faith. He believed that there was something to the promise of God, and he respected his father's faith, although as yet he really possessed none of it. He believed that the inheritance promised to the fathers would be bestowed, but he had so little spiritual knowledge that he supposed the gift of God might be purchased with money. We know that even Abraham thought at one time that he himself must fulfill the promise of God. So Jacob doubtless thought, as many do still, that "God helps those who help themselves." Afterwards he learned better, and was truly converted, and exercised as sincere faith as Abraham and Isaac. His case should be an encouragement to us, in that it shows what God can do with one who has a very unlovely disposition, provided he yields to Him.

The case of Esau is set thus forth before us as a warning: –

"Follow peace with all men, and holiness, without which no man shall see the Lord; looking diligently lest any man fail of the grace of God; lest any root of bitterness springing up trouble you, and thereby many be defiled; lest there be any fornicator, or profane person, as Esau, who for one morsel of meat sold his birthright. For ye know how that afterward, when he would have inherited the blessing, he was rejected; for he found no place of repentance, though he sought it carefully with tears." Hebrews 12:14-17.

Esau was not the only foolish and profane person there has been in the world. Thousands have done the same thing that he did, even while blaming him for his folly.

The Lord has called us all to share the glory of the inheritance, which he promised to Abraham. By the resurrection of Jesus Christ from the dead He has begotten us again to a living hope, "to an inheritance incorruptible, undefiled, and that fadeth not away, reserved in heaven for you, who are kept by the power of God through faith unto salvation ready to be revealed in the last time." 1 Peter 1:3-5. This inheritance of righteousness we are to have through the obedience of faith – obedience to God's holy law, the Ten Commandments. But when men learn that it requires the observance of the seventh day, the Sabbath kept by Abraham, Isaac, and Jacob, and all Israel, they shake their heads. "No," say they, "I cannot do that; I should like to, and I see that it is a duty; but if I should keep it I could not make a living. I should be thrown out of employment, and should starve together with my family."

That is just the way Esau reasoned. He was about to starve, or, at least, he thought that he was, and so he deliberately parted with his birthright for something to eat. But most men do not even wait until they are apparently at the point of death, before they sell their right to the inheritance for something to eat. They imagine dangers that do not exist. Men do not starve to death for serving the Lord. We are entirely dependent upon Him for our life under all circumstances, and if He keeps us when we are trampling on His law, He surely is as able to keep us when we are serving Him. The Saviour says that to worry over the future, fearing lest we should starve, is a characteristic of heathenism, and gives us this positive assurance, "Seek ye first the kingdom of God, and His righteousness, and all these things shall be added unto you." Matthew 6:21-23. The Psalmist says, "I have been young, and now am old; yet have I not seen the righteous forsaken nor his seed begging bread." Even though we should lose our lives for the sake of the truth of God, we should be in good company. See Hebrews 11:32-38. Let us beware of so lightly esteeming the rich promises of God that we shall part with an eternal inheritance for a morsel of bread, and when it is too late find that there is no place for repentance.

"My Father is rich in houses and lands,
He holds the wealth of the world in His hands;
Of rubies and diamonds, of silver and gold,
His coffers are full – He has riches untold.

Refrain:
"I'm the child of a King, the child of a King;
With Jesus, my Saviour, I'm the child of a King.

"My Father's own Son, the Saviour of men,
Once wandered o'er earth as the poorest of them;
But now He is reigning forever on high,
And will give me a home in heaven by and by.

"I once was an outcast stranger on earth,
A sinner by choice, and an alien by birth;
But I've been adopted, my name's written down –
An heir to a mansion, robe, and a crown.

"A tent or a cottage, why should I care?
They're building a palace for me over there!
Though exiled from home, yet still I may sing,
All glory to God, I'm the child of a King!"

Chapter 13

The Promises to Israel - Israel, A Prince of God

The Present Truth, July 30, 1896

JACOB had bought the birthright from Esau for a mess of pottage, and ha through deceit obtained the blessing of the first-born from his father. But not by such means may anybody obtain the inheritance, which God promised, to Abraham and his seed. It was made sure to Abraham through faith, and no one need think to inherit it through force or fraud. "No lie is of the truth." Truth can never be served by falsehood. The inheritance promised to Abraham and his seed was an inheritance of righteousness, and therefore it could not be gained by anything unrighteous. Earthly possessions are often gained and held by fraud, for a time, but not so the heavenly inheritance. The only thing that Jacob gained by his sharpness and deceit was to make his brother an everlasting enemy, and to be an exile from his father's house for more than twenty years, never again seeing his mother.

Yet God had said long before that Jacob should be the heir instead of his elder brother. The trouble with Jacob and his mother was that they thought they could work out the promises of God in their own way. It was the same kind of mistake that Abraham and Sarah had made. They could not wait for God to work out His own plans in His own way. Rebekah knew what God had said concerning Jacob. She heard Isaac promise the blessing to Esau and thought that unless she interfered; the Lord's plan would fail. She forgot that the inheritance was wholly in the Lord's power, and that no man could have anything to do with the disposing of it, except to reject it for himself. Even though Esau had obtained the blessing from his father, God would have brought His own plan about in good time.

God's Choice

So Jacob became doubly an exile. Not only was he a stranger in the earth, but he was a fugitive. But God did not forsake him. There was hope for him, sinful as he was. To some it may seem strange that God should thus prefer Jacob to Esau, for Jacob's character does not at that time seem any better than Esau's. Let us remember that God does not choose any man because of his good character. "For we also were aforetime foolish, disobedient, deceived, serving divers lusts and pleasures, living in malice and envy, hateful, hating one another. But when the kindness of God our Saviour, and His love toward man, appeared, not by works done in righteousness, which we did ourselves, but according to His mercy He saved us, through the washing of regeneration and renewing of the Holy Ghost, which He poured out upon us richly, through Jesus Christ our Saviour; that being justified by His grace, we might be made heirs according to the hope of eternal life." Titus 3:3-7 R.V.

God chooses men, not for what they are, but for what He can make of them. And there is no limit to what He can make of even the meanest and most depraved, if they are only willing, and believe His Word. A gift cannot be forced upon one, and therefore those who would receive God's righteousness, and the inheritance of righteousness, must be willing to receive it. "All things are possible to him that believeth." God can do "exceeding abundantly above all that we ask or think," if we but believe His Word, which effectually worketh in them that believe. The Pharisees were much more respectable people than the publicans and harlots, and yet Christ said that these would go into the kingdom of heaven before they did; and the reason was that the Pharisees trusted in themselves, and disbelieved God, while the publicans and harlots believed the Lord, and yielded themselves to Him. So with Jacob and Esau. Esau was an infidel. He regarded the word of God with contempt. Jacob was no better by nature, but he believed the promise of God, which is able to make the believer a partaker of the Divine nature.

God chose Jacob in the same way that He does everybody else. "Blessed be the God and Father of our Lord Jesus Christ, who hath blessed us with all spiritual blessings in heavenly places in Christ; according as He hath chosen us in Him before the foundation of the world, that we should be holy and without blame before Him in love." Ephesians 1:3, 4. We are chosen in Christ. And since all things were created in Christ, and in Him all things consist, it is evident that we are not required to get ourselves into Christ, but only to acknowledge Him, and abide in Him by faith. There was no more partiality in the choice of Jacob before he was born than there is in the choice of all others. The choice is not arbitrary, but in Christ, and if none rejected and spurned Christ, none would be lost.

> *"How rich the grace! The gift how free!*
> *'Tis only 'ask' – it shall be given;*
> *'Tis only 'knock' and thou shalt see*
> *The opening door that leads to heaven.*
> *O then arise, and take the good,*
> *So full and freely proffered thee,*
> *Remembering that it cost the blood*
> *Of Him who died on Calvary."*

Jacob's First Lesson

While Jacob believed the promise of God sufficiently to enable him to endeavor to secure its fulfillment by his own efforts, he did not understand its nature well enough to know that God alone could fulfill it through righteousness. So the Lord began to instruct him. Jacob was on his lonely way to Syria, fleeing from the wrath of his offended brother, "and he lighted upon a certain place, and tarried there all night, because the sun was set; and he took one of the stones[7] of that place, and put it under his head, and lay down in that place to sleep. "And he dreamed, and behold a ladder set up on the earth, and the top of it reached to heaven; and behold the angels of God ascending and descending on it. And, behold, the Lord stood above it, and said, I am the Lord, the God of Abraham thy father, and the God of Isaac; the land whereon thou liest, to the will I give it, and to thy seed; and thy seed shall be as the dust of the earth, and thou shalt spread abroad to the west, and to the east, and to the north, and to the south; and in thee and in thy seed shall all the families of the earth be blessed. And, behold, I am with thee, and will keep thee whithersoever thou goest, and will bring thee again into this land; for I will not leave thee until I have done that which I have spoken to thee of. And Jacob awaked out of his sleep, and he said, Surely the Lord is in this place; and I knew it not. And he was afraid, and said, How dreadful is this place! This is none other but the house of God, and this is the gate of heaven." Genesis 28:11-17, R.V.

This was a great lesson for Jacob. Before this his ideas of God had been very crude. He had supposed that God was confined to one place. But now that God had appeared to him, he began to realize that "God is a Spirit; and they that worship Him must worship Him in Spirit and in truth." John 4:24. He began to realize what Jesus told the Samaritan woman long afterwards that the worship of God does not depend upon any place, but upon the soul's reaching out and finding Him, wherever it is.

Moreover, Jacob began to learn that the inheritance that God had promised to his fathers, and which he had thought to get by a sharp bargain, was something to be gained in an entirely different manner. How much of the lesson he grasped at this time, we cannot tell; but we know that in this revelation God proclaimed the Gospel to him.

---

[7] I beg the pardon of the intelligent reader for referring in this connection to the stone in the coronation chair in Westminster Abbey, which is by some supposed to be the stone on which Jacob slept, and which, by its position in the coronation chair, is supposed to identify England with Israel, and to make the Anglo-Saxon race heirs of the promise to Jacob. Saying nothing of the unfounded and unprovable assertion that the stone in question is the one on which Jacob slept, the absurdity of the idea that the possession of it could make any people heirs of the promises to Israel is paralleled only by the medieval superstition that a man could inherit the sanity of a departed saint by wearing his old shirt.

All this was indicated by that which Jacob saw, as well as by that which he heard. There was a ladder set up on the earth, reaching up to heaven, connecting God with man. Jesus Christ, the only begotten Son of God, is the connecting link between heaven and earth, between God and man. The ladder connecting heaven with earth, upon which the angels of God were ascending and descending, was a representation of that which Christ said to Nathanael, that true Israelite: "Hereafter ye shall see heaven open, and the angels of God ascending and descending upon the Son of man." John 1:51. The way to heaven is the way of the cross, and this is that which was indicated to Jacob that night. Not by self-assertion, but by self-denial, are the inheritance and the blessing to be gained. "He that will lose his life," and all that life contains, "shall save it."

We have learned that God preached the Gospel to Abraham in the words, "In thee shall all the families of the earth be blessed." Therefore, we are sure that when the Lord said to Jacob, "In thee and in thy seed shall all the families of the earth be blessed," He was preaching the same Gospel.

Connected with this statement, was the promise of land, and of an innumerable posterity. The promise made to Jacob was identical with that made to Abraham. The blessing to come through Jacob and his seed was identical with that to come through Abraham and his seed. The seed is the same, namely, Christ and those who are His through the Spirit; and the blessing comes through the cross of Christ.

Applying the Lesson

Of Jacob's sojourn in the land of Syria, we need not speak particularly. In the twenty years that he served his uncle Laban, he had ample opportunity to learn that deception and sharp dealing do not profit. The course that he had pursued came back upon himself; but God was with him, and prospered him. Jacob seems to have laid to heart the lesson that had been given him, for we see very little indication of his natural disposition to overreach in his dealing with his uncle. He seems to have trusted his case quite fully to the Lord, and to have submitted to all manner of ill treatment without retaliation. In his reply to Laban's charge that he had stolen, Jacob said: –

"This twenty years have I been with thee; thy ewes and thy she-goats have not cast their young, and the rams of thy flock have I not eaten. That which was torn of beasts, I brought not unto thee; I bare the loss of it; of my hand didst thou require it, whether stolen by day, or stolen by night. Thus I was; in the day the drought consumed me, and the frost by night; and my sleep departed from mine eyes. Thus have I been twenty years in thine house; I served thee fourteen years for thy two daughters, and six years for thy cattle; and thou hast changed my wages ten times. Except the God of my father, the God of Abraham, and the fear of Isaac, had been with me; surely thou hadst sent me away now empty. God hath seen mine affliction and the labor of my hands, and rebuked thee yesternight." Genesis 31:38-42.

This was a calm and dignified statement, and showed that the fear of Isaac, and the same spirit, had actuated him. The preaching of the Gospel had not been in vain in Jacob's case; a great change had come over him.

Let it be noted here that Jacob gained nothing whatever from the birthright which he had so shrewdly bought from his brother. His property was due to the direct blessing of God. And in this connection we may recall the fact that Isaac's blessing was to the effect that God would bless him. The inheritance was not one, which could be transmitted from father to son, as ordinary inheritances, but one, which must be to each one by the direct, personal promise and blessing of God.

To be "Abraham's seed, and heirs according to the promise," we must be Christ's; but if we are Christ's, and joint-heirs with Him, we are "heirs of God."

The Final Test

But Jacob had made a grievous failure in his earlier life, and so God as a faithful Teacher, must necessarily bring him over the same ground again. He had thought to win by guile: he must completely learn that "this is the victory that overcometh the world, even our faith." 1 John 5:4.

When Rebecca proposed to send Jacob away from home, because Esau sought to kill him, she said, "Now therefore, my son obey my voice; and arise, flee thou to Laban my brother to Haran; and tarry with him a few days, until thy brother's fury turn away; until thy brother's anger turn from thee, and he forget that which thou hast done to him; then will I send and fetch thee from thence." Genesis 27:43-45. But she did not know the nature of Esau. He was bitter and unrelenting. "Thus saith the Lord. For three transgressions of Edom, and for four, I will not turn away the punishment thereof; because he did pursue his brother with the sword, and did cast off all pity, and his anger did tear perpetually, and he kept his wrath for ever." Amos 1:11. (Edom is Esau. See Genesis 25:30; 36:1.) Here we see that, bad as Jacob's natural disposition was, Esau's character was most despicable.

Although twenty years had passed, Esau's anger was as fresh as ever. When Jacob sent messengers before him to Esau, to speak peaceably to him, and to conciliate him, they brought back the news that Esau was coming with four hundred men. Jacob could not hope to make any stand against these trained warriors; but he had learned to trust in the Lord, and so we find him pleading the promises in this manner: –

"O God of my father Abraham, and God of my father Isaac, the Lord which saidst unto me, Return unto thy country, and to thy kindred, and I will deal well with thee; I am not worthy of the least of all the mercies, and of all the truth which Thou hast showed unto Thy servant; for with my staff I passed over this Jordan; and now I am become two bands. Deliver me, I pray Thee, from the hand of my brother, from the hand of Esau; for I fear him, lest he will come and smite me, and the mother with the children. And Thou saidst, I will surely do thee good, and make thy seed as the sand of the sea, which cannot be numbered for multitude." Genesis 32:9-12.

Jacob had once tried to get the better of his brother by fraud. He had thought that thus he could become an heir of the promise of God. Now he had learned that it could be gained only by faith, and he betook himself to prayer in order to be delivered from the wrath of his brother. Having made the best possible disposition of his family and flocks, he remained alone to continue his prayer to God. He realized that he was not worthy of anything, and that if left to his deserts he should perish, and he felt that he must still further cast himself upon the mercy of God.

"And Jacob was left alone; and there wrestled a man with him until the breaking of the day. And when He saw that He prevailed not against him, He touched the hollow of his thigh; and the hollow of Jacob's thigh was out of joint, as he wrestled with Him. And He said, Let Me go, for the day breaketh. And he said, I will not let Thee go, except Thou bless me. And He said unto him, What is thy name? And he said, Jacob. And He said, Thy name shall be called no more Jacob, but Israel; for as a prince hast thou power with God and with man, and hast prevailed. And Jacob asked Him and said, Tell me, I pray Thee, Thy name. And He said, Wherefore is it that thou dost ask after My name? And He blessed him there. And Jacob called the name of the place Peniel; for I have seen God face to face, and my life is preserved." Genesis 32:24-30.

People often speak of wrestling with God in prayer, as Jacob did. There is no evidence that Jacob knew that it was the Lord that was wrestling with him, until the morning broke, and his thigh was put out of joint by the touch of his antagonist. Indeed, we very well know that no man would have the hardihood to engage in a contest of strength with the Lord, if he knew Him to be the Lord. The angel appeared to him as a man, and Jacob doubtless thought that a robber was attacking him. We can well conceive that Jacob was in sore trouble all night. The time was fast approaching when he must face his angry brother, and he dared not meet him without the full assurance that all was right between himself and God. He must know that he was pardoned for his past wicked course. Yet the hours that he had designed to spend in communing with God were being spent in wrestling with a supposed enemy. So we may be sure that while his strength was all engaged in resisting his antagonist, his heart was uplifted to God in bitter anguish. The suspense and anxiety of that night must have been terrible.

Jacob was a man of great physical power and endurance. Watching the flocks night and day for years had demonstrated this, and had, at the same time hardened his frame. So he continued the struggle, and held his ground all night. But it was not thus that he gained the victory.

We read that "by his strength he had power with God; yea, he had power, over the angel, and prevailed; he wept, and made supplication unto Him; he found Him in Bethel, and there He spake with us; even the Lord of hosts; the Lord is His memorial." Hosea 12:3-5.

By his power Jacob prevailed with God, but it was not by his power and skill as a wrestler. His strength was in his weakness, as we shall see. Notice that the first intimation that Jacob had that his opponent was other than an ordinary man was when his thigh was put out of joint by the Divine touch. That revealed in an instant who his supposed enemy was. It was no human touch, but the hand of the Lord that he felt. What did he then do? What could a man do in his condition? Picture to yourself a man wrestling, where so much depends upon the strength of his legs, and having one of them suddenly dislocated. Even if he were merely walking, or simply standing still, and one of his legs should suddenly be put out of joint, he would instantly fall to the ground. Much more would he fall if he were wrestling. Such would have been the case with Jacob, if he had not at once thrown himself upon the Lord, with a firm grasp. He would most naturally grasp the nearest object for support; but the knowledge that here was the One whom he had been longing to meet, would make his grasp more than an involuntary action. His opportunity had come, and he would not let it slip.

That Jacob did at once cease wrestling, and cling to the Lord, is not only most apparent from the fact that he could do nothing else, but also from the words of the Lord, "Let Me go." "No," said Jacob. "I will not let Thee go, except Thou bless me." It was a case of life and death. His life and salvation depended upon his holding on to the Lord. The words, "Let Me go," were only to test him, for the Lord does not willingly leave any man. But Jacob was determined to find a blessing indeed, and he prevailed. It was by his strength that he prevailed, but it was by the strength of faith. "When I am weak, then am I strong." In that hour Jacob fully learned the lesson that the blessing and the inheritance come not by might, nor by strength, but by the Spirit of the Lord.

A New Name

The new name was a pledge to Jacob that he was accepted. It did not confer anything upon him, but was a token of what he had already gained. Resting upon God, he had ceased from his own works, so that he was no more the supplanter, seeking to further his own ends, but the prince of God, who had fought the good fight of faith, and had laid hold on eternal life. As Israel he was henceforth to be known.

Now he could go forth to meet his brother. He who has seen God face to face has no need to fear the face of man. He, who has power with God, will most certainly prevail with men. This is the secret of power.

Let the servant of God know that if he would have power with men he must first be able to prevail with God. He must know the Lord, and have talked with Him face to face. To such the Lord says, "I will give you a mouth and wisdom, which all your adversaries shall not be able to gainsay nor resist." Luke 21:15. Stephen knew the Lord, and held communion with Him, and the haters of truth "were not able to resist the wisdom and the Spirit by which he spake." What then must have been his power with those whose hearts were open to receive the truth?

In this story of Jacob, we learn anew how the inheritance, which God promised to Abraham and to his seed, is to be obtained. It is by faith alone. Repentance and faith are the only means of deliverance. By no other means could he hope to have any share in the inheritance. His whole salvation lay in his dependence upon the promise of God. It was thus that he was fully made partaker of the Divine nature.

Who Are Israelites?

We learn also who Israel is. The name was given to Jacob in token of the victory, which he had gained, by faith. It did not bestow any grace upon him, but was a token of grace already possessed. So it will be bestowed upon all those who through faith overcome, and upon no others. To be called an Israelite does not add anything to anybody. It is not the name that brings the blessing, but the blessing that brings the name. As Jacob did not possess the name by nature, so nobody else can. The true Israelite is he in whom is no guile. Such ones alone please God; but "without faith it is impossible to please Him." So the Israelite is only the one who has personal faith in the Lord. "They are not all Israel, which are of Israel;" "but the children of the promise are counted for the seed." Romans 9:6, 8.

Let every one who would fain be known as an Israelite consider how Jacob received the name, and realize that only so can it be worthily carried by anyone. Christ, as the promised seed, had to go through the same struggle. He fought and won through His trust in the word of the Father, and so He is of right the King of Israel. Only Israelites will share the kingdom with Him; for Israelites are Overcomers, and the promise is, "To him that overcometh will I grant to sit with Me in My Throne, even as I also overcame, and am set down with My Father in His Throne." Revelation 3:21.

Chapter 14

The Promises to Israel - Israel in Egypt

The Present Truth, August 6, 1896

It will be remembered that when God made the covenant with Abraham, He told him that he himself should die without having received the inheritance, and that his descendants should be oppressed and afflicted in a strange land, and that afterwards, in the fourth generation, they should come into the promised land.

"And He gave him the covenant of circumcision; and so Abraham begat Isaac, and circumcised him the eighth day; and Isaac begat Jacob; and Jacob begat the twelve patriarchs. And the patriarchs, moved with envy, sold Joseph into Egypt; but God was with him, and delivered him out of all his afflictions, and gave him favor and wisdom in the sight of Pharaoh king of Egypt; and he made him governor over Egypt and all his house. . . Then sent Joseph, and called his father Jacob to him, and all his kindred, threescore and fifteen souls. So Jacob went down into Egypt, and died, he, and our fathers, and were carried over into Sychem, and laid in the sepulcher that Abraham had bought for a sum of money of the sons of Emmor, the father of Sychem. But when the time of the promise drew nigh, which God had sworn to Abraham, the people grew and multiplied in Egypt, till another king arose who knew not Joseph. The same dealt subtly with our fathers, so that they cast out their young children, to the end they might not live." Acts 7:8-19.

The king "who knew not Joseph," was one of another dynasty, a people from the East which conquered Egypt.

"For thus saith the Lord, Ye were sold for naught, and ye shall be redeemed without money. For thus saith the Lord God, My people went down at the first into Egypt to sojourn there; and the Assyrian oppressed them without cause. Now, therefore, what do I here saith the Lord, seeing that My people is taken away for naught? They that rule over them do howl; saith the Lord; and My name continually all the day is blasphemed. Therefore My people shall know My name; therefore they shall know in that day that am He that doth speak; behold, it is I." Isaiah 52:3-6. R.V.

What Egypt Signifies

From the text last quoted we learn that the oppression of Israel in Egypt was opposition and blasphemy against God; that contempt for their God and their religion had a great deal to do with its rigor. We learn also that their deliverance from Egypt was identical with the deliverance, which comes to all who are "sold under sin." "Ye have sold yourselves for naught; and ye shall be redeemed without money." "Knowing that ye were redeemed, not with corruptible things, with silver or gold, from your vain manner of life handed down from your fathers; but with precious blood, as of a lamb without blemish and without spot, even the blood of Christ." 1 Peter 1:18, 19 R.V. A brief study therefore of what Egypt stands for in the Bible, and of the real condition of the Israelites while there, will enable us to understand what was involved in their deliverance.

Egyptian Idolatry

Of all the idolatry of ancient times, that of Egypt was undoubtedly the grossest and most complete. The number of the gods of Egypt was almost beyond computation. "Every town in Egypt had its sacred animal, or fetish, and every town its local divinities." – *Encyc. Brit.* But "the sun was the kernel of the State Religion. In various forms he stood at the head of each hierarchy." – 'Sun Images and the Sun of Righteousness', in *O. T. Student*, Jan. 1886. "Ra, the sun, is usually represented as a hawk-headed man, occasionally as a man, in both cases generally bearing on his head the solar disc."

The union of Church and State was perfect in Egypt, the two being really identical. This is set forth in *Religions of the Ancient World* (Rawlinson) page 20: –

Ra was the Egyptian sun god, and was especially worshipped at Heliopolis. Obelisks, according to some, represented his rays, and were always, or usually, erected in his honor. . . . The kings for the most part considered Ra their special patron and protector; may, they went so far as to identify themselves with him; to use his titles as their own, and to adopt his name as the ordinary prefix to their own names and titles. This is believed by many to have been the origin of the word Pharaoh, which was, it is thought, the Hebrew rendering of Ph' Ra – the sun.

Besides the sun and moon, named Osiris and Isis, "the Egyptians worshipped a great number of beasts, as the ox, the dog, the wolf, the hawk, the crocodile, the ibis, the cat, etc." "Of all these animals, the bull Apis, called Epapris by the Greeks, was the most famous. Magnificent temples were erected to him while he lived, and still greater after his death. Egypt then went into general mourning. His obsequies were solemnized with such pomp as is hardly credible. In the reign of Ptolemy Lagus, the bull Apis dying of old age, the funeral pomp, besides the ordinary expenses, amounted to upwards of fifty thousand French crowns. After the last honors had been paid to the deceased, the next care was to provide him a successor, and all Egypt was sought through for that purpose. He was known by certain signs which distinguished him from all other animals of that species: upon his forehead was to be a white spot, in form of a crescent; on his back, the figure of an eagle; upon his tongue, that of a beetle. As soon as he was found, mourning gave way to joy; and nothing was heard in all parts of Egypt but festivals and rejoicings. The new god was brought to Memphis to take possession of his dignity, and there installed with a great number of ceremonies." *Rollin's Ancient History,* Book 1, part 2, chap. 2, sec. 1.

These ceremonies, it is hardly necessary to say, were of an obscene character; for sun-worship when carried out to its full was nothing else but the practice of vice as a religious duty.

So strong a hold had superstition upon the Egyptians that they worshipped even leeks and onions. In this we are reminded that superstition and abominable idolatry are not necessarily connected with a low order of intellect, for the ancient Egyptians cultivated the arts and sciences to a high degree. The practice of idolatry did, however, cause them to fall from their former high position.

The very name Egypt is a synonym for wickedness and opposition to the religion of Jesus Christ, and is coupled with Sodom. Of the Lord's "two witnesses," it is said that "their dead bodies shall lie in the street of that great city, which spiritually is called Sodom and Egypt, where also our Lord was crucified." Revelation 11:8. That the Israelites in Egypt took part in its wickedness and idolatry, and that they were prevented by force from serving the Lord, is evident from several texts of Scripture.

In the first place, when Moses was sent to deliver Israel, his message to Pharaoh was, "Thus saith the Lord, Israel is My son, even My firstborn; and I say unto thee, Let My son go, that he may serve Me." Exodus 4:22, 23. The object of the deliverance from Egypt was that Israel might serve the Lord, evidence that they were not serving Him there.

So again we read, "He remembered His holy promise, and Abraham His servant. And He brought forth His people with joy, and His chosen with gladness; and gave them the lands of the heathen; and they inherited the labor of the people; that they might observe His statutes, and keep His laws." Psalm 105:42-45.

But strongest of all the evidence that Israel had joined in the idolatry of Egypt is found in the reproach for their not forsaking it. "Thus saith the Lord God: In the day when I chose Israel, and lifted up Mine hand unto the seed of the house of Jacob, and made Myself known unto them in the land of Egypt . . . then said I unto them, Cast ye away every man the abominations of his eyes, and defile not yourselves with the idols of Egypt; I am the Lord your God. But they rebelled against Me, and would not hearken unto Me; they did not every man cast away the abominations of their eyes, neither did they forsake the idols of Egypt." Ezekiel 20:5-8.

Still in Egyptian Bondage

Neither has it been done unto this day. The darkness that overspread Egypt at the time of the plagues was no denser than the darkness that Egypt has cast over the whole earth. That physical darkness was but a vivid representation of the moral darkness into which the people had fallen, and of that which has since come from that wicked country. The story of the apostasy in the Christian church is but the record of the errors, which were brought from Egypt.

Near the close of the second century of the Christian era, a new system of philosophy sprung up in Egypt. "This philosophy was adopted by such of the learned at Alexandria as wished to be accounted Christians, and yet to retain the name, the garb, and the rank of philosophers. In particular, all those who in this century presided in the schools of the Christians at Alexandria – Athenagoras, Pantaenus, and Clemens Alexandrinus – are said to have approved of it. These men were persuaded that true philosophy, the great and most salutary gift of God, lay in scattered fragments among all the sects of philosophers; and, therefore, that it was the duty of every wise man, and especially of a Christian teacher, to collect these fragments from all quarters, and to use them for the defense of religion and the confutation of impiety."

"This mode of philosophizing received some modification, when Ammonius Saccas, at the close of the century, opened a school at Alexandria, and laid the foundation of the sect called the New Platonic. This man was born and educated a Christian, and perhaps made pretensions to Christianity all his life. Being possessed of great fecundity of genius as well as eloquence, he undertook to bring all systems of philosophy and religion into harmony, or attempted to teach a philosophy by which all philosophers, and the men of all religions, the Christian not excepted, might unite together and have fellowship. And here, especially, lies the difference between this new sect and the eclectic philosophy, which had before flourished in Egypt. For the eclectics held that there was a mixture of good and bad, true and false, in all the systems; and therefore they selected out of all, what appeared to them consonant with reason, and rejected the rest. But Ammonius held that all sects professed one and the same system of truth, with only some difference in the mode of stating it, and some minute difference in their conceptions; so that by means of suitable explanations they might with little difficulty be brought into one body. He, moreover, held this new and singular principle, that the popular religions, and likewise the Christian, must be understood and explained according to the common philosophy." – Mosheim's *Eccl. Hist.*, Cent. 2, part, ch. 1, Secs. 6, 7.

"Clement of Alexandria has been mentioned as one of the Christian teachers who was devoted to this philosophy. Mosheim tells us that "Clement is to be ranked among the first and principal Christian defenders and teachers of philosophic science, indeed that he may even be placed at the head of those who devoted themselves to the cultivation of philosophy with an ardor that knew no bounds, and were so blind and misguided as to engage in the hopeless attempt of producing an accommodation between the principles of philosophic science and those of the Christian religion." – Mosheim's *Commentaries*, Cent. 2, Section 25, Note 2.

Let it be remembered that the only philosophy was pagan philosophy, and it will be very easy to imagine the inevitable results of such devotion to it on the part of those who were the teachers in the Christian church. Mosheim tells us that "by the Christian disciples of Ammonius, and more particularly by Origen, who in the succeeding century (the third) attained to a degree of eminence scarcely credible, the doctrines which they had derived from their master were sedulously instilled into the minds of the youth with whose education they were entrusted, and by the efforts of these again, who were subsequently for the most part called to the ministry, the love of philosophy became pretty generally diffused throughout a considerable portion of the church." Origen was at the head of the "Catechetical School" or theological seminary of Alexandria, which was the seat of learning. He stood at the head of the interpreters of the Bible in that century, and was closely copied by the youth who flocked to that seminary. "Half the sermons of the day," says Farrar, "were borrowed, consciously or unconsciously, directly or indirectly, from the thoughts and methods of Origen" – *Lives of the Fathers*, chap. 16, sec. 8.

Origen's skill as an "interpreter" of the Bible was due to his skill as a philosopher, which consisted in making evident things that had no existence. The Bible was used by him and his companions, as were the writings of the philosophers, as a thing upon which to display their mental skill. To read a simple statement, and to believe it as it reads, and to set plain truth before the minds of students, leading the minds of the people to the Word of God, was considered too childish, and altogether beneath the dignity of a great teacher. Anybody could do that, they thought. Their work was to seem to draw from the Sacred Word something, which the common people would never find there, for the reason that it was not there, but was the invention of their own minds.

In order to keep their prestige as deep scholars and great teachers, they taught the people that the Bible does not mean what it says, and that whoever follows the plain letter of Scripture will certainly be led astray; and that it could be explained only by those who had exercised their faculties by the study of philosophy. Thus they effectually took the Bible from the hands of the common people. With the Bible practically out of their hands, there was no way by which the people could distinguish between Christianity and paganism. The result was not only that those who already professed Christianity were in a large measure corrupted, but that the heathen came into the church without changing their principles or practices. "It came to pass that the greater part of these Platonists, upon comparing the Christian religion with the system of

Ammonius, were led to imagine that nothing could be more easy than a transition from the one to the other, and, to the great detriment of the Christian cause, were induced to embrace Christianity without feeling it necessary to abandon scarcely any of their former principles."

Thus it came to pass that "nearly all those corruptions by which, in the second and subsequent centuries, Christianity was disfigured, and its pristine simplicity and innocence almost wholly effaced, had their origin in Egypt, and were thence communicated to the other churches." "Observing that in Egypt, as well as in other countries, the heathen worshipers, in addition to their public religious ceremonies, to which everyone was admitted without distinction, had certain secret and most sacred rites, to which they gave the name of mysteries, and at the celebration of which none except persons of the most approved faith and discretion were permitted to be present; the Alexandrian Christians first, and after them others, were beguiled into a notion that they could not do better than make the Christian discipline accommodate itself to this model. The multitude professing Christianity were therefore divided by them into the profane, or those who were not as yet admitted to the mysteries, and the initiated, or faithful and perfect. . . . From this constitution of things it came to pass, not only that many terms and phrases made use of in the heathen mysteries were transferred and applied to different parts of the Christian worship, particularly to the sacraments of baptism and the Lord's Supper, but that, in not a few instances, the sacred rites of the church were contaminated by the introduction of various pagan forms and ceremonies."

The Call to Come Out of Egypt

It is not necessary to enumerate the various false doctrines and practices that were thus introduced into the church. Suffice it to say that there was not a thing that was not corrupted, and there was scarcely a heathen dogma or ceremony that was not either adopted or to a greater or less extent copied. The light of God's Word being thus obscured, the "Dark Ages" necessarily resulted, continuing until at the time of the Reformation the Bible was once more put into the hands of the people, for them to read for themselves.

The Reformation, however, did not complete the work. A true reformation never ends; but when it has corrected the abuse, which first called it forth, it must go on with the good work. But those who came after the Reformers were not filled with the same spirit, and were content to believe no more than the Reformers had believed. Consequently, the same story was repeated. The word of men came to be received as the word of God, and therefore errors still remained in the church. To day the current is setting strongly downward, as the result of the widespread acceptance of the doctrine of Evolution, and of the influence of the so-called "Higher Criticism." Several years ago the historian Merivale, Dean of Ely, said, "Paganism was assimilated, not extirpated, and Christendom has suffered from it more or less ever since." – *Epochs of Church History*, p. 169.

It may easily be seen, from this brief outline, that the darkness that at any time covers the earth, and the gross darkness that envelops the people, is the darkness of Egypt. It was not merely from physical bondage that God set Himself to deliver His people, but from the spiritual darkness that was far worse. And since this darkness still remains to a great extent, that work of deliverance is still going on. Ancient Israel "in their hearts turned back again into Egypt." Throughout their whole history they were warned against Egypt, evidence that they were never fully free for any length of time from its blighting influence. Christ came to earth to deliver men from every species of bondage, and to that end He placed Himself to the fullest extent in man's position. There was therefore a deep significance in His going down into Egypt, that it might be fulfilled which was spoken by the Lord through the prophet, "Out of Egypt have I called my Son." Since Christ was called out of Egypt, all who are Christ's, that is, all the seed of Abraham, must likewise be called out of Egypt. This is the work of the Gospel.

Chapter 15

The Promises to Israel - The Time of the Promise

The Present Truth, August 13, 1896

WE have Israel in Egypt, and we know something of what that signifies. The bondage, as well as the deliverance, had been foretold to Abraham when the covenant was made with him; and that covenant had been confirmed by an oath of God.

Now let us turn again to some of the words spoken by Stephen when, full of the Holy Ghost, he stood before the Jewish Council. He began his discourse by a positive proof that the resurrection was necessary to the fulfillment of the promise to Abraham; for having repeated the promise, he declared that Abraham had not so much as a footbreadth of the land that was promised, although God had said that both he and his seed should possess it.

Since Abraham died without inheriting it, as did also a vast number of his descendants even those who, like him, had faith, the conclusion was inevitable that the fulfillment could be only through the resurrection. The only reason why so many of the Jews rejected the Gospel was that they persisted in ignoring the plain evidence of the Scriptures, that the promise to Abraham was not temporal, but eternal. Even so at the present time the belief that the promises to Israel convey an earthly and temporal inheritance, is incompatible with a full belief in Christ.

Stephen next recalled the word of the Lord to Abraham, that his seed should sojourn in a strange land, and be afflicted, and afterwards delivered. Then he said, "But when the time of the promise drew nigh, which God had sworn to Abraham, the people grew and multiplied in Egypt." Acts 7:17. Then followed the oppression, and the birth of Moses. What is meant by the drawing near of the time of the promise, which God had sworn to Abraham? A brief review of some of the Scriptures already studied will make this question very clear.

In the account of the making of the covenant with Abraham we read the words of the Lord to him, "I am the Lord that brought thee out of Ur of the Chaldees, to give thee this land to inherit it." Then follow the details of the making of the covenant, and then the words, "Know of a surety that thy seed shall be a stranger in a land that is not theirs, and shall serve them; and they shall afflict them four hundred years; and also that nation whom they shall serve, will I judge; and afterwards they shall come out with great substance. And thou shalt go to thy fathers in peace; thou shalt be buried in a good old age. But in the fourth generation they shall come hither again; for the iniquity of the Amorites is not yet full." Genesis 15:13-16.

That covenant was afterwards sealed with circumcision, and then when Abraham had shown his faith by the offering up of Isaac, the Lord added His oath to the promise, saying, "By Myself have I sworn, saith the Lord, for because thou hast done this thing, and hast not withheld thy son, thine only son; that in blessing I will bless thee, and in multiplying I will multiply thy seed as the stars of heaven, and as the sand which is upon the sea shore; and thy seed shall possess the gate of his enemies." Genesis 22:16, 17.

This is the only promise concerning which God swore to Abraham. It was a confirmation of the original promise. But, as we have already seen, it involved nothing less than the resurrection of the dead through Christ, who is the seed. "The last enemy that shall be destroyed is death," that the words of God by the prophet may be fulfilled, "I will ransom them from the power of the grave; I will redeem them from death; O death, I will be thy plagues; O grave, I will be thy destruction." Hosea 13:14. Not till then will the promise be fulfilled, which God swore to Abraham, for not till then will all his seed possess the gate of his enemies.

To the weeping mothers who mourned the loss of their children that had been slain by the command of Herod, the Lord said, "Refrain thy voice from weeping, and thine eyes from tears; for thy work shall be rewarded, saith the Lord; and they shall come again from the land of the enemy. And there is hope in thine end, saith the Lord, that thy children shall come again to their own border." Jeremiah 31:16, 17. Only through the resurrection can the seed of Abraham, Isaac, and Jacob come again to their own border. This was indicated to Abraham when he was told that before his seed should possess the land they should be afflicted in a strange land, and that he should die; "but in the fourth generation they shall come hither again."

There can therefore be no doubt but that God designed that the return of Israel from Egyptian bondage should be the time of the resurrection and restoration of all things. The time of the promise drew nigh. How long it would have been after the going forth from Egypt, before the full restoration would have taken place, we have no means of knowing. There was of course much to be done in the way of warning the people of the earth; and the time depended upon the faithfulness of the children of Israel. We need not speculate upon how all things would have been fulfilled, since the Israelites were not faithful. All that concerns us now is the fact that the deliverance from Egypt meant nothing less than the complete deliverance of all God's people from the bondage of sin and death, and the restoration of all things as they were in the beginning.

Chapter 16

The Promises to Israel - The Reproach of Christ

The Present Truth, August 20, 1896

"By faith Moses, when he was come to years, refused to be called the son of Pharaoh's daughter; choosing rather to suffer affliction with the people of God, than to enjoy the pleasures of sin for a season; esteeming the reproach of Christ greater riches than the treasures in Egypt." Hebrews 11:24, 25.

Here we are told most positively that the treasures of Egypt were the pleasures of sin; that refusing the treasures of Egypt was to refuse to live in sin; that to cast in one's lot with the Israelites, was to suffer the reproach of Christ. This demonstrates that Christ was the real leader of that people, and that that which had been promised them, and to share which they were to be delivered from Egypt, was to be theirs only through Him, and that, too, through His reproach. Now the reproach of Christ is the cross. Thus we are again brought face to face with the fact that the seed of Abraham, – the true Israel, – are those who are Christ's through faith in His blood.

Very few stop to think what it was that Moses gave up for the sake of Christ. He was the adopted son of Pharaoh's daughter, and was heir to the throne of Egypt. All the treasures of Egypt were therefore at his command. He "was learned in all the wisdom of the Egyptians, and was mighty in words and in deeds." Acts 7:22. The crown prince, a scholar, a general, and an orator, with every flattering worldly prospect open before him, – he gave up everything to cast in his lot with a despised class of people for the sake of Christ.

He "refused to be called the son of Pharaoh's daughter." That implies that he was urged to retain his position. It was in the face of opposition that he gave up his worldly prospects, and chose to suffer affliction with the people of God. We cannot over-estimate the contempt with which his action would be regarded, nor the epithets of scorn that must have been heaped upon him, among which that of "fool" must have been the mildest. When people in these days are called upon to accept an unpopular truth at the expense of their position, it will be well for them to remember the case of Moses.

What led him to make the "sacrifice?" "He had respect unto the recompense of the reward." It was not merely that he sacrificed present position for the hope of something better in the future. No; he got more than an equivalent as he went along. He esteemed the reproach of Christ, of which he had a full share, greater riches than the treasures in Egypt. That shows that he knew the Lord. He understood the sacrifice of Christ for man, and he simply chose to share it. He could not have done this if he had not known much of the joy of the Lord. That alone could strengthen him in such a case. Probably no other man has ever sacrificed so great worldly prospects for the sake of Christ, and therefore we may be sure that Moses had such knowledge of Christ and his work as few other men have ever had. The step that he took is evidence that he already knew much of the Lord; the sharing of the reproach and the sufferings of Christ must have made very close the bond of sympathy between the two.

When Moses refused to be called the son of Pharaoh's daughter, he did it for the sake of Christ and the Gospel. But his case, like that of Jacob, as well as of many others, shows that the most sincere believers often have much to learn. God calls men to His work, not because they are perfect, but in order that He may give them the necessary training for it. At the first Moses had to learn what thousands of professed Christians have not yet learned in this age. He had to learn that "the wrath of man worketh not the righteousness of God." James 1:20.

He had to learn that the cause of God is never advanced by human methods; that "the weapons of our warfare are not carnal, but mighty through God to the pulling down of strongholds; casting down imaginations, and every high thing that exalteth itself against the knowledge of God, and bringing into captivity every thought to the obedience of Christ." 2 Corinthians 10:4, 5.

"And when he was full forty years old, it came into his heart to visit his brethren the children of Israel. And seeing one of them suffer wrong, he defended him, and avenged him that was oppressed, and smote the Egyptian; for he supposed that his brethren would have understood how that God by his hand would deliver them; but they understood not. And the next day he showed himself unto them as they strove, and would have set them at one again, saying, Sirs, ye are brethren; Why do ye wrong one to another? But he that did his neighbor wrong thrust him away, saying, Who made thee a ruler and a judge over us? Wilt thou kill me, as thou diddest the Egyptian yesterday? Then fled Moses at this saying, and was a stranger in the land of Midian, where he begat two sons." Acts 7:23-29.

It was true that the Lord designed that the hand of Moses should deliver the people of Israel. Moses himself knew this, and he supposed that his brethren would also understand the matter. But they did not. His attempt to deliver them was a sad failure, and the reason for the failure lay in him as much as in them. They did not understand that God would deliver them by his hand; he understood that fact, but he had not yet learned the method. He supposed that the deliverance was to be affected by force; that under his generalship the children of Israel were to rise and conquer their oppressors. But that was not the Lord's way. The deliverance, which God had planned for His people, was such a deliverance as could not be gained by human efforts.

By this failure of Moses we learn much as to the nature of the work which God proposed to do for the Israelites, and of the inheritance to which he was about to lead them. If it had been a deliverance from mere physical bondage that He designed for them, and if they were to be led only to an earthly, temporal inheritance, then it might possibly have been accomplished in the way that Moses began. The Israelites were numerous, and under the generalship of Moses they might have conquered. That is the way in which earthly possessions are gained. History affords many instances in which a small people threw off the yoke of a great one. But God had promised to Abraham and his seed a heavenly inheritance, and not an earthly, and therefore it could be gained only through heavenly agencies.

Labour Troubles and Their Remedy

At the present day we find very much the same conditions that existed in the case of the children of Israel. Surely the "sweating system" prevailed at that time as much as it ever has since. Long hours, hard work, and little or no pay, was the rule. Capital has never oppressed labor more than at that time, and the natural thought of the oppressed then, as now, was that the only way to secure their rights was to meet force with force. But man's way is not God's way; and God's way is the only right way. No one can deny that the poor are grossly abused and trodden down; but very few of them are willing to accept God's method of deliverance. No one can condemn the oppression of the poor by the rich any more strongly than it is done in the Bible, for God is the poor man's friend.

The Lord cares for the poor and the afflicted. He has identified Himself so closely with them that whosoever gives to the poor is considered as lending to the Lord.

Jesus Christ was on this earth as a poor man, so that "he that oppresseth the poor reproacheth his Maker." Proverbs 14:31. "The Lord heareth the poor." Psalm 69:33. "The needy shall not alway be forgotten; the expectation of the poor shall not perish for ever." Psalm 9:15. "The Lord will maintain the cause of the afflicted, and the right of the poor." Psalm 140:12. "For the oppression of the poor, for the sighing of the needy, now will I arise, saith the Lord; I will set him in safety from him that puffeth at him." Psalm 12:5. "Lord, who is like unto Thee, which deliverest the poor from him that is too strong for him, yea, the poor and the needy from him that spoileth him?" Psalm 35:10. With the Almighty God so interested in their case, what a pity it is that the poor are so ill-advised as to seek to right their own wrongs.

The Lord says:

"Go to now, ye rich men, weep and howl for your miseries that shall come upon you. Your riches are corrupted, and your garments are moth-eaten. Your old and silver is cankered; and the rust of them shall be a witness against you, and shall eat your flesh as it were fire. Ye have heaped treasure together for the last days. Behold the hire of the laborers who have reaped down your fields, which is of you kept back by fraud, crieth; and the cries of them which have reaped are entered into the ears of the Lord of Sabbath. Ye have lived in pleasure on the earth, and been wanton; ye have nourished your hearts as in a day of slaughter. Ye have condemned and killed the just, and he doth not resist you." James 5:1-6.

This is a terrible indictment against the oppressors of the poor, and those who have defrauded them of their rightful wages. It is also a promise of sure judgment against them. The Lord hears the cry of the poor, and He does not forget. Every act of oppression He considers as directed against Himself. But when the poor take matters into their own hands, meeting monopoly with monopoly, and force with force, they put themselves in the same class with their oppressors, and thus deprive themselves of the good offices of God in their behalf.

To the rich oppressors God says, "Ye have condemned and killed the just, and he doth not resist you." The injunction, "I say unto you, That ye resist not evil," means just that, and nothing else; and it is not out of date. It is just as applicable to day as it was eighteen hundred years ago. The world has not changed in its character; the greed of men is the same now as then; and God is the same. Those who heed that injunction, God calls "the just." The just do not resist when they are unjustly condemned and defrauded, and even killed.

"But how then can there ever be any remedy for these wrongs, if the poor suffer even to death?" Listen further to what the Lord says to the poor themselves. He is not ashamed to call them brethren, and He says, "Be patient, therefore, brethren, until the coming of the Lord. Behold, the husbandman waiteth for the precious fruit of the earth, and hath long patience for it, until he receive the early and latter rain. Be ye also patient; establish your hearts; for the coming of the Lord draweth nigh." James 5:7, 8.

The coming of the Lord is the time when all oppression shall cease. The trouble is that, like Esau, people do not have faith nor patience to wait.

So a lesson is drawn from the farmer. He sows his seed, and does not become impatient because he does not reap the harvest the same day. He has long patience in waiting for the fruit of the earth. "The harvest is the end of the world." Matthew 13:39. Then those who have committed their cause to the Lord will receive ample return for their trust and patience. Then will be proclaimed claimed liberty throughout all the land, and to all the inhabitants thereof.

That which makes known this deliverance, and which gives even now the joy of it, although grievous trials oppress, is the Gospel of Jesus Christ. That is the power of God unto salvation to every one that believeth. The worldly-wise scoff at the preaching of the Gospel as the remedy for the labor troubles of the present day. But the labor troubles of to day are no greater than they were in the days of Moses; and the proclamation of the Gospel was the only means that God then approved of and used for their betterment. When Christ came, the strongest proof of the Divinity of His mission was that the Gospel was preached to the poor. Matthew 11:5. He knew the needs of the poor as no other ever can, and His remedy was the Gospel. There are possibilities in the Gospel that have scarcely been dreamed of as yet. The right understanding of the inheritance, which the Gospel promises, can alone make man patient under earthly oppression.

Chapter 17

The Promises to Israel - Giving the Commission

The Present Truth, August 27, 1896

FORTY years passed by after that first ill-advised attempt, when the Egyptian was killed, before the Lord was ready to deliver His people by the hand of Moses. It took that length of time to fit Moses for the important work. We read of Moses, at a later period of his life, that he was meek above all other men; but that was not his natural disposition. An education at court is not calculated to develop the quality of meekness. From the way in which Moses at the first proceeded to settle the labor troubles of his people, we see that he was impulsive and arbitrary. The blow closely followed the word. But the man who should lead the children of Abraham into the promised inheritance must have very different characteristics.

The inheritance promised to Abraham was the earth. It was to be gained through the righteousness of faith. But the righteousness of faith is inseparable from meekness of spirit. "Behold, his soul which is lifted up is not upright in him; but the just shall live by his faith." Habakkuk 2:4.

Therefore the Saviour said, "Blessed are the meek, for they shall inherit the earth." Matthew 5:5. "Hearken my beloved brethren, Hath not God chosen the poor of this world, rich in faith, and heirs of the kingdom which He hath promised to them that love Him?" James 2:5. The promised inheritance, to which the Israelites were to be led, could be possessed only by the meek, and therefore he who should conduct them on the way must necessarily possess that virtue. Forty years' retirement in the wilderness as a shepherd, wrought the desired change in Moses.

"And it came to pass in process of time, that the king of Egypt died; and the children of Israel sighed by reason of the bondage, and they cried, and their cry came up unto God by reason of the bondage. And God heard their groaning, and God remembered His covenant with Abraham, with Isaac, and with Jacob." Exodus 2:23, 24.

This covenant, as we have seen, was confirmed in Christ. It was the covenant, which God made with the fathers, saying unto Abraham, "And in thy seed shall all the kindreds of the earth be blessed." Acts 3:25.

And this blessing consisted in turning them away from their iniquities. It was the covenant which God remembered in sending John the Baptist, the forerunner of Christ, who should deliver His people from the hand of their enemies, so that they might "serve Him without fear, in holiness and righteousness before Him" all the days of their lives. It was the covenant, which assured to Abraham and his seed the possession of land, through personal faith in Christ.

But faith in Christ does not assure any man an earthly possession. Those who are heirs of God are the poor of this world, rich in faith. Christ Himself had not a place of His own on this earth, where he could lay His head; therefore, none need think that following Him in truth will assure them worldly possessions. It is more likely to be the contrary.

These points are necessary to be borne in mind as we consider the deliverance of Israel from Egypt, and their journey to the land of Canaan. They should be borne in mind in the study of the entire history of Israel, or else we shall be continually making the same mistake that was made by His own who received Him not when He came, because He did not come to advance their worldly interests.

"Now Moses kept the flock of Jethro his father-in-law, the priest of Midian; and he led the flock to the back side of the desert, and came to the mountain of God, even to Horeb. And the angel of the Lord appeared unto him in a flame of fire out of the midst of a bush; and he looked, and, behold, the bush burned with fire, and the bush was not consumed. And Moses said, I will now turn aside, and see this great sight, why the bush is not burnt. And when the Lord saw that he turned aside to see, God called unto him out of the midst of the bush, and said, Moses, Moses. And he said, Here am I. And He said, Draw not nigh hither; put off thy shoes from off thy feet, for the place whereon thou standest is holy ground. Moreover, He said, I am the God of thy father, the God of Abraham, the God of Isaac, and the God of Jacob. And Moses hid his face; for he was afraid to look upon God. And the Lord said, I have surely seen the affliction of My people which are in Egypt, and have heard their cry by reason of their taskmasters; for I know their sorrows; and I am come down to deliver them out of the hand of the Egyptians, and to bring them up out of that land unto a good land and a large, unto a land flowing with milk and honey; unto the place of the Canaanites, and the Hittites, and the Amorites, and the Perizzites, and the Hivites, and the Jebusites. Now therefore, behold, the cry of the children of Israel is come unto Me; and I have also seen the oppression wherewith the Egyptians oppress them. Come now, therefore, and I will send thee unto Pharaoh, that thou mayest bring forth My people the children of Israel out of Egypt." Exodus 3:1-10.

We do not need to go into the details of the refusal of Moses, and of his final acceptance of the Divine commission. Now that he was actually fitted for the task, he shrank from it. It is sufficient to note that in the commission the power by which the deliverance was to be affected was made very clear. It was such a deliverance as could be accomplished only by the power of the Lord. Moses was to be simply the agent in His hands.

Notice also the credentials, which Moses carried. "Moses said unto God Behold, when I come unto the children of Israel, and shall say unto them, the God of your fathers hath sent me unto you; and they shall say to me, What is His name? What shall I say unto them? And God said unto Moses, I AM THAT I AM; and He said, Thus shalt thou say unto the children of Israel, I AM hath sent me unto you." Exodus 3:13, 14.

This is "the glorious and fearful name" of the Lord, which no man can ever comprehend, because it expresses His infinity and eternity. Look at the renderings that are given in the margin of the Revision: "I am because I am," or "I am who I am," or "I will be that I will be." No one of these renderings is complete in itself, but all of them together are necessary to give something of an idea of the title. Together they represent "The Lord which is, and which was, and which is to come, the Almighty." Revelation 1:8.

How fitting that when the Lord was about to deliver the people, not simply from temporal bondage, but from spiritual bondage as well, and give to them that inheritance which could be possessed only by the coming of the Lord and the resurrection, He should make Himself known not only as the self-existent Creator, but as The Coming One, the same title by which He reveals Himself in the last book of the Bible, which is wholly devoted to the coming of the Lord and the final deliverance of His people from their great enemy, death.

"And God said, moreover, unto Moses. Thus shalt thou say unto the children of Israel, the Lord God of your fathers, the God of Abraham, the God of Isaac, and the God of Jacob, hath sent me unto you; this is My name for ever, and this is My memorial unto all generations." Exodus 3:15. Continually are we reminded that all this deliverance is but the fulfillment of the promise made through Christ to Abraham, Isaac, and Jacob. Notice also the significance of the fact that some of the most powerful Gospel sermons recorded in the New Testament, refer to God as the God of Abraham and Isaac and Jacob, an evidence that He is to be known to us by the same title, and that the promises made to the fathers hold good to us, if we will but receive them in the same faith. "This is My name for ever, and this is My memorial unto all generations."

With this name for his support, with the assurance that God would be with him and would teach him what to say, armed with the power to work miracles, and comforted with the assurance that Aaron his brother would join him in the work, Moses set out for Egypt.

Chapter 18

The Promises to Israel - Preaching the Gospel in Egypt

The Present Truth, September 3, 1896

"And Moses and Aaron went and gathered together all the elders of the children of Israel; and Aaron spake all the words which the Lord had spoken unto Moses, and did the signs in the sight of the people. And the people believed; and when they heard that the Lord had visited the children of Israel, and that He had looked upon their affliction, then they bowed their heads and worshipped." Exodus 4:29-31.

But they were not yet ready to leave Egypt. They were as yet but stony ground hearers of the Word. They received it with joy at the first, but as soon as persecution arose they became offended. If they could have left Egypt without any hindrance, and could have had an easy passage to the Promised Land, they doubtless would not have murmured; but "we must through much tribulation enter into the kingdom of God," (Acts 14:22), and those who do enter in must learn to rejoice even in tribulation. This lesson the Israelites had yet to learn.

The message to Pharaoh, "Thus saith the Lord God of Israel, Let My people go," of which we shall speak more particularly later on, resulted in a still more grievous oppression of the Israelites. This was really a necessity for them, that they might be the more anxious to leave, and afterward have less desire to return, and that they might see the power of God. The plagues that came upon the land of Egypt were as necessary to teach the Israelites the power of God, that they might be willing to go, as they were for the Egyptians, that they might be willing to let them go. The Israelites needed to learn that it was not by any human power that they were delivered, but that it was wholly the work of the Lord. They needed to learn to trust themselves completely to His care and guidance. And as "whatsoever things were written aforetime were written for our learning, that we through patience and comfort of the Scriptures might have hope," (Romans 15:4), we should learn the same lesson as we read the story.

It is not at all to be wondered at that the people complained at the first when persecution increased as the result of the message brought by Moses. Moses himself seems to have been perplexed by it, and went to ask the Lord about it.

"Then the Lord said unto Moses, Now shalt thou see what I will do to Pharaoh; for with a strong hand shall he let them go and with a strong hand shall he drive them out of his land. And God spake unto Moses, and said unto him, I am Jehovah; and I appeared unto Abraham, unto Isaac, and unto Jacob, by the name of God Almighty, but by My name Jehovah I was not known to them. And I have also established My covenant with them, to give them the land of Canaan, the land of their sojourning, wherein they were strangers. And I have also heard the groaning of the children of Israel, whom the Egyptians keep in bondage; and I have remembered My covenant. Wherefore say unto the children of Israel, I am Jehovah, and I will bring you out from under the burdens of the Egyptians, and I will rid you out of their bondage, and I will redeem you with a stretched out arm, and with great judgments; and I will take you to Me for a people, and I will be to you a God; and ye shall know that I am Jehovah your God, which bringeth you out from under the burdens of the Egyptians. And I will bring you into the land concerning the which I did swear to give it to Abraham, to Isaac, and to Jacob; and I will give it to you for an inheritance; I am Jehovah." Exodus 6:1-8, R.V.

The Gospel of Deliverance

We have learned that when God made the promise to Abraham He preached the Gospel to him; it follows, therefore, that when the time comes for the fulfillment of the promise, the seed to whom it is fulfilled must know at least as much of the Gospel as was revealed to Abraham; and we should expect to find the same Gospel preached to them. This was the case. We learn from the Epistle to the Hebrews that the Gospel, which is now preached to us, is the same that was then preached to them, and in the Scripture last quoted we find it. Note the following points: –

1. God said of Abraham, Isaac, and Jacob, "I have also established My covenant with them, to give them the land of Canaan, the land of their pilgrimage, wherein they were strangers."

2. Then He added, "And I have also heard the groaning of the children of Israel, whom the Egyptians keep in bondage; and I have remembered My covenant."

3. When the Lord says that he remembers a certain thing, He does not imply that that thing has ever passed from His mind, for that is impossible. Nothing can ever escape Him. But, as we find in various instances, He thus indicates that He is about to perform that thing. In the final judgment of Babylon it is said, "God hath remembered her iniquities." Revelation 18:5. "And great Babylon came in remembrance before God, to give unto her the cup of the wine of the fierceness of His wrath." Revelation 16:19. "God remembered Noah," and caused the flood to cease, but we know that not for one moment while Noah was in the ark was he forgotten, for not even a sparrow is forgotten. See also Genesis 19:29; 30:22; and I Samuel 1:19, for the use of the word "remember" in the sense of being about to fulfill the thing promised.

4. It is evident, therefore, from the sixth of Exodus that the Lord was about to fulfill the promise to Abraham and his seed. But as Abraham was dead, that could be done only by the resurrection. The time of the promise, which God had sworn to Abraham, was very near. But this is evidence that the Gospel was being preached, since only the Gospel of the kingdom prepares for the end.

5. God was making Himself known to the people. But it is only in the Gospel that God is made known. The things, which reveal the power of God, make known His Divinity.

6. God said, "I will take you to Me for a people, and I will be to you a God; and ye shall know that I am the Lord your God." Compare with this the promise of the new covenant, "I will be their God, and they shall be my people. And they shall teach no more every man his neighbor, and every man his brother, saying, Know the Lord; for they shall all know Me, from the least of them unto the greatest of them, saith the Lord." Jeremiah 31:33, 34. No one questions that this is the proclamation of the Gospel; but it is the very same thing that was proclaimed to the Israelites in Egypt.

7. The fact that the deliverance of the children of Israel was such deliverance as could be affected only through the preaching of the Gospel, is evidence that it was no ordinary deliverance from physical bondage to a temporal inheritance. A most wonderful prospect was opened before the children of Israel, if they had but known the day of their visitation, and had continued faithful.

Preaching to Pharaoh

It is a truth that "God is no respecter of persons; but in every nation he that feareth Him, and worketh righteousness, is accepted with Him." Acts 10:34, 35. This was not a new truth in the days of Peter, but has ever been true, for God is always the same. The fact that men have usually been slow to perceive it, makes no difference with the fact. Men may fail to recognize the power of God, but that does not make Him any the less powerful; so the fact that the great mass of God's professed followers have usually failed to recognize that He is perfectly impartial, and have supposed that He loved them to the exclusion of other people, has not narrowed His character.

The promise was to Abraham and his seed. But the promise and the blessing came to Abraham before he was circumcised, "that he might be the father of all them that believe, though they be not circumcised; that righteousness might be imputed unto them also." Romans 4:11. "There is neither Jew nor Greek, there is neither bond nor free, there is neither male nor female; for ye are all one in Christ Jesus. And if ye be Christ's, then are ye Abraham's seed, and heirs according to the promise." Galatians 3:28, 29. Therefore the promise embraced even the Egyptians, as well as the Israelites, provided they believed. And it did not embrace unbelieving Israelites any more than it did unbelieving Egyptians. Abraham is the father of those who are circumcised, but only of those who "are not of the circumcision only, but who also walk in the steps of that faith of our father Abraham, which he had being yet uncircumcised." If the uncircumcision keeps the righteousness of the law, their uncircumcision is counted for circumcision. See Romans 2:25-29.

It should not be forgotten that God did not begin at once to send the plagues upon Pharaoh and his people. He did not propose to deliver the Israelites by killing their oppressors, but rather by converting them, if it were possible. God is "not willing that any should perish, but that all should come to repentance." 2 Peter 3:9. He "will have all men to be saved, and to come to the knowledge of the truth." 1 Timothy 2:4. "As I live, saith the Lord God, I have no pleasure in the death of the wicked; but that the wicked turn from his way and live." Ezekiel 33:11. All men are God's creatures, and His children, and His great heart of love embraces them all, without respect to race or nationality.

Accordingly, at the first, the simple demand was made upon Pharaoh to let God's people go free. But he impudently and haughtily replied, "Who is the Lord, that I should obey His voice, to let Israel go? I know not the Lord, neither will I let Israel go." Exodus 5:2. Then miracles were wrought before him. These were not at the first judgments, but simply manifestations of God's power. But the magicians of Pharaoh, the servants of Satan, counterfeited these miracles, and Pharaoh's heart became harder than before. Yet the careful reader will see that even in the miracles that were counterfeited by the magicians, the superior power of the Lord was manifested.

The next article in this series of studies on the Everlasting Gospel will deal with that much-talked-of question of how Pharaoh's heart was hardened.

Chapter 19

The Promises to Israel - How Pharaoh's Heart Was Hardened

The Present Truth, September 10, 1896

WHEN mild measures failed to cause Pharaoh to acknowledge the power of God, judgments were sent. God, who knows the end from the beginning, had said that Pharaoh's heart would be hardened, and even that He Himself would harden it; and so it was. Yet it must not be supposed that God set about deliberately to harden Pharaoh's heart against his will, so that he could not have relented if he had wished. God sends strong delusion, that men should believe a lie, only upon those who have rejected the truth, and who love a lie. Every one has just what he most desires. If any man wishes to do the will of God, he shall know of the doctrine; but to him who rejects truth, there is nothing left but darkness and deception.

It is interesting to note that it was the manifestation of the mercy of God that hardened Pharaoh's heart. The simple request of the Lord was scornfully denied. Then the plagues began to come, yet not immediately, but with interval enough to allow Pharaoh to think. But as long as the power of the magicians appeared to be as great as that exercised by Moses and Aaron, Pharaoh would not yield. Then it became manifest that there was a power greater than that with his magicians. They brought frogs upon the land, but they could not drive them away. "Then Pharaoh called for Moses and Aaron, and said, Entreat the Lord, that he may take away the frogs from me, and from my people; and I will let the people go, that they may do sacrifice unto the Lord." Exodus 8:8. He had already learned enough of the Lord to call Him by His name.

"And Moses and Aaron went out from Pharaoh; and Moses cried unto the Lord because of the frogs which He had brought against Pharaoh. And the Lord did according to the word of Moses; and the frogs died out of the houses, out of the villages, and out of the fields. And they gathered them together upon heaps; and the land stank. But when Pharaoh saw that there was respite, he hardened his heart, and hearkened not unto them; as the Lord had said." Verses 12-15.

"Let favor be shown to the wicked, yet will he not learn righteousness; in the land of uprightness will he deal unjustly, and will not behold the majesty of the Lord." Isaiah 26:10.

Thus it was with Pharaoh. The judgment of God caused his haughty purpose to weaken; but "when he saw that there was respite, he hardened his heart."

Again there came swarms of flies, at the command of the Lord, and Pharaoh said, "I will let you go, that you may sacrifice to the Lord your God in the wilderness; only ye shall not go very far away; entreat for me. And Moses said, Behold I go out from thee, and I will entreat the Lord that the swarms of flies may depart from Pharaoh, from his servants, and from his people, to-morrow; but let not Pharaoh deal deceitfully any more in not letting the people go to sacrifice to the Lord. And Moses went out from Pharaoh, and entreated the Lord. And the Lord did according to the word of Moses; and He removed the swarms of flies from Pharaoh, and from his servants, and from his people; there remained not one. And Pharaoh hardened his heart at this time also, neither would he let the people go." Exodus 8:28-32.

And so it went on throughout the plagues. All the steps in each case are not recorded, but we see that it was the longsuffering and mercy of God that hardened Pharaoh's heart. The same preaching that comforted the hearts of many in the days of Jesus, made others more bitter against Him. The raising of Lazarus from the dead fixed the determination in the hearts of the unbelieving Jews to kill him. The Judgment will reveal the fact that every one who has in hardness of heart rejected the Lord has done so in the face of the revelation of His mercy.

God's Purpose with Pharaoh

"And the Lord said unto Moses, Rise up early in the morning, and stand before Pharaoh, and say unto him, Thus saith the Lord, the God of the Hebrews, Let My people go, that they may serve Me. For I will this time send all My plagues upon thine heart, and upon thy servants, and upon thy people; that thou mayest know that there is none like Me in all the earth. For now I had put forth My hand, and smitten thee and they people with pestilence, and thou hadst been cut off from the earth; but in very deed for this cause have I made thee to stand, for to show thee My power, and that My name may be declared throughout all the earth." Exodus ix. 13-16, R.V.

The still more literal rendering of the Hebrew by Dr. Kalisch, reads thus:

"For now I might have stretched out My hand, and might have smitten thee and thy people with pestilence; and thou wouldst have been cut off from the earth. But only for this cause have I let thee exist, in order to show thee My power, and that My name may be acknowledged throughout all the earth." A close comparison will show that this idea is expressed in the Revised Version, as quoted above, but not so clearly.

It is not the case, as is too often lightly supposed, that God brought Pharaoh into existence for the express purpose of wreaking His vengeance upon him. Such an idea is most dishonoring to the character of the Lord. But the true idea is that God might have cut Pharaoh off at the very first, and so have delivered His people without any delay. That, however, would not have been in keeping with the Lord's invariable course, which is to give every man ample opportunity to repent. God had borne long with Pharaoh's stubbornness, and now proposed to send severer judgments; yet He gives him fair warning, that even yet he may turn from his wickedness.

God had kept Pharaoh alive, and had delayed to send His severest judgments upon him, in order that He might show unto him His power. But the power of God was being manifested at that time for the salvation of His people, and the power of God unto salvation is the Gospel. Therefore God was keeping Pharaoh alive, in spite of his stubbornness, to give him ample opportunity to learn the Gospel. That Gospel was as powerful to save Pharaoh, as it was to save the Israelites.

The revised renderings have been used because they are clearer than those of the common version, and not because the same truth is not set forth in each. Take the common rendering, "In very deed for this cause have I raised thee up, for to show in thee My power; and that My name may be declared throughout all the earth," and grant that it refers to the bringing of Pharaoh to the throne. Even then it is far from showing that God raised him up for the purpose of plaguing and killing him. The text says that it was for the purpose of showing God's power, and causing His name to be known throughout all the earth. To infer that God can show His power and make known His name only by the destruction of men, is dishonoring to Him, and contrary to the Gospel. "His mercy endureth for ever."

God's purpose was that His name should be declared throughout all the earth. This is what was done, for we read that forty years later the people of Canaan were terrified at the approach of the Israelites, because they remembered what God had done in delivering them from Egypt. But the purpose of God would have been accomplished just the same if Pharaoh had yielded to the wishes of the Lord. Suppose that Pharaoh had acknowledged the Lord, and had accepted the Gospel that was preached to him; what would have been the result? He would have done as Moses did, and have exchanged the throne of Egypt for the reproach of Christ, and a place in the everlasting inheritance. And so he would have been a most powerful agent in declaring the name of the Lord throughout all the earth. The very fact of the acceptance of the Gospel by a mighty king, would have made known the power of the Lord as effectually as did the plagues. And Pharaoh himself, from being a persecutor of God's people, might, like Paul, have become a preacher of the faith. Sad to say, he did not know the day of his visitation.

Take particular notice of the fact that the purpose of God was that His name should be declared throughout all the earth. This affair was not to be done in a corner. The deliverance from Egypt was not something that concerned only a few people in one portion of the earth. It was to "be to all people."

In accordance with the promise to Abraham, God was delivering the children of Israel from bondage; but the deliverance was not for their sakes alone. Through their deliverance His name and power was to be made known to the uttermost parts of the earth. The time of the promise, which God had sworn to Abraham, was drawing near; but since that promise included the whole earth, it was necessary that the Gospel should be proclaimed as extensively. The children of Israel were God's chosen agents to perform this work. Around them, as the nucleus, the kingdom of God was to centre. That they proved unfaithful to their trust, only delayed, but did not change God's plan. Although they failed to proclaim the name of the Lord, and even denied it, God said, "As truly as I live, all the earth shall be filled with the glory of the Lord."

Chapter 20

The Promises to Israel - Saved by the Life

The Present Truth, September 17, 1896

OF Moses we read, "By faith he forsook Egypt, not fearing the wrath of the king; for he endured as seeing Him who is invisible. Through faith he kept the Passover, and the sprinkling of blood, lest he that destroyed the first-born should touch them." Hebrews 11:27, 28.

It was not at the first, when he fled in fear, that Moses forsook Egypt in faith, but when he went out after having kept the Passover. Then the wrath of the king was nothing to him, because "he endured as seeing Him who is invisible." He was under the protection of the King of kings.

Although this text speaks only of Moses, we need not suppose that he was the only one of the children of Israel who had faith; for we read in the next verse of the whole company "by faith they passed through the Red Sea." But even if it were true that Moses alone of all the company left Egypt by faith, that fact would prove that all ought to have left it in the same manner, and that the entire deliverance was a work of faith.

"He endured as seeing Him who is invisible." Moses lived in the same way that true Christians of the present day live. Here is the parallel: "Blessed be the God and Father of our Lord Jesus Christ, which according to His abundant mercy hath begotten us again unto a lively hope by the resurrection of Jesus Christ from the dead, to an inheritance incorruptible, undefiled, and that fadeth not away, reserved in heaven for you, who are kept by the power of God through faith unto salvation ready to be revealed in the last time. Wherein ye greatly rejoice, though now for a season, if need be, ye are in heaviness through manifold temptations; that the trial of your faith, being much more precious than of gold that perisheth, though it be tried in the fire, might be found unto praise and honor and glory at the appearing of Jesus Christ; whom having not seen, ye love; in whom, though now ye see Him not; yet believing, ye rejoice with joy unspeakable and full of glory; receiving the end of your faith, even the salvation of your souls." 1 Peter 1:3-9.

Moses and the children of Israel were called to the same inheritance that is reserved for us. The promise was to them in Christ, as well as to us. It was an inheritance to be gained only by faith in Christ, and that faith was to be such as would make Christ a real, personal presence, although invisible. And more, the basis of the faith and hope was the resurrection of Jesus Christ from the dead. Christ then, as now, was the head of the church. The true church has not and never has had any other than an invisible head. "The Holy One of Israel" was given to be "a leader and commander to the people" ages before He was born a babe in Bethlehem.

We see therefore that personal faith in Christ was the basis of the deliverance of Israel from Egypt. This was shown in the institution of the Passover. Matters had then come to a crisis. Pharaoh had persisted in stubborn resistance until the mercy of the Lord had no effect upon him. His own statement shows that Pharaoh had acted deliberately, and had sinned against light, after the locusts had been sent. He called for Moses and Aaron, and said, "I have sinned against the Lord your God, and against you. Now therefore forgive, I pray thee, my sin only this once, and entreat the Lord your God, that He may take away from me this death only." Exodus 10:16, 17. He had come to acknowledge the Lord, and he knew that rebellion against him was sin, yet as soon as there was respite he was as stubborn as ever. He definitely and fully rejected all the Lord's advances, and now nothing remained but to execute such judgment upon him as would compel him to desist from his oppression, and to let Israel go.

The First Passover

It was the last night that the children of Israel were to spend in Egypt. The Lord was about to bring His last great judgment upon the king and people, in the destruction of the first-born. The children of Israel were instructed to take a lamb "without blemish," and to kill it in the evening, and to eat the flesh. "And they shall take of the blood, and strike it on the two side posts and on the upper door post of the houses, wherein they shall eat it." "It is the Lord's Passover. For I will pass through the land of Egypt this night, and will smite all the first-born in the land of Egypt, both man and beast; and against all the gods of Egypt will I execute judgment; I am the Lord. And the blood shall be to you for a token upon the houses where ye are; and when I see the blood, I will pass over you, and the plague shall not be upon you to destroy you, when I smite the land of Egypt." Exodus 12:5-13

The blood of that lamb did not save them, and they well knew that. The Lord told them that it was but a token. It was simply a sign of their faith in that which it represented, namely, "the precious blood of Christ, as of a lamb without blemish and without spot," for "Christ our Passover is sacrificed for us." 1 Corinthians 5:7. The blood of the lamb was therefore only a token of the Lamb of God; and they who "endured as seeing Him who is invisible" understood this.

"The life of the flesh is in the blood." Leviticus 17:11. In the blood of Christ, that is, in His life, we have redemption, even the forgiveness of sins; because God hath set him forth, "to be a propitiation through faith, by His blood, to show His righteousness, because of the passing over of the sins done aforetime, in the forbearance of God." Romans 3:25, R.V. God passes over sins, not in that He compromises with them, but because "the blood of Jesus Christ His son cleanseth us from all sin." 1 John 1:7. The life of Christ is the righteousness of God, for out of the heart are the issues of life, and the law of God was in His heart as perfect righteousness. The application of the blood or the life of Christ is therefore the application of the life of God in Christ; and that is the taking away of sin.

The sprinkling of the blood upon the doorposts signified what was said later: "The Lord our God is one Lord; and thou shalt love the Lord thy God with all thine heart, and with all thy soul, and with all thy might. And these words, which I command thee this day, shall be in thine heart; . . . and thou shalt write them upon the posts of thy house, and on thy gates." Deuteronomy 6:4-9. The righteousness of the law of God is found only in the life of Christ. It can be in the heart only as the life of God in Christ is in the heart, to cleanse it from all sin. Putting the blood on the posts of the door of the house was the same as writing the law of God on the posts of the house and on the gates; and it indicated nothing else but dwelling in Christ – being encompassed with His life.

Christ is the Son of God, whose delight was found in doing His Father's will. As He was the Passover of the children of Israel in Egypt, so He is ours, because His life is everlasting and indestructible, and those who are dwelling in it by faith share its safety. Neither man nor devil could take His life from Him; and the Father loved Him, and had no desire to take His life from Him. He laid it down of His own free will, and took it again. He laid it down that we might take it, and He took it again, that He might take us with it. The dwelling in Him, therefore, which was signified by the sprinkling of the blood upon the door posts, means being made free from sin, and so being saved from the wrath of God which cometh upon the children of disobedience.

Jesus Christ is "the same yesterday and to-day and for ever." Hebrews 13:8. Faith in His blood, which was signified by the sprinkling of the blood of the lamb upon the doors of the houses, accomplishes the same result to day that it ever did. When we celebrate the Lord's Supper, which was instituted at the time of the Passover at which Christ was betrayed and crucified, we celebrate the same thing that the Israelites did in Egypt. They were yet in Egypt when they celebrated that first Passover. It was an act of faith, showing their confidence in Christ as their Deliverer. So we, through the blood of the covenant, show our faith in the power of His life to preserve us from sin and from the destruction that is coming upon the earth because of sin. In that day the Lord will spare those whose life is hid with Christ in God, "as a man spareth his own son that serveth him." Malachi 3:17. And it will be for the same reason, because God spares His own Son, and men are spared in Him.

The Last Passover

When Christ celebrated that last Passover with His disciples, He said, "With desire have I desired to eat this Passover with you before I suffer; for I say unto you, I will not any more eat thereof, until it be fulfilled in the kingdom of God." Luke 22:15, 16. From this we learn that the institution of the Passover had direct reference to the coming of the Lord to punish the wicked and to deliver His people. So we are told, "As often as ye eat this bread and drink this cup, ye do show the Lord's death till He come." 1 Corinthians 11:6. The death of Christ is nothing without the resurrection; and the resurrection of Christ means simply the resurrection of all those whose lives are hidden in His life. It is by His resurrection that He begets us to a lively hope of the inheritance incorruptible, undefiled, and that fadeth not away; and the same faith and hope, laying hold of the same inheritance, was shown by the true Israel in Egypt. The inheritance for which we look is one that is reserved in heaven; and the inheritance that was promised to Abraham, Isaac, and Jacob, to which God was prepared to lead the children of Israel, was "a better country, that is, an heavenly."

"The sprinkling of the blood" (compare Exodus 12:5-14; Hebrews 11:27, 28; 12:24; and 1 Peter 1:2-10) is the grand link that unites us in our Christian experience with ancient Israel. It shows that the deliverance that God was working for them was identical with that which He is now working for us. It unites us with them in the one Lord and the one faith. Christ was as really present with them as He is with us. They could endure as seeing Him who is invisible, and we can do no more. He was "slain from the foundation of the world," and therefore risen from the foundation of the world, so that all the benefits of His death and resurrection might be grasped by them as well as by us. And the deliverance that He was working for them was very real. Their hope was in the coming of the Lord to raise the dead, and thus to complete the deliverance, and we have the same blessed hope. Let us take warning from their subsequent failures, and "hold the beginning of our confidence steadfast unto the end."

From this point on, our way will be much more plain, because at every step we shall see clearly that we are only studying the dealings of God with His people in the plan of salvation, and are learning his power to save and to carry on the work of proclaiming the Gospel. "Whatsoever things are written aforetime were written for our learning, that we through patience and comfort of the Scriptures might have hope."

Chapter 21

The Promises to Israel - The Final Deliverance

The Present Truth, September 24, 1896

*"Sound the loud timbrel o'er Egypt's dark sea;
Jehovah has triumphed; His people are free."*

LET us read in brief the story of Israel's deliverance, as recorded by inspiration. "And it came to pass at midnight, that the Lord smote all the first-born in the land of Egypt, from the first-born of Pharaoh that sat on his throne unto the first-born of the captive that was in the dungeon; and all the first-born of cattle. And Pharaoh rose up in the night, he, and all his servants, and all the Egyptians; and there was a great cry in Egypt; for there was not a house where there was not one dead. And he called for Moses and Aaron by night, and said, Rise up, get you forth from among my people, both ye and the children of Israel; and go, serve the Lord, as ye have said. Take both your flocks and your herds, as ye have said, and be gone; and bless me also. And the Egyptians were urgent upon the people, to send them out of the land in haste; for they said, We be all dead men. And the people took their dough before it was leavened, their kneading-troughs being bound up in their clothes upon their shoulders. And the children of Israel did according to the word of Moses; and they asked[8] of the Egyptians jewels of silver, and jewels of gold, and raiment; and the Lord gave the people favor in the sight of the Egyptians, so that they let them have what they asked. And they spoiled the Egyptians.

"And the children of Israel journeyed from Rameses to Succoth, about six hundred thousand on foot that were men, beside children. And a mixed multitude went up also with them; and flocks, and herds, even very much cattle." Exodus 12:29-38, R.V.

"And it came to pass, when Pharaoh had let the people go, that God led them not through the way of the land of the Philistines, although that way was near; for God said, Lest peradventure the people repent when they see war, and they return to Egypt.

---

[8] Many hard speeches have been uttered against the children of Israel, and even against the Lord, because of the word "borrowed," which is found in the common version. It is a mistaken rendering of the original. The children of Israel had worked hard and long for nothing, and now they asked for something in return, and it was given them. What they received was theirs by right.

But God led the people about, through the way of the wilderness of the Red Sea." Exodus 13:17, 18.

"And they took their journey from Succoth, and encamped in Etham, in the edge of the wilderness. And the Lord went before them by day in a pillar of cloud, to lead them the way; and by night in a pillar of fire, to give them light; to go by day and night: He took not away the pillar of the cloud by day, nor the pillar of fire by night, from before the people." Verses 20-22.

"And the Lord spake unto Moses, saying, Speak unto the children of Israel, that they turn and encamp before Pi-hahiroth, between Migdol and the sea, over against Baal-zephon; before it ye shall encamp by the sea. For Pharaoh will say of the children of Israel, They are entangled in the land; the wilderness hath shut them in. And I will harden Pharaoh's heart that he shall follow after them; and I will be honored upon Pharaoh, and upon all his host; that the Egyptians may know that I am the Lord. And they did so."

"And it was told the king of Egypt that the people fled; and the heart of Pharaoh and of his servants was turned against the people, and they said, Why have we done this, that we have let Israel go from serving us? And he made ready his chariot, and took his people with him; and he took six hundred chosen chariots, and all the chariots of Egypt, and captains over every one of them. And the Lord hardened the heart of Pharaoh king of Egypt, and he pursued after the children of Israel; and the children of Israel went but with an high hand. But the Egyptians pursued after them, all the horses and chariots of Pharaoh, and his horsemen, and his army, and overtook them encamping by the sea." Exodus 14:1-9.

"And when Pharaoh drew nigh, the children of Israel lifted up their eyes, and, behold, the Egyptians marched after them; and they were sore afraid; and the children of Israel cried out unto the Lord. And they said unto Moses, because there were no graves in Egypt, hast thou taken us away to die in the wilderness? Wherefore has thou dealt thus with us, to carry us forth out of Egypt; is not this the word that we did tell thee in Egypt, saying, Let us alone that we may serve the Egyptians? For it had been better for us to serve the Egyptians, than that we should die in the wilderness.

"And Moses said unto the people, Fear not, stand still, and see the salvation of the Lord, which He will show you to-day; for the Egyptians whom ye have seen to-day, ye shall see them no more again for ever. The Lord shall fight for you, and ye shall hold your peace." Verses 10-14.

With the manner of their deliverance, everybody is familiar; how at the command of the Lord the sea went back and left a path through the midst of it, so that the children of Israel went through dry-shod, and how when the Egyptians attempted to do the same thing, the sea rushed back and swallowed them up. "By faith they passed through the

Red Sea as by dry land; which the Egyptians assaying to do were drowned." Hebrews 11:29. Let us note a few lessons that we are to learn from this history.

1. It was God that was leading the people. "And it came to pass, when Pharaoh had let the people go, that God led them not through the way of the land of the Philistines." Moses no more knew what to do, or which way to go, than the people did, only as the Lord told him. God could tell Moses, because "Moses was faithful in all His house."

2. When the people murmured, they were murmuring against God, instead of against Moses. When they said to Moses, "Wherefore hast thou dealt thus with us, to carry us forth out of Egypt?" they were really denying the agency of God in the matter, although they had well known that it was God who had sent Moses to them.

3. At the first sight of danger the faith of the people oozed away. They forgot what God had already done for them, and how powerfully He had wrought for their deliverance. The last judgment upon the Egyptians should have been sufficient of itself to teach them to trust in the Lord, and that He was abundantly able to save them from those of the Egyptians who yet remained alive.

4. God did not design that the people should do any fighting. He led them through the wilderness, in order that they might not see war. Yet He knew that if they went the way that they did, the Egyptians would surely pursue them. The children of Israel never had any greater need of fighting than they did when the Egyptians closed in on them by the Red Sea; yet the word then was, "The Lord shall fight for you, and ye shall hold your peace." It may be said that the reason why the Lord did not wish them to see war was because they were as yet unprepared for fighting; but we must remember that on other occasions when they had many trained warriors, God often delivered them without their striking a blow. When we consider the circumstances of their deliverance from Egypt – how it was all accomplished by the direct power of God, without any human power, their part being only to follow and obey His word – we must be convinced that it was not according to the plan of God that they should do any fighting, even in self-defense.

5. We are also to learn that the shortest and the apparently easiest way is not always the best way. The route through the land of the Philistines was the shortest, but it was not the best one for the Israelites to take. The fact that we get into difficult places, where we cannot see our way out, is no evidence that God has not been leading us. God led the children of Israel into that narrow place in the wilderness, between the mountains and the sea, just as surely as He led them out of Egypt. He knew that they could not help themselves in such a trap, and He led them there deliberately, in order that they might see as never before that it was God Himself who was responsible for their safety, and that He was fully able to discharge the task which He had undertaken. Their trouble was designed to give them an ineffaceable lesson of trust in God.

6. Lastly, we must learn not to condemn them for their unbelief. "Thou art inexcusable, O man, whosoever thou art that judgest; for wherein thou judgest another, thou condemnest thyself; for thou that judgest doest the same things." Romans 2:1. When we condemn them for not trusting the Lord, we show that we know that there is no excuse for our murmuring and fear. We have all the evidence of the power of God that they had, and a great deal more besides. If we can see clearly how foolish their fear was, and how wicked their murmurings, then let us see to it that we do not show ourselves still more foolish and wicked. There is one more lesson that we must note in this connection, and it is of so much importance that special attention must be called to it, for it includes all the others. We learn it from the eleventh chapter of Isaiah. That chapter gives in few words the whole story of the Gospel, from the birth of Christ till the final deliverance of the saints in the kingdom of God, and the destruction of the wicked.

"The Second Time"

There is one more lesson that we must note in this connection, and it is of so much importance that special attention must be called to it, for it includes all the others. We learn it from the eleventh chapter of Isaiah. That chapter contains in few words the whole story of the Gospel, from the birth of Christ till the final deliverance of the saints in the kingdom of God, and the destruction of the wicked.

"There shall come forth a rod out of the stem of Jesse, and a Branch shall grow out of his roots; and the Spirit of the Lord shall rest upon Him, the Spirit of wisdom and understanding, the Spirit of counsel and might, the Spirit of knowledge and of the fear of the Lord; and He shall not judge after the sight of His eyes, neither reprove after the hearing of His ears; but with righteousness shall He judge the poor, and reprove with equity for the meek of the earth; and He shall smite the earth with the rod of His mouth, and with the breath of His lips shall He slay the wicked. And righteousness shall be the girdle of His loins, and faithfulness the girdle of His reins." Isaiah 11:1-5.

Compare the first part of the above with Luke 4:16-18, and the last part with Revelation 19:11-21, and we shall see how much it covers. It brings us down to the destruction of the wicked. It covers the entire day of salvation.

"And in that day there shall be a root of Jesse, which shall stand for an ensign of the people; to it shall the Gentiles seek; and His rest shall be glorious. And it shall come to pass in that day, that the Lord shall set His hand again the second time to recover the remnant of His people, which shall be left from Assyria, and from Egypt, and from Pathros, and from Cush, and from Elam, and from Shinar, and from Hamath, and from the islands of the sea. And He shall set up an ensign for the nations, and shall assemble the outcasts of Israel, and gather together the dispersed of Judah from the four corners of the earth." Verses 10-12.

Here again we have the deliverance of God's people brought to view. It is the second time that God sets His hand to the task, and it will be successful. He set His hand to the task the first time in the days of Moses; but the people entered not in because of unbelief. The second time will result in the everlasting salvation of His people. Notice that the final gathering of His people is through Christ, who is the ensign for the nations; for God is visiting the Gentiles to take out of them a people for His name. They are to be gathered "from the four corners of the earth;" for "He shall send His angels with a great sound of a trumpet, and they shall gather together His elect from the four winds, from one end of heaven to the other." Matthew 24:31.

That this deliverance is to be in the last days, even at the very close of time, is apparent from the fact that He gathers "the remnant" of His people, that is, the very last one of them. And now note this promise and reminder: "And there shall be an highway for the remnant of His people, which shall be left, from Assyria, like as it was to Israel in the day that the came up out of the land of Egypt." Isaiah 11:16.

Bear in mind the fact that the work of delivering Israel from Egypt began a long time before the day that they left that land. It began the very day that Moses reached Egypt and began to tell the people about the purpose of God to fulfill the promise to Abraham. All the display of the power of God in Egypt, which was but the proclamation of the Gospel, was a part of the work of deliverance. Even so will it be in the day when the Lord sets His hand the second time to deliver the remnant of His people. That day is now, for "behold, now is the accepted time; behold, now is the day of salvation." 2 Corinthians 6:2. All Israel shall be saved, because "There shall come out of Sion the Deliverer, and shall turn away ungodliness from Jacob." Romans 11:26. The work of delivering God's people from the bondage of sin is the same as the final deliverance. When the Lord comes the second time He "shall change our vile body, that it may be fashioned like unto His glorious body, according to the working whereby He is able to subdue all things unto Himself." Philippians 3:21. The power by which our bodies will be change – the power of the resurrection – is the power by which our sins are subdued, and we are delivered from their control. It is by the same power that was displayed in the deliverance of Israel from Egypt.

"I am not ashamed of the Gospel of Christ; for it is the power of God unto salvation to every one that believeth; to the Jew first, and also to the Greek." Romans 1:16. Whoever wishes to know how great that power is, has only to look at the deliverance of Israel from Egypt, and the dividing of the Red Sea, to see a practical example of it. That is the power that will accompany the preaching of the complete Gospel until the coming of the Lord Jesus.

Chapter 22

The Promises to Israel - The Song of Deliverance

The Present Truth, October 1, 1896

"THEN sang Moses and the children of Israel this song unto the Lord, and spake, saying,
I will sing unto the Lord, for He hath triumphed gloriously;
The horse and his rider hath He thrown into the sea.
The Lord is my strength and song,
And He is become my salvation;
This is my God, and I will praise Him;
My father's God, and I will exalt Him;
The Lord is a Man of War;
The Lord is His name.
Pharaoh's chariots and his host bath He cast into the sea;
And his chosen captains are sunk in the Red Sea.
The deeps cover them;
They went down into the depths like a stone.
Thy right hand, O Lord, is glorious in power,
Thy right hand, O Lord, dasheth in pieces the enemy.
And in the greatness of thine excellency Thou over-throwest them
that rise up against Thee;
Thou sendest forth thy wrath, it consumeth them as stubble.
And with the blast of Thy nostrils the waters were piled up,
The enemy said, I will pursue, I will overtake, I will divide the spoil;
My lust shall be satisfied upon them;
I will draw my sword, my hand shall destroy them;
Thou didst blow with Thy wind, the sea covered them;
They sank as lead in the mighty waters.
Who is like unto Thee, O Lord, among the gods?
Who is like Thee, glorious in holiness,
Fearful in praises, doing wonders?
Thou stretchedst out Thy right hand,
The earth swallowed them.

> *Thou in Thy mercy hast led the people, which Thou hast redeemed;*
> *Thou hast guided them in Thy strength to Thy holy habitation.*
> *The peoples have heard, they tremble;*
> *Pangs have taken hold on the inhabitants of Philistia.*
> *Then were the dukes of Edom amazed;*
> *The mighty men of Moab, trembling hath taken hold upon them;*
> *All the inhabitants of Canaan are melted away.*
> *Terror and dread falleth upon them;*
> *By the greatness of Thine arm they are as still as a stone;*
> *Till thy people pass over, O Lord,*
> *Till the people pass over which Thou hast purchased.*
> *Thou shalt bring them in, and plant them in the mountain of Thine inheritance,*
> *In the place, O Lord, which Thou hast made for Thee to dwell in,*
> *The sanctuary, O Lord, which Thy hands have established.*
> *The Lord shall reign for ever and ever."*
> Exodus 15:1-18

And now let us see what instruction and encouragement and hope there is in this record for us.

1. The power by which the Red Sea was divided, and the people passed over in safety, was the power by which their enemies were to be kept from attacking them. Compare Exodus 15:14-16 and Joshua 2:9-11. If they had gone forward in the faith that they had at the moment of their deliverance, there would have been no need of their fighting. No enemy would have dared to attack them. Now we can see why the Lord led them the way He did. By one final act of deliverance He designed to teach them never to be afraid of man.

2. In this same power they were to make known the name of the Lord – to preach the Gospel of the kingdom – in all the earth, as a preparation for the end. That was a work, which they had to do before the promise could be completely fulfilled. If they had kept the faith, it would not have taken long to complete the work.

3. The object of their deliverance was that they should be brought in and planted in the mountain of the Lord's inheritance – a land of their own, where they might dwell forever in safety. This had not been fulfilled in the days of King David, even when his kingdom was at its height; for it was at the time when he had rest from all his enemies, and proposed to build a temple for the Lord, that the Lord said to him, "Moreover, I will appoint a place for My people Israel, and will plant them, that they may dwell in a place of their own, and move no more; neither shall the children of wickedness afflict them any more as before time." Compare this also with Luke 1:67-75.

4. God's plan in delivering Israel from Egypt was thus set forth in the inspired song:

"Thou shalt bring them in, and plant them in the mountain of Thine inheritance, in the place, O Lord, which Thou hast made for Thee to dwell in, in the sanctuary, O Lord, which Thy hands have established." No man can build a dwelling-place for the Lord, for "the Most High dwelleth not in temples made with hands." Acts 7:48. "The Lord's throne is in heaven." Psalm 11:4. The true sanctuary, the real dwelling-place of God, "which the Lord pitched, and not man," (Hebrews 8:1, 2), is in heaven upon Mount Zion. This is in harmony with the promise made to Abraham, Isaac, and Jacob, and which led them to count themselves strangers on this earth, and to look for a heavenly country, and "for a city that hath foundations, whose builder and maker is God." Hebrews 11:10. This long-deferred hope was now about to be fulfilled, and it would have been fulfilled speedily if the children of Israel had kept the faith of their song.

5. The deliverance of Israel from Egypt and the dividing of the Red Sea is the encouragement of the people of God in the last days of the Gospel, when the salvation of the Lord is gone forth. These are the words, which the Lord teaches His people to say: –

"Awake, awake, put on strength, O arm of the Lord; awake as in the ancient days, in the generations of old. Art Thou not it that hath cut Rahab, and wounded the dragon? Art Thou not it which hath dried the sea, the waters of the great deep; that hath made the depths of the sea a way for the ransomed to pass over? Therefore the redeemed of the Lord shall return, and come with singing unto Zion; and everlasting joy shall be upon their head; they shall obtain gladness and joy; and sorrow and mourning shall flee away." Isaiah 51:9-11.

If the ancient Israelites had gone on singing, and had not once stopped to murmur, they would speedily have reached Zion, the city whose builder and maker is God.

6. When the redeemed of the Lord do at last stand on Mount Zion, having the harps of God, they will "sing the song of Moses the servant of God, and the song of the Lamb, saying, Great and marvelous are Thy works, Lord God Almighty; just and true are Thy ways, Thou King of saints. Who shall not fear Thee, O Lord, and glorify Thy name? for Thou only art holy; for all nations shall come and worship before Thee; for Thy judgments are made manifest." Revelation 15:3, 4. It is the song of deliverance, the song of victory.

7. Even as the children of Israel sang the song of victory while upon the shore of the Red Sea, before they reached the Promised Land, so the children of God in the last days will sing the song of victory before they reach the heavenly Canaan. Here is the song, and as we read it, compare it with the opening part of the song of Moses by the Red Sea. We have already read that when the Lord sets His hand the second time to recover the remnant of His people, "there shall be an highway for the remnant of His people, which shall be left from Assyria, like as it was to Israel in the day that he came up out of the land of Egypt." Isaiah 11:16.

"And in that day Thou shalt say, O Lord, I will praise Thee; though Thou wast angry with me, Thine anger is turned away, and Thou comfortedst me. Behold, God is my salvation; I will trust and not be afraid; for the Lord JEHOVAH is my strength and my song; He also is become my salvation. Therefore with joy shall ye draw water out of the wells of salvation. And in that day shall ye say. Praise the Lord, call upon His name, declare His doings among the people, make mention that His name is exalted. Sing unto the Lord; for He hath done excellent things; this is known in all the earth. Cry out and shout, thou inhabitant of Zion; for great is the Holy One of Israel in the midst of thee." Isaiah 12

This is the song with which the redeemed of the Lord are to come to Zion. It is a song of victory, but they can sing it now, for "this is the victory that hath overcome the world, even our faith." Only as they proclaim the salvation of the Lord, they do not share it. While being conducted to Zion, they learn the song that they will sing when they reach that place. Thus

"When, in scenes of glory,
I sing the NEW, NEW SONG,
'Twill be the OLD, OLD STORY
That I have loved so long."

Chapter 23

The Promises to Israel - Bread from Heaven

The Present Truth, October 8, 1896

It is with singing that the ransomed of the Lord will return and come to Zion. The song of victory is an evidence of faith, by which the just shall live. The exhortation is, "Cast not away therefore your confidence, which hath great recompense of reward." Hebrews 10:35. "We are made partakers of Christ, if we hold the beginning of our confidence steadfast unto the end." Hebrews 3:14. The Israelites had started well. "By faith they passed through the Red Sea as by dry land." On the other shore they had sung the song of victory. True, they were still in the wilderness; but faith is "the victory that hath overcome the world," and they had just received the most wonderful evidence of the power of God to carry them safely through. Had they but gone on singing that song of victory, they would speedily have come to Zion.

But they had not yet perfectly learned the lesson. They could trust the Lord as far as they could see Him, but no further. They "provoked Him at the sea, even at the Red Sea. Nevertheless He saved them for His name's sake, that He might make His mighty power to be known. He rebuked the Red Sea also, and it was dried up; so He led them through the depths, as through the wilderness. And he saved them from the hand of him that hated them, and redeemed them from the hand of the enemy. And the waters covered their enemies; there was not one of them left. Then believed they His words; they sang His praise; they soon forgot His works; they waited not for His counsel." Psalm 111:7-13.

Only three days' journey in the wilderness without water sufficed to make them forget all that the Lord had done for them.

When they found water, it was so bitter that they could not drink it, and then they murmured. This difficulty was easily remedied by the Lord, who showed Moses a tree which, when cast into the bitter waters, made them sweet. "There He made for them a statute and an ordinance, and there He proved them." Exodus 15:25.

Encamped by the palm trees and wells of Elim, they had nothing to vex them, so that it must have been nearly a month before they murmured again. During that time they doubtless felt very well satisfied with themselves, as well as with their surroundings.

Now they surely trusted the Lord! It is so easy for us to imagine that we are making progress when we are only lying at anchor, and the tide is flowing past us; so natural to think that we have learned to trust the Lord, when there are no trials to test our faith.

It was not long before the people not only forgot the power of the Lord, but they were ready to deny that He had ever had anything to do with them. It was only a month and a half after their leaving Egypt that they came to the wilderness of Sin, "which is between Elim and Sinai," "and the whole congregation of the children of Israel murmured against Moses and Aaron in the wilderness; and the children of Israel said unto them, Would to God we had died by the hand of the Lord in the land of Egypt, when we sat by the flesh pots, and when we did eat bread to the full; for ye have brought us forth into this wilderness, to kill this whole assembly with hunger.

"Then said the Lord unto Moses, Behold, I will rain bread from heaven for you; and the people shall go out and gather a certain rate every day, that I may prove them, whether they will walk in my law, or no. And it shall come to pass, that on the sixth day they shall prepare that which they bring in; and it shall be twice as much as they gather daily. And Moses and Aaron said unto all the children of Israel, At even, then ye shall know that the Lord hath brought you out from the land of Egypt; and in the morning, then ye shall see the glory of the Lord; for that He heareth your murmurings against the Lord; and what are we, that ye murmur against us?" Verses 4-7.

The next morning when the dew was gone, "behold, upon the face of the wilderness there lay a small round thing, as small as the hoar frost upon the ground. And when the children of Israel saw it, they said one to another, It is manna; for they wist not what it was. And Moses said unto them, This is the bread which the Lord hath given you to eat. This is the thing which the Lord hath commanded, Gather of it every man according to his eating, an omer for every man, according to the number of your persons; take ye every man for them which are in his tents. And the children of Israel did so, and gathered, some more, some less. And when they did mete it with an omer, he that gathered much had nothing over, and he that gathered little had no lack; they gathered every man according to his eating." Verses 14-18.

"And Moses said, Let no man leave of it till the morning. Notwithstanding they hearkened not unto Moses; but some of them left of it until the morning, and it bred worms, and stank; and Moses was wroth with them. And they gathered it every man according to his eating; and when the sun waxed hot it melted." Verses 19-21.

"And it came to pass, that on the sixth day they gathered twice as much bread, two omers for every man; and all the rulers of the congregation came and told Moses. And he said unto them, This is that which the Lord hath said, To-morrow is the rest of the holy Sabbath unto the Lord; bake that which ye will bake to-day, and seethe that ye will seethe; and that which remaineth over lay up for you to be kept until the morning.

And they laid it up till the morning, as Moses bade; and it did not stink, neither was there any worm therein. And Moses said, eat that to day: for to day is a Sabbath unto the Lord; to day ye shall not find it in the field. Six days ye shall gather it; but on the seventh day, which is the Sabbath, in it there shall be none." Verses 22-26.

"And it came to pass, that there went out some of the people on the seventh day for to gather, and they found none. And the Lord said unto Moses, How long refuse ye to keep My commandments and My laws? See, for that the Lord hath given you the Sabbath, therefore He giveth you on the Sabbath the bread of two days; abide ye every man in his place, let no man go out of His place on the seventh day. So the people rested on the seventh day." Verses 27-30.

We now have the entire story before us, and can study its lessons in detail.

Remember that this was not written for the sake of those who participated in it, but for us. "Whatsoever things were written aforetime were written for our learning, that we through patience and comfort of the Scriptures might have hope."

If they failed to learn the lesson that God designed they should from the event, there is so much the more reason for us to learn it from the record.

The Test

The Lord said that He would prove the people, whether they would walk in His law or not. And the special thing upon which they were tested was the Sabbath. If they would keep this, there was no doubt that they would keep the whole law.

The Sabbath, therefore, was the crucial test of the law of God, Even so it is now, as the following points that we have already learned will show: –

1. The people were being delivered in pursuance of the covenant made with Abraham. See Exodus 6:3, 4. That covenant had been confirmed with an oath, and the time of the promise, which God had sworn to Abraham, had come near. Abraham kept God's law, and it was on this account that the promise was continued to his descendants. Genesis 26:3-5. The Lord said to Isaac that He would perform all the oath that He swore unto Abraham his father, "Because that Abraham obeyed My voice, and kept My charge, My commandments, My statutes, and My laws." Now when God was bringing the children of Abraham out of Egypt, in fulfillment of that oath, He proposed to test them to see if they also would walk in His law; and the point upon which He tested them was the Sabbath. This therefore proves beyond all controversy that the Sabbath was kept by Abraham, and that it was in the covenant made with him. It was a part of the righteousness of the faith which Abraham had before he was circumcised.

2. "If ye are Christ's, then are ye Abraham's seed, and heirs according to the promise."

Now since the Sabbath – the very same one that the Israelites kept in the wilderness, and which the descendants of Jacob have kept, or professed to, until this day – was in the covenant made with Abraham, it follows that it is the Sabbath for Christians to keep.

3. We have already learned that our hope is the very same that was set before Abraham, Isaac, and Jacob, and all the children of Israel. "The hope of the promise made of God unto the fathers," was that for which the Apostle Paul was judged (Acts 26:6); and the promise to the faithful is that they shall sit down with Abraham, Isaac, and Jacob in the kingdom of God. The Lord has set His hand the second time to deliver the remnant of His people and therefore the test of obedience at this time is the same that it was at the beginning. The Sabbath is the memorial of God's power as Creator and Sanctifier; and in the message that announces the hour of God's Judgment at hand, the everlasting Gospel, which is the preparation for the end, is preached in the words, "Worship Him that made heaven, and earth, and the sea, and the fountains of waters." Revelation 14:6, 7.

This test was made before the law was spoken from Sinai, and before the people had reached that place. Yet we find that every feature of the law was already known. So far was the giving of the law from Sinai from being the first announcement of it, that more than a month before that event the children of Israel were tasted upon it; and the words, "How long refuse ye to keep My commandments and My laws?" show that they had known it a long time, and had often broken it through their unbelief.

When we come to the events connected with the giving of the law, we shall be able to see more clearly than now that the Sabbath, which the Jews were, expected to keep could not by any possibility be affected by the death of Christ, but that it was for ever identified with the Gospel, centuries before the crucifixion. In this connection, however, we must note one point in regard to the definiteness of the Sabbath day.

The people were told, "Six days shall ye gather it; but on the seventh day, which is the Sabbath, in it there shall be none." This is the very same expression that is used in the fourth commandment, "Six days shalt thou labor, and do all thy work; but the seventh day is the Sabbath of the Lord thy God; in it thou shalt not do any work." Many people have been led to believe that the commandment is not definite in its requirement, and that the Sabbath is not by it fixed to one particular day of the week, but that any day of the week will answer, provided it is preceded by six days of labor. The account of the giving of the manna shows that this is a mistaken idea, and that the commandment requires not simply an indefinite seventh part of time, but the seventh day of the week.

The giving of the manna showed most positively that the Sabbath day was definite, and that it was not left for man to decide which day it is. Moreover, it showed that "the seventh day" does not mean the seventh part of time, but a definitely recurring day.

If "the seventh day" means one seventh part of time, then "the sixth day" would at the same time mean the sixth part of time; but if the children of Israel had proceeded upon that assumption, they would have been in difficulty the first thing.

There is but one period of seven days, and that is the week, which was known from the creation. God worked six days, and in those first six days He finished the work of creation; "and He rested the seventh day from His work which He had made. And God blessed the seventh day, and sanctified it; because that in it He had rested from all His work which God created and made." Genesis 2:2, 3. Therefore, when God says that the seventh day is the Sabbath, He means that the Sabbath is the seventh day of the week, the day that is commonly known as Saturday. The sixth day, upon which the children of Israel were to prepare for the Sabbath, is the sixth day of the week, commonly called Friday.

This is also settled beyond all controversy by the account of the crucifixion and burial of Christ, where we are told that the women came to the sepulcher "in the end of the Sabbath, as it began to dawn toward the first day of the week" (Matthew 28:1); and by another writer that it was "when the Sabbath was past." Mark 16:1. We refer to these texts to show that the first day of the week immediately follows the Sabbath, and that no time intervened between the close of the Sabbath and the visit of the women to the sepulcher. Now when we read the record in Luke, we learn that when Christ was buried "that day was the preparation, and the Sabbath drew on." The women came and saw where He was laid, "and they returned, and prepared spices and ointments, and rested the Sabbath day according to the commandment." And "upon the first day of the week, very early in the morning, they came unto the sepulcher." Luke 23:54-56; 24:1.

The Sabbath followed "the preparation," and immediately preceded "the first day of the week." Therefore, the Sabbath was the seventh day of the week. And it was "the Sabbath day according to the commandment." Therefore, the Sabbath of the commandment is none other than the seventh day of the week. This was the day, which God marked out in the most special manner as the Sabbath, by performing wonderful miracles in its honor for forty years. Let this fact be well considered. Let it be remembered that whenever in the Bible the Sabbath is spoken of, the seventh day of the week, and that only, is meant. That long before the days of Moses, this Sabbath of the fourth commandment, together with the whole law, was inseparably connected with the Gospel of Jesus Christ, will be very apparent as we proceed in our study.

Chapter 24

The Promises to Israel - Life from God

The Present Truth, October 15, 1896

At the close of the wandering in the wilderness, Moses said to the people, "All the commandments which I command thee this day shall ye observe to do, that ye may live, and multiply, and go in and possess the land which the Lord swore unto your fathers. And thou shalt remember all the way which the Lord thy God led thee these forty years in the wilderness, to humble thee, and to prove thee, to know what was in thine heart, whether thou wouldst keep His commandments, or no. And He humbled thee, and suffered thee to hunger; and fed thee with manna, which thou knewest not, neither did thy fathers know; that He might make thee know that man doth not live by bread only, but by every word that proceedeth out of the mouth of the Lord doth man live." Deuteronomy 8:1-3.

"The word of God is living and active." Hebrews 4:12. Christ said, "The words that I speak unto you, they are spirit, and they are life." John 6:68. Through the prophet He says, "Incline your ear, and come unto Me; hear, and your soul shall live." Isaiah 55:3. "Verily, verily, I say unto you, The hour is coming, and now is, when the dead shall hear the voice of the Son of God; and they that hear shall live." John 5:25. That time had come in the days when the children of Israel were in the wilderness. In the giving of the manna He was teaching them that men could live only by "every word that proceedeth out of the mouth of God."

Note this well. God was proving them by the manna, whether they would walk in His law or not. But at the same time He was teaching them that the law is life. Jesus said, "I know that His commandment is life everlasting." John 12:50. They were to keep the commandments that they might live, but they could keep them only by hearing them. The life is in the commandments themselves, and not in the individual who tries to keep them. He can get no life from his own efforts, yet he is to get life through the commandments. Grace reigns through righteousness unto eternal life through Jesus Christ our Lord. The reason is that the word itself is life, and if we listen attentively to it, we shall be made alive by it. "O that thou hadst hearkened to My commandments! Then had thy peace been as a river, and thy righteousness as the waves of the sea." Isaiah 48:18.

Jesus said, "If thou wilt enter into life, keep the commandments." Matthew 19:17. But it is not by our efforts to conform to a certain standard, and by measuring ourselves by it to see what progress we are making, that we get righteousness and life. Such a course makes Pharisees, but not Christians. Abraham kept all the commandments of God, and yet not a line of them was written. How did He do it? – By hearkening unto the voice of God, and by trusting Him. God bore witness that he had the righteousness of faith.

In the same way that He had led Abraham, God was leading the children of Israel. He had spoken to them by His prophets, and by the miracles that He had wrought in delivering them from Egypt; He had shown them His power to work righteousness in them. If they had but listened to His voice, and believed Him, there would have been no difficulty in regard to their righteousness. If they would only trust God, and not trust in themselves, He would be responsible for their righteousness and life. "Hear, O My people, and I will testify unto thee; O Israel, if thou wilt hearken unto Me, there shall no strange god be in thee; neither shalt thou worship any strange god. I am the Lord thy God, which brought thee out of the land of Egypt; open thy mouth wide, and I will fill it." Psalm 81:8-10. "Blessed are they which do hunger and thirst after righteousness; for they shall be filled." Matthew 5:6. In the giving of the manna, God was trying to teach them this fact, and in the record of it He expects us to learn it. Let us therefore study it a little more closely.

Living Bread

The Apostle Paul tells us that the children of Israel in the wilderness "did all eat the same spiritual meat." 1 Corinthians 10:4. We have already read the words of the Lord when He promised to give them food, saying, "Behold, I will rain bread from heaven for you." He "commanded the clouds from above, and opened the doors of heaven;" He "rained down manna upon them to eat," and gave them "of the corn of heaven;" "man did eat angels' food." Psalm 78:23-25.

The food that they had to eat was not a product of the country through which they were passing. If it had been, they would have had it from the first. But the Scripture tells us that it was rained down from heaven. It came direct from God. It was "spiritual meat," "angels' food." What it was intended to be for them, if they had only believed it, we learn from the words of Christ, when on another occasion He fed a multitude of people in the desert.

In the sixth chapter of John we have the account of another miraculous provision of food for a multitude of people in the wilderness. There were "about five thousand men, beside women and children," and the entire amount of food in the company was five barley loaves and two fishes. One of the disciples said that two hundred penny-worth of bread would not be sufficient for every one to have even a little. Their "penny," we are told, was a coin equal to about eightpence-halfpenny, so that two hundred pence would be more than seven pounds, which would purchase much more than the same amount now. Yet even that would have afforded but a scanty meal. No wonder that Peter said of the paltry five loaves and fishes, "What are they among so many?"

Nevertheless Jesus "knew what He would do." He took the loaves into his hands, and gave thanks, and then gave the bread to the disciples, who passed it on to the multitude. The same was done with the fishes. The result was that from that insignificant amount which would not ordinarily have given them a taste, they were all satisfied, and there were twelve baskets full of fragments left. There was more food when they had finished than there was when they began.

Where did that bread come from? There is only one possible answer, namely, It came from the Lord Himself. The Divine life that was in Him, which is the source of all life, caused the bread to multiply, even as it had made the grain to grow, from which it was made. The multitude, therefore, ate from Christ Himself. It was His own life that was the nourishment of their bodies that day. The miracle was wrought for the purpose of satisfying their immediate physical wants; but it was also designed to teach them a most valuable spiritual lesson, which Jesus set before them the next day.

When the people found Jesus the next day, He reproved them for caring more for the loaves and the fishes than for the better food, which He had for them. He said, "Labor not for the meat which perisheth, but for that meat which endureth unto everlasting life, which the Son of man shall give unto you; for Him hath God the Father sealed." Then they said to Him, "What shall we do that we might work the works of God?" Jesus replied, "This is the work of God, that ye believe on Him whom He hath sent." John 6:28, 29. Then, notwithstanding all that they had seen and experienced, they asked Him for a sign, saying, "What sign showest Thou, then, that we may see and believe? What dost Thou work?" And then, not realizing that they had just had the same miracle repeated in effect for them, they referred to the giving of the manna, saying, "Our fathers did eat manna in the desert; as it is written, He gave them bread from heaven to eat." Verses 30, 31.

Jesus then reminded them that it was not Moses that gave them that bread in the desert, but that God alone gives the true bread from heaven. Said He, "The bread of God is He which cometh down from heaven, and giveth life unto the world." Still failing to see what Jesus meant, they asked that they might evermore have that bread of life, when He told them plainly that He Himself was the living bread, saying, "I am the bread of life; he that cometh to Me shall never hunger, and he that believeth on Me shall never thirst." Still later Jesus said, "Verily, verily, I say unto you, He that believeth on Me hath everlasting life. I am that bread of life. Your fathers did eat manna in the wilderness, and are dead. This is the bread which cometh down from heaven, that a man may eat thereof, and not die. I am the living bread which came down from heaven; if any man eat of this bread, he shall live for ever; and the bread that I will give is My flesh, which I will give for the life of the world." Verses 32-51.

Just as the people ate that bread which came from the Lord Jesus, and were strengthened by it, even so they might, if they had believed, have received spiritual life from Him. His life is righteousness, and all who eat of Him in faith must receive righteousness. Like ancient Israel, they were eating bread from heaven, and like them they did not appreciate it, so as to receive the full benefit of it.

Chapter 25

The Promises to Israel - Life from the Word

The Present Truth, October 22, 1896

The Jews found it difficult to believe the words of Christ, that He would give them Himself to eat. They said, "How can this man give us His flesh to eat?" Jesus repeated the statement still more emphatically, and then said, "It is the Spirit that quickeneth; the flesh profiteth nothing; the words that I speak unto you, they are Spirit, and they are life."

If each one of them could have eaten of the flesh of Christ as He stood there, and the flesh, which they ate, had been replaced, so that they could continue to eat of it, taking it into their stomachs, and assimilating it, they would have received no lasting benefit from it. No spiritual good would have come to them. That was what they had in reality already done, when they ate of the bread, which came from the life that was in His body; but they had not profited by it. So if the Romish claim were true, that the priests have power to transform the bread into the actual flesh of Christ, there would be no profit in it. People might eat of it, and be as wicked as ever. "The flesh profiteth nothing; the words that I speak unto you, they are Spirit, and they are life." John 6:63.

"By the word of the Lord were the heavens made; and all the host of them by the breath of His mouth." Psalm 33:6. He spoke and said, "Let the earth bring forth grass, the herb yielding seed, and the fruit tree yielding fruit after his kind, whose seed is in itself, upon the earth; and it was so." Genesis 1:11. All plant life is but the manifestation of the life of the word of the Lord. The life that was in His word caused the corn to grow in the beginning, and that same life has caused it to grow ever since. Therefore all the food that men have to eat is that which comes from the word of God. We cannot see the life in a grain of wheat, but when we eat the bread that is made from it, we experience it. But the physical strength, which we receive from the food, is but the working of the word of the Lord. Now if we do not recognize and acknowledge God in this, we get nothing but physical strength; but if in everything we see and acknowledge God, we receive of His life of righteousness. He says, "In all thy ways acknowledge Him, and He shall direct thy paths." Proverbs 3:6.

When God directs our paths, those ways will be right; for "as for God, His way is perfect." Psalm 18:30. The people who ate of the loaves in the desert, did not believe the Lord, and did not recognize His life, and so they derived no spiritual life from it. So it was with the children of Israel in the desert. "They believed not in God, and trusted not in His salvation; though He had commanded the clouds from above, and opened the doors of heaven, and had rained down upon them manna to eat, and had given them of the corn of heaven." Psalm 78:22-24. So although they were indeed feeding upon the life of Christ, they received no spiritual life, because of their blind unbelief. In the giving of the manna God was giving the same lesson that Christ gave the multitude in the desert, namely, that His word is life, and that "man doth not live by bread alone, but by every word that proceedeth out of the mouth of God."

The manna was the test of their loyalty to the law of God, and especially to the Sabbath as a seal of that law. But in the manna they were taking in Christ, if they had only realized it. Therefore we are to learn that if we but allow Christ to dwell in our hearts by faith in His word, – not a part only, but the whole, – He will bring into our lives the keeping of the whole law, including the Sabbath. Every word that proceeds out of the mouth of God is necessary for our lives.

It is customary among Christians to return thanks whenever they eat. There is just as much reason for giving thanks when we drink, or when we receive any other of God's blessings. "In everything give thanks; for this is the will of God in Christ Jesus concerning you." The trouble is that giving thanks is so often a mere form. It is often done because it has become the custom, and not from the heart. What does it really mean? Just this: That our food and drink, and everything necessary for our life, comes from God. It is all a manifestation of His love for us. But since "God is love," the manifestation of His love is but the manifestation of His life. In partaking of the bounties of His love, we are in reality partaking of Him. Now if we continually recognize this, and knowledge it, whether we eat, or drink, or whatsoever we do call, all will be done to the glory of God. We shall live as in His immediate presence. Knowing that His life is righteousness, and that His word is His life, our thanks for food will be thanks for His word.

Who cannot see that such a life must necessarily be a righteous life? With our daily food we shall be feeding upon Christ, and so of course upon His righteousness. This is what God wishes us to learn from the account of the giving of the manna. It was their life, and if they had recognized Christ in it, their life would have been the righteousness of the law. But our daily food comes from God just as surely as theirs did. May we learn a lesson that they neglected.

A Lesson of Equality

In the account of the giving of the manna, we find the statement often repeated, "they gathered it every man according to his eating." They were also told to gather it for them that were in the tents. "And the children of Israel did so, and gathered, some more, some less. And when they did mete it with an omer, he that gathered much had nothing over, and he that gathered little had no lack." Exodus 16:17, 18.

There is something wonderful about this. It seems as though there was a miracle in it, and so there was in a sense; but the miracle did not consist in one man's large amount suddenly shrinking in the measure, and another man's half empty measure mysteriously filling up. The Apostle Paul helps us to an understanding of it. Writing to the Corinthian brethren, concerning giving, he said: "I mean not that other men be eased, and ye burdened; but by an equality, that now at this time your abundance may be a supply for their want, that their abundance may also be a supply for your want; that there may be equality; as it is written, He that had gathered much had nothing over; and he that had gathered little had no lack." 2 Corinthians 13:13-15.

The miracle was a miracle of the grace of God in giving. He that gathered much had nothing over; because he divided with some one who had little, or who had not been able to gather any; and thus he that gathered little had no lack. And so we find that there in the wilderness there was the same principle acted upon that was in the church after the day of Pentecost. "And the multitude of them that believed were of one heart and of one soul; neither said any of them that aught of the things which he possessed was his own; but they had all things common. And with great power gave the apostles witness of the resurrection of the Lord Jesus; and great grace was upon them all. Neither was there any among them that lacked." Acts 4:32-34.

We talk much about the faults of the ancient Israelites; it is well sometimes to consider the other side. With all their faults, they had none except such as are common to men. They were no worse than people generally are, and they sometimes rose to heights of faith and trust that are rarely seen. We need not suppose that they always kept up this kindness, and that there were not greedy ones among them. Even so it was in the church whose history is given in the Acts of the Apostles. But it is enough for us to know what they did at least part of the time, and to know that God approved it. God gave them bread abundantly. Their part was simply to gather it. There was therefore no reason why they should not divide with their needy brethren. Indeed, as we look at it from this distance, it seems the most natural thing in the world to do.

But our condition is the same as theirs. We have nothing except that which comes from God. He gives it, and the most that we can do is to gather His bounty. Therefore we ought not to consider any of our possessions as our own, but to hold them simply in trust for Him. But take notice that this is far different from all modern schemes of communism. It is not a dividing of property by law, but a daily giving by the strong to the weak. No one laid up anything for the future, leaving others destitute of present provisions, but trusted God for his daily supply.

That sort of communism cannot be attained by any human plans. It is the result of the love of God in the heart. "Whoso hath this world's goods, and seeth his brother have need, and shutteth up his bowels of compassion from him, how dwelleth the love of God in him?" "For ye know the grace of our Lord Jesus Christ, that, though he was rich, yet for your sakes He became poor, that ye through His poverty might be rich." This grace and this love characterize the true Israel.

Chapter 26

The Promises to Israel - Living Water from the Rock

The Present Truth, October 29, 1896

"Rock of Ages cleft for me, Let me hide myself in Thee."

"And all the congregation of the children of Israel journeyed from the wilderness of Sin, by their journeys, according to the commandment of the Lord, and pitched in Rephidim; and there was no water for the people to drink. Wherefore the people strove with Moses, and said, Give us water that we may drink. And Moses said unto them, Why strive ye with me? Wherefore do ye tempt the Lord? And the people thirsted there for water; and the people murmured against Moses, and said.

Wherefore hast then brought us up out of Egypt, to kill us and our children and our cattle with thirst? And Moses cried unto the Lord, saying, What shall I do unto this people? They be almost ready to stone me. And the Lord said unto Moses, Pass on before the people, and take with thee of the elders of Israel; and thy rod, wherewith thou smotest the river, take in thine hand, and go. Behold, I will stand before thee there upon the rock in Horeb; and thou shalt smile the rock, and there shall come water out of it, that the people may drink. And Moses did so in the sight of the elders of Israel. And he called the name of the place Massah, and Meribah, because of the striving of the people of Israel, and because they tempted the Lord, saying, Is the Lord among us, or not?" Exodus 27:1-7.

We have seen that in the manna God was giving the people spiritual food. In like manner we read, with reference to the event just narrated, that they "did all drink the same spiritual drink; for they drank of that Rock that followed [margin, "went with"] them; and that Rock was Christ." 1 Corinthians 10:4.

Water is one of the things most essential to life. Indeed, it is life. It constitutes two-thirds of the human body. Without a proper supply of water, both animals and plants soon cease to exist. Those people in the desert would soon have perished, if water had not been provided for them. It was therefore life to them. Everybody who has suffered from thirst can vividly realize how the spirits of the children of Israel revived, and new life sprang up in them, as they drank of that fresh, sparkling living water that gushed forth from the smitten rock.

"And that Rock was Christ." Many times the Lord is represented as a Rock. "The Lord is my Rock, and my Fortress, and my Deliverer." Psalm 18:2. "The Lord is upright; He is my Rock, and there is no unrighteousness in Him." Psalm 92:15. "Ascribe ye greatness unto our God. He is the Rock, His work is perfect; for all His ways are judgment; a God of truth and without iniquity, just and right is He." Deuteronomy 32:3, 4. Jesus Christ is the Rock upon which the church is built – the "living stone, disallowed indeed of men, but chosen of God, and precious," upon whom, if we come to Him, we are "built up a spiritual house." 1 Peter 2:4, 5. Both prophets and apostles built on Him not only as "the chief corner stone," (Ephesians 2:20), but as the entire foundation, and the only one that can be laid. 1 Corinthians 3:11. Whosoever builds not on Him, builds on the shifting sand.

The rock, which the people saw in the desert, was but a figure of the Rock, Jesus Christ, who stood upon it, but whom they did not see. That flinty rock could not of itself furnish water. There was no exhaustless supply stored up within it, which, once given vent, would continue to flow ever fresh and sweet. It had no life. But Christ, "the Author of Life" stood upon it, and it was from Him that the water came. We do not need to theorize, for the Scripture plainly tells us that the people drank from Christ.

This must have been evident to every one who gave a moment's thought to the matter. Indeed, the water was given as a direct answer to the unbelieving question, "Is the Lord among us, or not?" By supplying them with water out of the solid, flinty rock in the dry and barren desert, the Lord showed the people that He was really among them; for none but He could have done it.

But it was not simply as a guest that He was among them. He was their life, and this miracle was designed to teach them that fact. They knew that water was their sole hope of life, and they could not help seeing that the water, which revived them, came directly from the Lord. Therefore those who stopped to think must have seen that He was their life and their support. Whether they knew it or not, they were drinking directly from Christ, that is, receiving of His life. With Him is "the fountain of life." Psalm 36:9.

It made all the difference in the world whether or not the people recognized Christ as the source of their life. If they did, if they drank in faith, they received spiritual life from the Rock. If they did not recognize the Lord in His gracious gift, then the water was no more to them than it was to their cattle. "Man that is in honor, and understandeth not, is like the beasts that perish." Psalm xlix. 20. But when the people with their superior abilities did not recognize God in His gifts any more than their cattle did, they showed themselves even less discerning than the cattle. "The ox knoweth his owner, and the ass his master's crib; but Israel doth not know, My people doth not consider." Isaiah 1:3.

In view of the miracle of the water from the Rock, the Lord Himself, we can better understand the force of His words when He afterward thus expressed the greatness of their sin in departing from Him: "Be astonished, O ye heavens, at this, and be horribly afraid, be ye very desolate, saith the Lord. For My people have committed two evils; they have forsaken Me, the fountain of living waters, and hewed them out cisterns, broken cisterns, that can hold no water." Jeremiah 2:12, 13.

The Psalmist said of the Lord, "He is my Rock, and there is no unrighteousness in Him." His life is righteousness. Therefore those who live by faith in Him live righteous lives. The water, which came from the Rock, in the desert, was for the life of the people. It was Christ's own life. If, therefore, in drinking it they had recognized the source whence it came, they would have been drinking in righteousness, and would have been blessed with righteousness; for it is written, "Blessed are they which do hunger and thirst after righteousness; for they shall be filled." Matthew 5:6. If we thirst for righteousness, and are filled, it is only by drinking in the righteousness for which we thirst.

Jesus Christ is the fountain of living water. So when the woman of Samaria expressed surprise that He should ask her for a drink as she came to draw from Jacob's well, He said to her: "If thou knewest the gift of God, and who it is that saith to thee, Give me to drink, thou wouldst have asked of Him, and He would have given thee living water." And then, as she still wondered at His words, He added, "Whosoever drinketh of this water shall thirst again; but whosoever drinketh of the water that I shall give him shall never thirst; but the water that I shall give him shall be in him a well of water springing up into everlasting life." John 4:10-14.

This living water may be drunk now by "whosoever will." For "the Spirit and the Bride say, Come. And let him that heareth say, Come. And let him that is athirst come. And whosoever will, let him take the water of life freely." Revelation 22:17.

This water of life of which all are invited to drink freely, is the "pure river of water of life, clear as crystal, proceeding out of the throne of God and of the Lamb." Revelation 22:1. It proceeds from Christ, for when John saw the throne, from which the water of life comes, he saw "in the midst of the throne" "a Lamb as it had been slain, having seven eyes, which are the Seven Spirits of God sent forth into all the earth." Revelation 5:6.

If we look to Calvary we shall see this made still plainer. As Jesus hung upon the cross, "one of the soldiers with a spear pierced His side, and forthwith came there out blood and water." John 19:34. Now "there are three who bear witness, the Spirit, and the water, and the blood; and the three agree in one." 1 John 5:8, R.V. We know that "the blood is the life," (Leviticus 17:11, 14), and that "the Spirit is life because of righteousness;" (Romans 8:10); therefore since the Spirit and the water and the blood agree in one, the water must also be the water of life. On the cross Christ poured out His life for mankind. His body was the temple of God, and in His heart God was enthroned; so the water of life, which flowed from His wounded side, was the same water of life that flows from the throne of God, from which we may all drink and live. His heart is the fountain opened "for sin and for uncleanness." Zechariah 13:1.

It is the Spirit of God that brings this water of life to us; or, rather, it is by receiving the Holy Spirit that we receive the water of life; and this we do by faith in Christ, who is represented by the Holy Spirit. On the last day of the feast of tabernacles, "Jesus stood and cried, saying, If any man thirst, let him come unto Me, and drink. He that believeth on Me, as the Scripture hath said, out of his belly shall flow rivers of living water. But this spake He of the Spirit, which they that believe on Him should receive." John 7:37-39.

The Holy Spirit received into the heart brings to us the very life of Christ, even "that eternal life which was with the Father, and was manifested unto us." 1 John 1:2. Whoever willingly receives the Holy Spirit receives the water of life, which is identical with the blood of Christ, which cleanses from all sin. This would have been the portion of the Israelites in the desert, if they had but drank in faith. In the rock, which Moses smote, they had, even as did the Galatians in Paul's day, Jesus Christ "evidently set forth crucified" among them. Galatians 3:1. They stood at the foot of the cross of Christ as really as did the Jews who flocked out from Jerusalem to Calvary. Many of them did not know the day of their visitation, and so perished in the wilderness, even as the later Jews did not know the crucified Christ, and so perished in their sins in the destruction of Jerusalem. "But as many as received Him, to them gave He power to become the sons of God, even to them that believe on His name." John 1:12.

The Israelites, in the days of Moses, had no excuse for not knowing the Lord, for He made Himself known unto them by many mighty miracles. There was no excuse for their not recognizing Him as "the Lamb of God, which taketh away the sin of the world," for they had daily evidence that He was their life; the smitten rock continually spoke to them of the Rock of their salvation pouring out His life for them from His smitten side.

The ransomed of the Lord are to come to Zion with songs, but they are not to be forced songs. They will sing because they are happy; because nothing but song will express their joy. This joy is the joy of the Lord. He feeds them with bread from heaven and makes them drink of the river of His pleasures. That is, He gives them Himself. But when the Lord gives us Himself, there is nothing more to give. "He that spared not His own Son, but delivered Him up for us all, how shall He not with Him also freely give us all things?" Romans 8:32. God gives Himself to us in giving us His life in Christ; and this was expressed to the Israelites in the giving of the water of life, which came from Christ. Therefore we know that everything, which the Gospel of Christ has for men, was there for the children of Israel in the desert.

We have already learned that the promise to Abraham was the Gospel. The oath, which confirmed that promise, is the oath that gives us strong consolation when we flee for refuge to Christ, in the holy place of God. It was to assure the Israelites of the free grace of God, and that they could drink in the life of Christ, if they would believe, that the water came from the Rock. It was to assure them that the blessing of Abraham, which is the forgiveness of sins through the righteousness of God in Christ, was for them. This is shown by the words, "He opened the rock, and the waters gushed out; they ran in the dry places like a river. For He remembered His holy promise, and Abraham His servant." Psalm 105:41, 42.

Jesus Christ is "the Lamb slain from the foundation of the world," (Revelation 13:8), "who verily was foreordained before the foundation of the world." 1 Peter 1:20. The cross of Christ is not a thing of a day, but stands wherever there are sinners to be saved, ever since the fall. It is always present, so that continually believers may say with Paul, "I am crucified with Christ, nevertheless I live." Galatians 2:20. We have not to look backward to see the cross, even as the men of the most ancient times had not to look forward to see it. It stands with its outstretched arms spanning the centuries from Eden lost till Eden restored, and always and everywhere men have only to look up, to see Christ "lifted up from the earth" drawing them to Him by His everlasting love, which flows out to them in a living stream.

The Real Presence

In their murmuring for water the people had said, "Is the Lord among us, or not?" The Lord answered that question in a most practical way. He stood upon the rock in Horeb, and gave them water that they might drink and live. He was really there in person. It was His Real Presence. He was there nonetheless because they could not see Him. And as He was giving them evidence that He was not far from every one of them, so, if they had felt after Him by faith they would have found and received Him, and His real presence would have been in them as truly as was the water, which they drank.

In the manna, the bread from heaven, which the Israelites were eating every day, and in the water from the Rock Christ Jesus, we have the exact counterpart of the Lord's Supper. The bread and the water were not Christ, even as the bread and the wine cannot by any means be changed into the body and blood of Christ. It would be of no use even if they could be thus changed, for "the flesh profiteth nothing." But they showed the real presence, to all who had eyes of faith to discern the Lord's body. They showed that Christ dwells in the heart by faith just as freely as the emblems are received into the body; and that just as really as those emblems are assimilated, and become flesh, so really does Christ, the Word, become flesh in all those receive Him by faith. Christ is formed within by the power of the Spirit.

God is not a myth. The Holy Spirit is not a myth. His presence is just as real as He Himself. When Christ says, "Behold, I stand at the door, and knock; if any man hear My voice, and open the door, I will come in to him, and sup with him," (Revelation 3:20), He means it for an actual fact; and when He says, "If any man love Me, he will keep My word; and My Father will love him, and we will come unto him, and make our abode with him," (John 14:22), He does not intend to deceive us with a phantom. He comes in the flesh to-day as really as He did in Judea. His appearance then was simply to show all men the possibility and the perfection of it. And just as He comes in the flesh now, to all who receive Him, so He did in the days of old, when Israel was in the wilderness; yea, even in the days of Abraham and Abel. We may weary ourselves in speculations as to how it is possible, and die in spiritual starvation by this means, or we may "taste and see that the Lord is good," and find in His presence satisfaction and "fullness of joy."

Chapter 27

The Promises to Israel - Object Teaching

The Present Truth, November 5, 1896

God deals with us as with children, and teaches us by object lessons. By the things that we can see, He teaches us the things that mortal eye cannot see. So in the water that flowed from the rock, and in the water and the blood, which flowed from the side of Christ, we learn the reality of the life that Christ gives those who believe on Him. Spiritual things are not imaginary, but real. The people in the desert could know that the water that refreshed their bodies came direct from Christ, and from that they could know that He can actually give life. They could not know how, but that was not necessary. It was sufficient for them to know the fact.

If we believe the Word, we may know that we drink as directly from Christ as did the Israelites in the wilderness. He made the heaven, and the earth, and the sea, and the fountains of water. "In Him all things consist." The water, which we drink, coming forth from the ground, is as truly from Him as that which gushed from the rock in Horeb. "He layeth up the depth in storehouses." Psalm 33:7.

People speak of the water on the earth as a "natural product," almost with the thought that it is self-existent. The falling rain and the flowing spring are referred to "natural causes." Convenient terms are these to avoid giving God the glory. Stand by a stream of clear, sparkling water as it rushes on its way from its birthplace in the mountains. It is ever changing, yet ever the same. Unceasing in its flow, why does it not exhaust the supply? Is there a reservoir of infinite capacity in the heart of the earth that enables the brook to "go on forever," without ever diminishing the quantity. Is there not something marvelous about that constant flow? "Oh no," says the man who knows it all, "it is a very simple matter; the water on the earth's surface is drawn up to the clouds, and these give rain which keeps the supply constantly good." But who causes the rain? "The Lord is the true God, He is the living God, and an everlasting King; . . . when He uttereth His voice, there is a multitude of waters in the heavens, and He causeth the vapors to ascend from the ends of the earth." Jeremiah 10:10-13. He is the "living God" and the operations of "nature" are but manifestations of His ceaseless activity.

No doubt the Israelites in the desert soon ceased to look upon the flow of water from the rock as miraculous. No doubt many of them never, even at the first, gave a single thought to it, save that it afforded a supply for their thirst. But as it flowed on year after year, and became a familiar thing, the wonder of it diminished, and at last ceased altogether. Children were born, to whom it was as though it always had been; to them it seemed but a product of "natural causes" as do the springs which we may now see coming from the earth; and so the Great Source was forgotten, even as He is now.

Be assured that those who credit everything to "Nature," and who do not acknowledge and glorify God as the immediate source of all earthly gifts, would do the same in heaven, if they were admitted to that place. To them the river of life eternally flowing from the throne of God, would be but "one of the phenomena of nature." They did not see it begin to flow and they would look upon it as a matter of course, and would not glorify God for it. The man who does not recognize and acknowledge God in His works in this world, would be as unmindful of Him in the world to come. The praise to God that will come from the lips of the redeemed in eternity will be but the full chorus of the song whose first strains they practiced on earth.

Acknowledging God

"In all thy ways acknowledge Him, and He shall direct thy paths." Proverbs 3:6. When God directs a man's ways they are all perfect; even as God's own ways. "What man is he that feareth the Lord? Him shall he teach in the way that He shall choose." The man who sees and acknowledges God in all His works, and who in everything gives thanks, will live a righteous life.

Take the gift of water, which we are continually using. If as often as we need water we thought of God as the provider of it, and as often as we saw it or used it we thought of Christ as the giver of the water of life, and remembered that in that water we receive His own life, what would be the result? – Simply this that our lives would be continually subject to His control. Acknowledging that our life comes from Him, we should realize that He alone has the right to order it; and we should allow Him to live His own life in us. Thus we should drink in righteousness. For us truth would spring out of the earth, and righteousness look down from heaven. Psalm 85:11. Even the skies would "pour down righteousness." Isaiah 45:8.

This acknowledgment of God in all our ways would keep us from selfish pride, and from boastful trust in our own "natural abilities." We should continually heed the words, "Who maketh thee to differ from another? and what hast thou that thou didst not receive? Now if thou didst receive it, why dost thou glory, as if thou hadst not received it?" This would keep us in the right way, for the promise is, "The meek will He guide in judgment; and the meek will He teach His way." Psalm 25:9. Instead of our own weak, foolish wisdom, we should have the wisdom of God to guide us.

We learn the same truth by looking at the opposite side. Men became degraded heathen simply through not acknowledging God as He is revealed in "the things that are made." For the gross darkness into which they fell there is no excuse, "because that when they knew God, they glorified Him not as God, neither were thankful; but became vain they became fools, and changed the glory of the uncorruptible God into an image made like to corruptible man, and to birds, and fourfooted beasts, and creeping things." "And even as they did not like to retain God in their knowledge, God gave them over to a reprobate mind [a mind void of judgment], to do those things which are not convenient; being filled with all unrighteousness," etc. Romans 1:21-23, 28, 29.

Even so it was with the Israelites, who were in a most wonderful manner permitted to see some of God's wonderful works, but who did not acknowledge Him in them. "They made a calf in those days, and offered sacrifice unto the idol, and rejoiced in the works of their own hands." Acts. 8:40. "Thus they changed their glory into the similitude of an ox that eateth grass. They forgot God their Saviour, which had done great things in Egypt; wondrous works in the land of Ham, and terrible things by the Red Sea." Psalm 106:20-22.

But this need not have been; it need not be now. God was bringing the children of Israel to plant them in the mountain of His own inheritance, in the place which He had made for Himself to dwell in, the Sanctuary, which His hands had established; and while they were on the way He would have them partake of the delights of that place. So He gave them water direct from Himself, to show them that by faith they could even then approach His throne, and drink the water of life that flows from it.

The same lesson is for us. God does not wish us to wait until immortality is bestowed upon us before we can share the joys of the heavenly city. By the blood of Christ we have boldness to enter even into the Most Holy place of His sanctuary. We are invited to come boldly to His throne of grace to find mercy. His grace, or favor, is life, and it flows in a living stream. Surely, since we are permitted to come to the throne of God, whence the river of life flows, there is nothing to hinder our drinking of it, especially when He offers it freely. Revelation 12:17.

"Blessed are they that dwell in Thy house; they will be still praising Thee." Psalm 84:4. If in the things that we see we learn of the things that are unseen; if we behold and acknowledge God in all His works and in all our ways, we shall indeed, even on this earth, be dwelling in God's immediate presence, and will be continually praising Him, even as do the angels in heaven.

"Those that be planted in the house of the Lord shall flourish in the courts of our God. They shall still bring forth fruit in old age; they shall be fat and flourishing; to show that the Lord is upright; He is my Rock, and there is no unrighteousness in Him." Psalm 92:13-15. "How excellent is Thy loving-kindness, O God! Therefore the children of men put their trust under the shadow of Thy wings. They shall be abundantly satisfied with the fatness of Thy house; and Thou shalt make them drink of the river of Thy pleasures. For with Thee is the fountain of life; in Thy light shall we see light." Psalm 36:7-9.

Eden Here Below

Mark that expression, "Thou shalt make them drink of the river of Thy pleasures." The Hebrew word rendered "pleasure" is Eden. Eden means pleasure, or delight. The garden of Eden is the garden of delight. So the text really says that those who dwell in the secret place of God, abiding under the shadow of the Almighty, shall be abundantly satisfied with the fatness of His house, and shall drink of the river of Eden, which is the living river of God.

This is the portion of believers even now; and we may know it as surely as the Israelites drank water from the rock or we live day by day from the bounties of His hand. Even now by faith we may refresh our souls by drinking from the river of the water of life, and eating of "the hidden manna." We may eat and drink righteousness by eating and drinking the flesh and blood of the Son of God.

"River of God, I greet thee,
Not now afar, but near;
My soul to thy still waters
Hastes in its thirstings here;
Holy River,
Let me ever
Drink of only thee."
"Rivers of Living Water"

But God blesses men only that they may in turn be a blessing to others. To Abraham God said, "I will bless thee, and make thy name great; and thou shalt be a blessing;" and even so it is to be with all his seed. So we read again the words of Christ, which may be fulfilled to us today and every day if we but believe them: –

"If any man thirst, let him come unto Me, and drink. He that believeth on Me, as the Scripture hath said, out of his belly shall flow rivers of living water. But this He spake of the Spirit, which they that believe on Him should receive." John 7:37-39.

As Christ was the temple of God, and His heart God's throne, so we are the temples of God that He should dwell in us. But God cannot be confined. The Holy Spirit cannot be hermetically sealed up in the heart. If He is there His glory will shine forth. If the water of life is in the soul it will flow out to others.

As God was in Christ reconciling the world unto Himself, so He takes up His abode in His true believers, putting into them the word of reconciliation, making them His representatives in Christ's stead to reconcile men to Himself. To His adopted sons is the wonderful privilege given of sharing the work of His only begotten Son. Like Him they may also become ministers of the Spirit; not merely ministers sent forth by the Spirit, but those who shall minister the Spirit. Thus as we become the dwelling-places of God, to reproduce Christ again before the world, and living streams flow from us to refresh the faint and weary, heaven is revealed on earth.

This is the lesson that God wished the Israelites to learn at the waters of Meribah, and it is what He is still patiently endeavoring to teach us, even though we like them have murmured and rebelled. Shall we not learn it now? "Happy is the people that is in such a case; yea, happy is the people whose God is the Lord."

Chapter 28

The Promises to Israel - The Entering of the Law (Part 1 of 2)

The Present Truth, November 12, 1896

"MOREOVER the law entered, that the offense might abound. But where sin abounded, grace did much more abound; that as sin hath reigned unto death, even so might grace reign through righteousness unto eternal life by Jesus Christ our Lord." Romans 5:20.

The object of the entering of the law at Sinai was "that the offense might abound." Not that there might be more sin; for since we are warned not to continue in sin that grace may abound, it is evident that the righteous God would not deliberately increase sin in order that He might have an opportunity of exhibiting more grace.

The law is not sin, but has the effect, by its own righteousness, of causing sin to "appear sin," "that sin by the commandment might become exceeding sinful." Romans 7:13.

The object, therefore, of the entering of the law at Sinai, was to cause the sin that already existed to stand out in its true nature and extent, so that the super abounding grace of God might be appreciated at its true value.

The entering of the law made the offence to abound. But the sin, which the law made to abound already, existed; "for until the law sin was in the world." Romans 10:13. Therefore the law was also in the world before it was given upon Sinai, as well as after, for "sin is not imputed when there is no law." To Isaac, God said, "Abraham obeyed My voice, and kept My charge, My commandments, My statues, and My laws." Genesis 26:5. The blessedness of Abraham was that of sins forgiven, "and he received the sign of circumcision, a seal of the righteousness of the faith which he had yet being uncircumcised; that he might be the father of all them that believe, though they be not circumcised; that righteousness might be imputed unto them also." Romans 4:11. Before the children of Israel had reached Sinai; when the manna first fell, God said that He was proving them "whether they will walk in My law or not." Exodus 16:4.

It is evident; therefore, that the giving of the law upon Sinai did not make any difference whatever in the relation that already existed between men and God. The very same law existed before that time, having the same effect, namely, to show men that they were sinners; and all the righteousness which the law demands, and all that it is possible for any man to have, had been possessed by men of faith, of whom Enoch and Abraham are notable instances. The only reason for the giving of the law upon Sinai, was to give men a more vivid sense of its awful importance, and of the terrible nature of sin which it forbids, and to lead them to trust in God, instead of in themselves.

This effect the circumstances attending the giving of the law were calculated to produce. No such event of awful majesty and power had ever been witnessed by man. Neither has its like been seen since. The event of the giving of the law upon Sinai will be paralleled and exceeded only by the second coming of Christ, "to take vengeance on them that know not God, and that obey not the Gospel of our Lord Jesus Christ," and "to be glorified in His saints, and to be admired in all them that believe." 2 Thessalonians 1:8-10.

Parallels

At the giving of the law, "Mount Sinai was altogether on a smoke, because the Lord descended upon it in fire." Exodus 19:18. At the Second Advent "the Lord Himself shall descend from heaven," "in flaming fire." 1 Thessalonians 4:16; 2 Thessalonians 1:8.

When God came to Sinai, sending forth from His right hand "a fiery law" for His people, "He came with ten thousands of saints." Deuteronomy 33:1, 2. The angels of God – the armies of heaven – were all present at the giving of the law. But long before that time, Enoch, the seventh from Adam, had prophesied of the second coming of Christ, saying, "Behold, the Lord cometh with ten thousands of His saints, to execute judgment." Jude 14, 15. At His coming in glory, He will have "all the holy angels with Him." Matthew 25:31.

God came down upon Sinai to proclaim His holy law to His people. "From His right hand went forth a fiery law for them." That law from Sinai was a verbal description of God's own righteousness. But when He comes the second time, "the heavens shall declare His righteousness; for God is Judge Himself." Psalm 50:6.

To announce the presence of God upon Sinai, in royal state, "the voice of the trumpet sounded long, and waxed louder and louder." Exodus 19:19. So Christ's second coming will be proclaimed by "the trump of God." "For the trumpet shall sound, and the dead shall be raised incorruptible, and we shall be changed," for "He shall send His angels with a great sound of a trumpet, and they shall gather together His elect from the four winds." 1 Corinthians 15:52; Matthew 24:31.

When the trumpet sounded long and loud upon Sinai, "Moses spake, and God answered him by a voice." Exodus 19:19. Then God spake all the words of the Ten

Commandments "out of the midst of the fire, of the cloud, and of the thick darkness, with a great voice; and He added no more." Deuteronomy 5:22. In like manner, "our God shall come, and shall not keep silence; a fire shall devour before Him, and it shall be very tempestuous round about Him. He shall call to the heavens from above, and to the earth, that He may judge His people." Psalm 50:3, 4. "The Lord Himself shall descend from heaven with a shout, with the voice of the Archangel, and with the trump of God." 1 Thessalonians 4:16.

But herein the Lord's coming to judgment will be greater than His coming to proclaim His law: for then none of the people saw Him. "The Lord spake unto you out of the midst of the fire; ye heard the voice of the words, but saw no similitude; only ye heard a voice." Deuteronomy 4:12. But when He comes the second time, "every eye shall see Him, and they also which pierced Him; and all kindred's of the earth shall wail because of Him." Revelation 1:7.

Lastly, a parallel as a difference in the effect of the voice of God: When God spoke His law from Sinai, "the whole mount quaked greatly." Exodus 19:18. "The earth shook, the heavens also dropped at the presence of God; even Sinai itself was moved at the presence of God, the God of Israel." Psalm 68:8. "The earth trembled and shook." Psalm 77:18. But even greater will be the effect of that voice at the Second Advent. From Sinai, His "voice then shook the earth; but now hath he promised, saying: Yet once more I shake not the earth only, but also heaven." Hebrews 12:26. "The heavens shall pass away with a great noise," (2 Peter 3:10), for "the powers of the heavens shall be shaken." Matthew 24:29.

Wonderful likenesses we find between the coming of the Lord to give the law at Sinai, and His coming to judgment in the end of the world; and we shall find as we study that the likenesses are by no means accidental.

The Ministration of Death

"The sting of death is sin; and the strength of sin is the law." 1 Corinthians 15:56.

The law entered for the purpose of making the sins of the people stand out in the boldest relief. The sin which lies dormant, and of whose power we are unconscious because we have never entered into mortal combat with it, springs into life and activity when the law enters. "Without the law sin was dead." Romans 7:8. The law sets forth sin in its true character and magnitude, and arms it with its power – the power of death. "By the law is the knowledge of sin." Romans 3:20. To point out sin, and to show its hideous strength, is the sole office of the law.

But death comes by sin. "By one man sin entered into the world, and death by sin; and so death passed upon all men, for that all have sinned." Romans 5:12. Where sin goes, there death goes. Sin does not merely bring death in its train; it carries it in its bosom. Sin and death are inseparable; each is a part of the other. It is impossible to set the door far enough ajar to allow sin to creep through, and to shut death out. Be the crevice never so small, if it be large enough to admit sin, death comes with it.

Since sin already existed before the law entered at Sinai, the entering of the law proclaimed a curse, for it is written, "Cursed is every one that continueth not in all things which are written in the book of the law to do them." Galatians 3:10. That curse was death, because it was the curse, which Christ bore for us. It is evident, therefore, that the giving of the law from Sinai was the ministration of death. "The law worketh wrath." All the attending circumstances proclaimed that fact. The thunders and lightning's, the devouring fire, the smoking mountain, and the quaking earth, all spoke death. Mount Sinai, itself a symbol of Divine law broken, was death to whoever should touch it. It needed not the barriers about the mountain to keep the people away, after the awful voice of God was heard proclaiming His law; for when they heard and saw, "they removed, and stood afar off," and said, "Let not God speak with us, lest we die." Exodus 20:18, 19.

"Sin, taking occasion by the commandment, deceived me, and by it slew me." (Romans 7:8); for "the sting of death is sin; and the strength of sin is the law." It was impossible that there could be a law given which could give life. But it was not necessary that there should be and this we shall see clearly when in the light of revelations previously made to Israel we consider the deeper reason.

Why the Law was Given

Did God wish to mock the people by giving to them a law, which could bring them nothing but death? Far from it. "Yea, He loved the people;" and never did He love them more than when "from His right hand went forth a fiery law for them." Deuteronomy 33:2, 3.

For be it remembered that although "the law entered that the offense might abound," yet "where sin abounded, grace did much more abound." Romans 5:20. Since it is the law that makes sin to abound, where can its hideous magnitude be more clearly defined than at Sinai? But since "where sin abounded, grace did much more abound," it is evident that at Sinai we may most clearly see the vastness of God's grace. No matter how greatly sin abounds, in that very place grace super abounds. What though "the mountain burned with fire unto the midst of heaven?" Still we have the assurance, "Thy mercy is great above the heavens; and Thy truth reaches unto the clouds." Psalm 107:4. "As the heaven is high above the earth, so great is His mercy toward them that fear Him." Psalm 103:11.

Jesus is the Comforter. "If any man sin, we have a Comforter with the Father, Jesus Christ the righteous." 1 John 2:1, R.V. margin. So when His disciples were sorrowing because of His announcement that He was going to leave them, He said, "I will pray the Father, and He shall give you another Comforter, that He may abide with you forever; even the Spirit of truth." John 14:16, 17. While Jesus was on earth, he was the embodiment of the Spirit; but He would not have His work limited, so He said: "It is expedient for you that I go away; for if I go not away, the Comforter will not come unto you; but if I go away, I will send Him unto you. And He, when He is come, will convict the world in respect of sin, and of righteousness, and of judgment." John 16:7, 8.

Mark well the fact that the first work of the Comforter is to convict of sin. The sword of the Spirit is the Word of God, which pierces "even to the dividing asunder of soul and spirit, and of the joints and marrow, and is a discerner of the thoughts and intents of the heart." Hebrews 4:12. Yet even while sending the keenest and deepest conviction, the Spirit is the Comforter. He is nonetheless the Comforter in convicting of sin, than in revealing the righteousness of God for the remission of the sin. There is comfort in the conviction, which God sends. The surgeon, who cuts to the very bone, that he may remove the poisonous death-breeding substance from the flesh, does it only that he may successfully apply the healing oil.

The great sin of the children of Israel was unbelief – trust in self rather than in God. This is common to all mankind. What is needed is something to destroy this vain self-confidence, so that faith may come in. The law entered in a way calculated to do this, and to emphasize the fact that only by faith, and not by works of man, does righteousness come. In the very giving of the law is shown man's dependence on God alone for righteousness and salvation, since men could not so much as touch the mountain where the law was spoken, without perishing. How, then, can it be supposed that God ever designed that any man should, for a single moment, imagine that he was to get righteousness by the law? At Sinai Christ the crucified One was preached in tones intended to reach all people, even as they shook the whole earth.

Chapter 29

The Promises to Israel - The Entering of the Law (Part 2 of 2)

The Present Truth, November 19, 1896

AFTER what we have already learned of the history of Israel, there is nothing that more concisely and simply states the purpose of God in speaking the law from Sinai than

The Third Chapter of Galatians

which we will briefly study. It is as simple as a child's storybook, yet it is as deep and comprehensive as the love of God.

The sixth and seventh verses of the first chapter reveal to us the fact that the Galatian brethren had begun to fall away from the faith, being deceived by false teaching – by a pretended Gospel. Whereupon the Apostle vehemently exclaims: "Though we, or an angel from heaven, preach any other Gospel unto you than that which we have preached unto you, let him be accursed. As I said before, so say I now again, If any man preach any other Gospel unto you than that ye have received, let him be accursed." Galatians 1:8, 9.

The only portion of the Scriptures that was written when Paul preached was that which consisted of the books commonly known as the Old Testament. When he preached he opened those Scriptures, and reasoned out of them; and the interested ones among his hearers searched the same Scriptures to see if the things, which he preached, were so. Acts 17:3, 11. When he was on trial for heresy and sedition, he solemnly declared that in all his ministry he had said "none other things than those which the prophets and Moses did say should come." Acts 26:22. Now when we read again his anathema against any who should presume to preach a different Gospel from what he had preached, we know that if any man preaches anything different from what is found in the Old Testament, he brings the curse of God upon himself. This is a strong reason why we should faithfully study Moses and the prophets.

Knowing therefore that Paul always and everywhere preached nothing "save Jesus Christ, and Him crucified," we are not surprised that he breaks out, "O foolish Galatians, who hath bewitched you, that ye should not obey the truth, before whose eyes Jesus Christ hath been evidently set forth, crucified among you?" Galatians 3:1. From the writings of Moses and the prophets they had been made to see Christ, not as one who was to be crucified, nor merely as one who had been crucified some years in the past, but as one plainly and visibly crucified among them. And it is from those ancient writings alone that he proceeded to revive their languishing faith and zeal.

Theirs had been a thorough conversion, for they had received the Spirit, and had suffered persecution for Christ's sake. So the Apostle asks, "Received ye the Spirit by the works of the law, or by the hearing of faith?" Verse 2. They had heard the words of the law, and had received them in faith, and thus the Spirit had worked the righteousness of the law in them. "This is the work of God, that ye believe on Him whom He hath sent." John 6:29. The Apostle was not depreciating the law, but only rebuking their changed relation to it. When they heard it in faith, they received the Spirit, and it was well with them; but when they began to trust in the flesh to perform the righteousness of the law, they ceased to obey the truth.

Again the Apostle asks, "He therefore that ministereth to you the Spirit, and worketh miracles among you, doeth he it by the works of the law, or by the hearing of faith?" Galatians 3:5. It is a question admitting but the obvious answer that it was through the hearing of faith, "even as Abraham believed God, and it was accounted to him for righteousness." Verse 6. They, like Abraham, had been justified – made righteous – by faith, not by works. Before we proceed further, let us have a few definitions. "Sin is the transgression of the law," (1 John 3:4), and "all unrighteousness is sin." 1 John 5:17 Therefore it follows that all unrighteousness is transgression (disobedience) of the law, and just as evidently that all righteousness is obedience to the law. So when we read that Abraham believed God, and it was accounted to him for righteousness, we may know that his faith was accounted to him for obedience to the law.

This accounting of faith for righteousness was not an empty form to Abraham, nor is it to us. Remember that the accounting is done by God, who cannot lie, yet who calls things that are not as though they were, by the power by which He makes the dead live. Abraham actually possessed righteousness. Faith works.

"This is the work of God, that ye believe on Him whom He hath sent." "With the heart man believeth unto righteousness." Romans 10:10.

This little digression will help us to bear in mind that in the chapter before us there is no disparagement of the law, but the righteousness, which is the fruit of faith, is always obedience to the law of God.

Abraham is the father of all that believe. "Know therefore that they which be of faith, the same are the sons of Abraham. And the Scripture, foreseeing that God would justify the Gentiles by faith, preached beforehand the Gospel unto Abraham, saying, "In thee shall all the nations be blessed." Galatians 3:7, 8. The Gospel, which was preached to Abraham is the same, that is for "all people," and which "shall be preached in all the world, for a witness unto all nations." To "every creature" it is to be preached, and whoever believes it and is baptized, shall be saved. But in the Gospel "the righteousness of God is revealed from faith to faith." The Gospel is preached "for the obedience of faith." Obedience carries a blessing with it, for it is written, "Blessed are they that do His commandments." "So then they which be of faith are blessed with faithful Abraham." Verse 9.

The Curse of the Law

"For as many as are of the works of the law are under the curse; for it is written, Cursed is every one that continueth not in all things which are written in the book of the law to do them." Galatians 3:10.

A careless reading of this verse, or, perhaps, of the first part only, has led some to believe that the law itself, and obedience to it, is a curse. But a thoughtful reading of the last portion of the verse shows that such an idea is a grave error. "For it is written, Cursed is every one that continueth not in all things which are written in the book of the law to do them." The curse is not for obedience, but for disobedience. Not the man who continues in all things that are written in the law, but the man who does not continually do all things written in the law, is the one who is cursed. Not a part only, but the whole, must be done, not a part of the time only, but continually. The one who doesn't do that is cursed: therefore the man who should do that would be blessed.

In the ninth and tenth verses of this chapter we have the same contrast of blessing and cursing that is presented in Deuteronomy 11:26-28: "Behold, I set before you this day a blessing and a curse; a blessing, if ye obey the commandments of the Lord your God, which I command you this day; and a curse if ye will not obey the commandments of the Lord your God." On the one hand we have in one group, faith, obedience, righteousness, blessing, life; on the other hand we find bound together in one bundle, unbelief, disobedience, sin, the curse, death. The grouping is not in the least affected by the age in which one lives.

"But that no man is justified by the law in the sight of God, it is evident; for, the just shall live by faith. And the law is not of faith; but the man that doeth them shall live in them." Galatians 3:11, 12.

"The man that doeth them shall live in them;" but no man has done them; "for all have sinned, and come short of the glory of God." Therefore no man can find life in the law.

Thus it is that "the commandment which was ordained unto life," is "found to be unto death." Romans 7:10. And so it is that whoever attempts to keep the law by his own works, is under the curse; and to set the law before people who do not receive it in faith, is but the ministration of death to them. The curse of the law is the death, which it inflicts upon the transgressors of it.

But "Christ hath redeemed us from the curse of the law, being made a curse for us; for it is written, Cursed is every one that hangeth on a tree." Galatians 3:13. Here we have fresh evidence that death is the curse of the law, since death was what Christ suffered on the tree. "The wages of sin is death;" and Christ was made "to be sin for us." 2 Corinthians 5:21. The Lord hath laid on Him the iniquity of us all," and "by His stripes we are healed." Isaiah 53:5, 6. It is not from obedience to the law, that Christ has redeemed us, but from (disobedience to the law) its transgression, and from death, which comes by sin. His sacrifice was in order "that the righteousness of the law might be fulfilled in us." Romans 8:4.

Now this truth, that "Christ hath redeemed us from the curse of the law, being made a curse for us," was as much a truth in the days of Israel at Sinai as it is to day. More than seven hundred years before the cross was raised on Calvary, Isaiah, whose own sin had been purged by a live coal from God's altar, and who knew whereof he spoke, said: Surely He hath borne our grief's, and carried our sorrows;" "He was wounded for our transgressions, He was bruised for our iniquities; the chastisement of our peace was upon Him; and with His stripes we are healed." This is identical with Galatians 3:13.

Again, Isaiah wrote, with special reference to the children of Israel in their wanderings in the wilderness: "In all their affliction He was afflicted, and the Angel of His presence saved them; in His love and in His pity He redeemed them; and He bare them, and carried them all the days of old." Isaiah 63:9. And it is to David, long before the days of Isaiah, that we are indebted for those soul-cheering words: "He hath not dwelt with us after our sins; nor rewarded us according to our iniquities." "As far as the east is from the west, so far hath he removed our transgressions from us." Psalm 53:10, 12. That language describes an accomplished fact. Salvation was as complete in those days as it is to day.

Christ is "the Lamb slain from the foundation of the world;" and from the days of Abel until now He has redeemed from the curse of the law all who have believed on Him. Abraham received the blessing of righteousness; and "they which be of faith are blessed with faithful Abraham."

This is made still more evident from the statement that Christ was made a curse for us, "that the blessing of Abraham might come on the Gentiles through Jesus Christ; that we might receive the promise of the Spirit through faith." Galatians 3:14. To Abraham, and to those who are his children by faith, no matter what their nation or language, belong all the blessings that come by means of Christ's cross; and all the blessings of the cross of Christ are only those, which Abraham had. No wonder that he rejoiced and was glad to see the day of Christ. Christ's death on the cross brings to us only the blessing of Abraham. Nothing more could be asked or imagined.

The Covenant Unaltered

"Brethren, I speak after the manner of men; though it be but a man's covenant, yet, if it be confirmed, no man disannulleth or addeth thereto. Now to Abraham and his seed were the promises made. He saith not, and to seeds, as of many; but as of one, And to thy seed, which is Christ. And this I say, that the covenant that was confirmed before of God in Christ, the law, which was four hundred and thirty years after, cannot disannul, that it should make the promise of none effect." Galatians 3:15-17.

The first statement is very simple: No man can disannul, take from, or add to, even a man's covenant, if it be once confirmed.

The conclusion is equally simple. God made a covenant with Abraham, and confirmed it with an oath. "Men verily swear by the greater; and an oath for confirmation is to them an end of all strife. Wherein God, willing more abundantly to show unto the heirs of promise the immutability of His council, confirmed it by an oath; that by two immutable things, in which it was impossible for God to lie, we might have a strong consolation, who have fled for refuge to lay hold on the hope set before us." Hebrews 6:16-18. Therefore that covenant, which was confirmed in Christ by God's oath pledging His own existence to its fulfillment, could never afterwards be changed one iota. Not one jot or tittle could pass from it or be added to it while God lives.

Note the statement that "to Abraham and his seed were the promises made." And the seed is Christ. All the promises to Abraham were confirmed in Christ. "Promises," remember, and not simply a promise. "For how many so ever be the promises of God, in Him is the yea; wherefore also through Him is the Amen, unto the glory of God through us." 2 Corinthians 1:20.

Our Hope Also

Note also again that the covenant made with Abraham, and confirmed in Christ by God's oath, is that which gives us our hope in Christ. It was confirmed by the oath, in order that we might have strong consolation in fleeing for refuge to lay hold on the hope set before us. The sum of the covenant was righteousness by faith in Jesus crucified, as shown by the words of Peter: "Ye are the children of the prophets, and of the covenant which God made with our fathers, saying unto Abraham, "And in thy seed shall all the kindred's of the earth be blessed." Unto you first God, having raised up His Son Jesus, sent Him to bless you, in turning away every one of you from his iniquities." Acts 3:25, 26.

The cross of Christ, and the blessing of sins forgiven, existed therefore, not only at Sinai but also in the days of Abraham. Salvation was no surer the day that Jesus rose from the tomb than it was the day that Isaac carried the wood for his own sacrifice up Mount Moriah; for God's promise and oath are two "immutable things." Though it be but a man's covenant, "yet if it be confirmed, no man disannulleth, or addeth thereto." How much more so, then, when it is God's own covenant, confirmed by an oath pledging his own life! That covenant embraced the salvation of mankind. Therefore it is a fact that, saying nothing of previous time, after God's promise and oath to Abraham not a single new feature could be introduced into the plan of salvation. Not one duty less or more could be enjoined or required, nor could there by any possibility be any variation in the conditions of salvation.

Therefore the entering of the law at Sinai could not contribute any new feature to the covenant made with Abraham and confirmed in Christ, nor could it in any way whatever interfere with the promise. The covenant, that was confirmed beforehand by God in Christ, cannot by any means be disannulled, or its promises made of none effect, by the law spoken four hundred and thirty years afterward.

Yet the law was to be kept, and if it was not kept, death was sure. Not one jot or one tittle could by any means be abated from the law. "Cursed is every one that continueth not in all things which are written in the book of the law to do them." Now since the giving of the law at Sinai added nothing to the covenant with Abraham, and yet that law must be perfectly kept, it follows that the law was in the covenant made with Abraham. The righteousness that was confirmed to Abraham by that covenant – the righteousness that Abraham had by faith – was the righteousness of the law that was proclaimed on Sinai. And this is further evident from the fact that Abraham received circumcision as a seal of the righteousness, which he had by faith, and circumcision stood simply for the keeping of the law. Romans 2:25-29.

The oath of God to Abraham pledged the putting of the righteousness of God, which is fully outlined in the Ten Commandments, into and upon every believer. The covenant being confirmed in Christ, and the law being in the covenant, it most surely follows that God's requirements for Christians in these days are not a particle different from what they were in the days of Abraham. The giving of the law introduced no new element.

---

[9] Some have thought to build an argument on the word "added," supposing that it indicates something entirely new added to the provisions, which God had previously made. A reference to Deuteronomy 5:22 will show the sense in which it is used. After having rehearsed the Ten Commandments, Moses said: "Those words the Lord spake unto all your assembly in the mount out of the midst of the fire, of the cloud, and of the thick darkness, with a great voice; and He added no more." That is, He spoke so much, and He spoke no more. The same thing is shown even more plainly in Hebrews 12:18,19: "For ye are not come unto the mount that might be touched, and that burned with fire, nor unto blackness, and darkness, and tempest, and the sound of a trumpet, and the voice of words; which voice they that heard entreated that the word should not be spoken to them any more." Compare Exodus 20:19. The Greek word rendered "spoken" in this instance is identical with that rendered "added" in Galatians 3:19, and the Septuagint rendering of Deuteronomy 22. So to the question, "What was the use of the law, since it made no change in the covenant? The answer is, "It was spoken because of transgression."

"Wherefore then the law?" A pertinent question, and one that is fairly answered. If the law made no change whatever in the terms of the covenant made with Abraham, what was the use of giving it? The answer is, "It was added[9] because of transgression;" (Galatians 3:19); it "entered that the offense might abound." Romans 5:20. It was not "against the promises of God," Galatians 3:21, but directly in harmony with them, for the promises of God are all through righteousness, and the law is the standard of righteousness. It was necessary for the offence to be made to abound, "that as sin hath reigned unto death, even so might grace reign through righteousness unto eternal life by Jesus Christ our Lord." Conviction necessarily precedes conversion. The inheritance could be obtained only through righteousness, although it was wholly by promise; for righteousness is the "gift of grace." But in order that men may appreciate the promises of God, they must be made to feel their need of them. The law, given in such as awful manner, was for the purpose of letting them know how impossible it was for them to get its righteousness by their own strength, and thus to let them know what God was anxious to supply them with."

Christ the Mediator

And this is emphasized by the fact that it was ordained "in the hands of a Mediator." Who was that Mediator? – "Now a Mediator is not a Mediator of one, but God is one." Galatians 3:20. "For there is one God, and one Mediator between God and men, the man Christ Jesus." 1 Timothy 2:5 Jesus Christ was therefore the One who gave the law upon Sinai; and He gave it in His capacity of Mediator between God and men. And so, although it was impossible that there could be a law given which could give life, the law which was death to unbelieving sinners was in the hands of a Mediator who gives His own life, which is the law in its living perfection. In Him death is swallowed up, and life takes its place; He bears the curse of the law, and the blessing of it comes to us. This brings us to the fact that at Sinai we find Calvary, for further consideration of which we must wait till another number.

Chapter 30

The Promises to Israel - Sinai and Calvary

The Present Truth, November 26, 1896

"Remember ye the law of Moses My servant, which I commanded unto him in Horeb for all Israel, with the statutes and Judgments. Behold, I will send you Elijah the prophet before the coming of the great and dreadful day of the Lord; and he shall turn the hearts of the fathers to the children, and the hearts of the children to their fathers, lest I come and smite the earth with a curse," or, literally, "with utter destruction." Malachi 4:5, 6.

Notice how intimately the tender, converting work of the Spirit of God is connected with the law that was spoken from Horeb. For Sinai is Horeb, as we learn from Deuteronomy 4:10-14, where we read the words of Moses, the servant of God: –

"Thou stoodest before the Lord thy God in Horeb, when the Lord said unto me. Gather Me the people together, and I will make them hear My words . . . and ye came near and stood under the mountain; and the mountain burned with fire unto the midst of heaven, with darkness, clouds, and thick darkness. And the Lord spake unto you out of the midst of the fire . . . and He declared unto you His covenant, which He commanded you to perform, even Ten Commandments; and He wrote them upon two tables of stone. And the Lord commanded me at that time to teach you statutes and judgments, that ye might do them in the land whither ye go over to possess it."

When the Lord tells us to remember the law which He commanded in Horeb, or Sinai, it is that we may know the power with which He will turn the hearts of the fathers to the children, that they may be prepared for the terrible day of His coming. "The law of the Lord is perfect, converting the soul." Psalm 19:7.

The Riven Rock

When God spoke the law from Sinai, that living stream of water, which gushed forth from the smitten rock in Horeb, was still flowing. If it had ceased to flow, the Israelites would have been in as bad a condition as before, for it was their only water supply, their only hope of life. It was from Horeb, whence the water came that restored their life, that God spoke the law. The law came from the same rock whence the water was already flowing, "and that Rock was Christ." 1 Corinthians 10:4.

Sinai is rightly regarded as a synonym for the law; but it is no more so than Christ is; nay, not so much, for in Him it is life. Jesus said, "I delight to do Thy will, O My God; yea, Thy law is within My heart." Psalm 40:8. The law was therefore Christ's life, for out of the heart are the issues of life. Proverbs 4:23.

"He was bruised for our iniquities;" and "with His stripes we are healed." When He was smitten and wounded on Calvary, the life-blood flowed from His heart, and that stream still flows for us. But in His heart is the law; and so as we drink by faith from the life-giving stream, we drink in the righteousness of the law of God. The law comes to us as a stream of grace, a river of life. Both "grace and truth come by Jesus Christ." John 1:17. When we believe in Him, the law is not to us merely "the voice of words," but a fountain of life.

Now all this was at Sinai. Christ, the giver of the law, was the Rock smitten in Horeb, which is Sinai. That stream was the life of those who drank, and none of those who received it in thoughtful gratitude could fail to know that it came direct from their Lord – the Lord of all the earth. They might have been assured of His tender love for them, and of the fact that He was their life, and hence their righteousness. So although they could not approach the mountain without dying – an evidence that the law is death to men out of Christ – they could drink of the stream that flowed from it, and thus in the life of Christ drink in the righteousness of the law.

The words spoken from Sinai, coming from the same Rock whence came the water which was the life of the people, showed the nature of the righteousness that Christ would impart to them. While it was "a fiery law," it was at the same time a gently flowing stream of life. Because the prophet Isaiah knew that Christ was the Rock smitten at Sinai, and that even then He was the One Mediator, "the man Christ Jesus; who gave Himself a ransom for all, to be testified in due time," he could say, "He was wounded for our transgressions," "and with His stripes we are healed."

For the ancient Israelites there was emphasized the lesson that the law comes as life to men only through the cross of Christ. For us there is the same lesson, together with the other side of it, namely, that the righteousness, which comes to us through the life given to us on the cross, is precisely, that which is required by the Ten Commandments, and none other. Let us read them: –

What God Spoke

1. "I am the Lord thy God, which have brought thee out of the Land of Egypt, out of the house of bondage; Thou shalt have no other gods before Me.

2. "Thou shalt not make unto thee any graven image, nor any likeness of anything that is in heaven above, or that is in the earth beneath, or that is in the water under the earth; thou shalt not bow down thyself to them, nor serve them, for I the Lord thy God am a jealous God, visiting the iniquities of the fathers upon the children unto the third and fourth generation[10] of them that hate Me; and showing mercy unto thousands of them that love Me, and keep My commandments.

3. "Thou shalt not take the name of the Lord thy God in vain; for the Lord will not hold him guiltless that taketh His name in vain.

4. "Remember the Sabbath day, to keep it holy. Six days shalt thou labor, and do all thy work; but the seventh day is the Sabbath of the Lord thy God; in it thou shalt not do any work, thou, nor thy son, nor thy daughter, thy manservant, nor thy maidservant, nor thy cattle, nor thy stranger that is within thy gates; for in six days the Lord made heaven and earth, the sea, and all that in them is, and rested the seventh day; wherefore the Lord blessed the Sabbath day, and hallowed it.

5. "Honor thy father and thy mother; that thy days may be long upon the land which the Lord thy God giveth thee.

6. "Thou shalt not kill.

7. "Thou shalt not commit adultery.

8. "Thou shalt not steal.

9. "Thou shalt not bear false witness against thy neighbor.

10. "Thou shalt not covet thy neighbor's house, thou shalt not covet thy neighbor's wife, nor his manservant, nor his maidservant, nor his ox, nor his ass, nor anything that is thy neighbor's."

This is the law that was uttered amid the terrors of Sinai, by the lips of Him whose life it was and is, and from whom had come the stream which was at that moment flowing – His own life given for the people. The Cross, – with its healing, life-giving stream was at Sinai, and hence the Cross – cannot possibly make any change in the law. The life proceeding from Christ at Sinai as at Calvary shows that the righteousness, which is revealed in the Gospel, is none other than that of the Ten Commandments. Not one jot or one tittle could pass away. The awfulness of Sinai was at Calvary, in the thick darkness, the earthquake, and the great voice of the Son of God. The smitten rock and the flowing stream at Sinai represented Calvary; Calvary was there, so that it is an actual fact that from Calvary the Ten Commandments are proclaimed in the identical

---

[10] There is in the Hebrew text of this passage no word indicating "generation," which is supplied by the translators. It is most evident, however, that it is the word required by the sense, and attention is called to it only to point out the fact that the construction is the same as in the next clause, where the word "generation" is not expressed, but where it belongs as surely as in the first. Some have hastily supposed that the "thousands" refers only to individuals, and so have erroneously concluded that God's chastisements outlast His mercy. Not so. He visits the iniquities of the fathers upon the children unto the third and fourth generation of them that hate Him, but shows mercy unto unnumbered thousands of generations of them that love Him and keep His commandments. His wrath is soon appeased, while His mercy flows on to eternity. Other versions than the English state it very plainly.

words that were heard from Sinai. Calvary, not less than Sinai, reveals the terrible and unchanging holiness of the law of God, so terrible and so unchangeable that it spared not even the Son of God when "He was reckoned among the transgressors." But however great the terror inspired by the law, the hope by grace is even greater; for "where sin abounded, grace did much more abound." Back of all stands the oath of God's covenant of grace, assuring the perfect righteousness and life of the law in Christ; so that although the law spoke death, it only showed what great things God had promised to do for those who believe. It teaches us to have no confidence in the flesh, but to worship God in the Spirit, and to rejoice in Christ Jesus. Thus God was proving His people that they might know that "man doth not live by bread only, but by every word that precedes out of the mouth of the Lord doth man live." Deuteronomy 8:3

So the law is not against the promises of God, even though it cannot give life. On the contrary, it backs up those promises in thunder tones; for with God's oath ever steadfast, the greatest requirement of the law is to the ear of faith but a promise of its fulfillment. And so, taught by the Lord Jesus, we may "know that His commandment is life everlasting."

Chapter 31

The Promises to Israel - Mount Sinai and Mount Zion

The Present Truth, December 3, 1896

"Great is the Lord, and greatly to be praised in the city of our God, in the mountain of His holiness. Beautiful for situation, the joy of the whole earth, is mount Zion, on the sides of the north, the city of the Great King. God is known in her palaces for a refuge." Psalm 48:1-3.

These words are sung in praise of the dwelling-place of God in heaven; for "the Lord is in His holy temple, the Lord's throne is in heaven" (Psalm 11:4), and of Christ "who is set on the right hand of the throne of the Majesty in the heavens," (Hebrews 8:1) the Lord says, "Yet have I set My King upon My holy hill of Zion," or, "upon Zion, the hill of My holiness." Psalm 2:6.

Jesus Christ, the anointed King in Zion, is High Priest as well, a "priest for ever, after the order of Melchizedek." The Lord has said of "the Man whose name is The BRANCH," that "He shall build the temple of the Lord; and He shall bear the glory, and shall sit and rule upon His throne; and He shall be a priest upon His throne; and the counsel of peace shall be between them both." Zechariah 6:12, 13. So as He sits upon His Father's throne in the heavens, he is "a Minister of the sanctuary, and of the true tabernacle which the Lord pitched, and not man." Hebrews 8:2.

It was to this place – to Mount Zion, the hill of God's holiness, and to the Sanctuary upon it, His dwelling place – that God was leading His people Israel when He delivered them from Egypt. When they had safely passed through the Red Sea, Moses sang these inspired words: "Thou shalt bring them in, and plant them in the mountain of Thine inheritance, in the place, O Lord, which Thou hast made for Thee to dwell in, in the Sanctuary, O Lord, which Thy hands have established." Exodus 15:17.

But they did not get to Mount Zion, because they did not "hold fast the confidence and the rejoicing of the hope firm unto the end." "So we see that they could not enter in because of unbelief." Yet God did not forsake them, for even "if we believe not, yet He abideth faithful; He cannot deny Himself." So He instructed Moses to tell the people to bring offerings of gold and silver and precious stones, together with other material, and said, "Let them make Me a sanctuary, that I may dwell among them. According to all that I show thee, after the pattern of the tabernacle, and the pattern of all the instruments thereof, even so shall ye make it." Exodus 25:8, 9.

This was not "the true tabernacle, which the Lord pitched," but one made by man. The tabernacle and its furniture were only "the patterns of things in the heavens," and not "the heavenly things themselves." Hebrews 9:23. It was but a shadow of the real substance. The cause of the shadow will be considered later on. But the believing ones of that olden time knew as well as Stephen did in later years, that "the Most High dwelleth not in temples made with hands," as saith the prophet, "Thus saith the Lord, The heaven is My throne, and the earth is My footstool; where is the house that ye build unto me? And where is the place of My rest? Acts 7:48, 49. Solomon, at the dedication of his grand temple, said, "But will God in very deed dwell with men on the earth? Behold, heaven and the heaven of heavens cannot contain Thee; how much less this house that I have built?" 2 Chronicles 6:18.

All of God's really faithful children understood that the earthly tabernacle or temple was not the real dwelling-place of God, but only a figure, a type. So of the furniture which the sanctuary contained.

As God's throne is in His holy temple in heaven, so in the type of that temple on earth there was a representation of His throne. A very feeble representation, it is true, as much inferior to the real as the works of man are inferior to those of God, yet a figure of it, nevertheless. That figure of God's throne was the ark, which contained the tables of the law. A few texts of Scripture will show this.

Exodus 25:10-22 contains the complete description of the ark. It was a box made of wood, but completely covered, within and without, with fine gold. Into this ark the Lord directed Moses to put the Testimony, which He should give him. This Moses did, for afterward, in recounting to Israel the circumstances of the giving of the law, together with their idolatry, which led to the breaking of the first tables, he said: –

"At that time the Lord said unto me, Hew thee two tables of stone like unto the first, and come up unto Me into the mount, and make thee an ark of wood. And I will write on the tables the words that were in the first tables, which thou brakest, and thou shalt put them in the ark. And I made an ark of shittim wood, and hewed two tables of stone like unto the first, and went up into the mount, having the two tables in mine hand. And He wrote on the tables, according to the first writing, the Ten Commandments, which the Lord spake unto you in the mount out of the midst of the fire in the day of the assembly; and the Lord gave them unto me. And I turned myself and came down from the mount, and put the tables in the ark which I had made; and there they be, as the Lord commanded me." Deuteronomy 10:1-5.

The cover of this ark was called the "mercy-seat." This was of solid, beaten gold, and upon each end of it, a part of the same piece of gold, there was a cherub with wings outstretched. "Toward the mercy-seat shall the faces of the cherubim be. After these directions, the Lord said: "Thou shalt put the mercy-seat above upon the ark; and in the ark thou shalt put the testimony that I shall give thee," which Moses did, as we have read. "And there I will meet with thee, and I will commune with thee from above the mercy-seat, from between the two cherubim which are upon the ark of the testimony, of all things which I will give thee in commandment unto the children of Israel." Exodus 25:7-22.

God said that He would speak to them from "between the cherubim." So we read, "The Lord reigneth; let the people tremble; He sitteth between the cherubim; let the earth be moved. The Lord is great in Zion; and He is high above all the people." Psalm 99:1, 2. The cherubim overshadowed the mercy seat, from which place God spoke to the people. Now mercy means grace, so that in the mercy seat of the earthly tabernacle we have the figure of "the throne of grace" unto which we are exhorted to come boldly, "that we may obtain mercy, and find grace to help in time of need." Hebrews 4:16.

Foundation of God's Government

The Ten Commandments on the two tables of stone were in the ark, under the mercy seat, thus showing that the law of God is the basis of His throne and government. Accordingly we read, "The Lord reigneth; let the earth rejoice; let the multitude of isles be glad thereof. Clouds and darkness are round about Him; righteousness and judgment are the foundation of His throne." "Justice and judgment are the foundation of Thy throne; mercy and truth go before Thy face." Psalm 97:1, 2; 89:14. R.V.

Since the tabernacle and all that it contained was to be made exactly like the pattern given to Moses, and they were "the patterns of things in the heavens," it necessarily follows that the ten commandments on the tables of stone were exact copies of the law which is the foundation of God's true throne in heaven. This enables us to understand more clearly how it is that "it is easier for heaven and earth to pass, than one tittle of the law to fail." Luke 16:17. As long as God's throne stands, so long must God's law as spoken from Sinai remain unchanged. "If the foundations be destroyed, what can the righteous do?" Psalm 11:3. If the Ten Commandments – the foundation stones of God's throne – were destroyed, the throne itself would fall, and the hope of the righteous would perish. But none need fear such a catastrophe. "The Lord is in His holy temple; the Lord's throne is in heaven," because His word is settled forever in heaven. That is one of "the things, which cannot be shaken."

Now we are able to see that Mount Sinai, which is a synonym for law, and which at the giving of the law was really the embodiment of the awful majesty of the law, is also a type of God's throne. Indeed, for the time being it was actually God's throne. God was present upon it with all His holy angels.

Moreover, the awful terror of Sinai is only the terror of God's throne in the heavens. John had a vision of the temple of God in heaven, and of the throne, with God seated in it; "and out of the throne proceeded lightning's and thundering and voices." "And the temple of God was opened in heaven; and there was seen in His temple the ark of His testament; and there were lightning's, and voices, and thundering, and an earthquake and great hail." "A fire goeth before Him."

The terror of God's throne is the same terror that was at Sinai – the terror of the law. Yet that same throne is "the throne of grace," to which we are exhorted to come with boldness. Even so "Moses drew near unto the thick darkness where God was" on Sinai. Exodus 20:21. Not only Moses, but "Aaron, Nadab, and Abihu, and seventy of the elders of Israel" went up into the mount; "and they saw the God of Israel; and there was under His feet as it were a paved work of a sapphire stone, and as it were the body of heaven in his clearness. And upon the nobles of Israel He laid not His hand; also they saw God, and did eat and drink." Exodus 24:9-11. If it had not been so, then we should not have had a positive demonstration of the fact that we may indeed come with boldness to the throne of grace – that awful throne whence comes lightning's and thundering and voices – and find mercy there. The law makes sin to abound, "but where sin abounded, grace did much more abound." The cross was at Sinai, so that even there was God's throne of grace.

For let it be remembered that it is only "by the blood of Jesus" that we have "boldness to enter into the holiest." Hebrews 10:19. But for that blood it would be as certain death for us to come to God's throne and take His name upon our lips, as it was for anyone who should lightly approach Sinai. But Moses and others did draw near to God on Sinai, even into the thick darkness, and did not die, sure evidence that the blood of Jesus saved them. The living stream from Christ was flowing at Sinai, even as "the pure river of water of life, clear as crystal" proceeds "from the throne of God and of the Lamb." Revelation 22:1.

That stream comes from the heart of Christ, in which the law was and is enshrined. Christ was the temple of God, and His heart was God's dwelling-place. We know that the stream – living water for the people – came from Christ at Sinai, and that the blood and the water, which agree in one, came from His side at Calvary – a living stream for the life of the world. Yet although the cross of Calvary is the highest possible manifestation of the tender mercy and love of God for man, it is a fact that the terrors of Sinai – the terrors of God's throne – were there. There was thick darkness and an earthquake, and the people were filled with an awful dread, because there God displayed the fearful consequences of violation of His law. The law in its terror to evildoers was at Calvary as well as at Sinai or in the midst of the throne of God.

When John saw the temple in heaven, and God's awful throne, he saw "in the midst of the throne" "a Lamb as it had been slain." Revelation 5:6. So the river of water of life from the midst of the throne of God proceeds from Christ, even as did the stream from Sinai and Calvary. Sinai, Calvary, and Zion, three sacred mountains of God, all agree in one to those who come to them in faith. In all we find the terrible, death-dealing law of God flowing to us in a sweet and refreshing stream of life, so that we may sing:

> *"There's a wideness in God's mercy,*
> *Like the wideness of the sea,*
> *There's a kindness in His justice*
> *That is more than liberty."*

Chapter 32

The Promises to Israel - The Covenants of Promise

The Present Truth, December 10, 1896

"Wherefore remember that ye being in time past Gentiles in the flesh, who are called uncircumcision by that which is called the circumcision in the flesh made by hands; that at that time ye were without Christ, being aliens from the commonwealth of Israel, and strangers from the covenants of promise, having no hope, and without God in the world." Ephesians 2:11, 12.

An idea that prevails quite extensively is that God has one covenant for Jews and another for Gentiles; that there was a time when the covenant with the Jews utterly excluded the Gentiles, but that now a new covenant has been made which concerns chiefly, if not wholly, the Gentiles; in short that the Jews are, or were, under the old covenant, and the Gentiles under the new. That this idea is a great error may readily be seen from the passage just quoted.

As a matter of fact, Gentiles, as Gentiles, have no part whatever in God's covenants of promise. In Christ is the yea. "For how many soever be the promises of God, in Him is the yea; wherefore also through Him is the Amen, unto the glory of God through us." 2 Corinthians 1:20. The Gentiles are those who are without Christ, and so they are "strangers from the covenants of promise." No Gentile has any part in any covenant of promise. But whosoever will may come to Christ, and may share in the promises; for Christ says, "Him that cometh to Me I will in no wise cast out." John 6:37. But when the Gentile does that, no matter what his nationality may be, he ceases to be a Gentile, and becomes a member of "the commonwealth of Israel."

But let it be noted also that the Jew, in the common acceptation of the term, that is, as a member of the Jewish nation, and a rejecter of Christ, has no more share in the promises of God, or the covenants of promise, than the Gentile has. That is only to say that nobody has any share in the promises, save those who accept them. Whoever is "without Christ," whether he be called Jew or Gentile, is also "without God in the world," and is a stranger from the covenants of promise, and an alien from the commonwealth of Israel. This text first quoted teaches us. One must be in Christ in order to share the benefits of "the covenants of promise," and be a member of "the commonwealth of Israel." To be "an Israelite indeed," therefore, is simply to be a Christian. This is as true of the men who lived in the days of Moses, as of those who lived in the days of Paul, or those who live to day.

Some one will probably think to ask, "How about the covenant made at Sinai? Do you mean to say that it was the same as that under which Christians live, or that it was as good? Are we not told that it was faulty? And if it was faulty, how could life and salvation have come through it?"

Very pertinent questions, and ones that are easily answered. It is an undeniable fact that grace abounded at Sinai – "the grace of God which bringeth salvation" – because Christ was there with all His fullness of grace and truth. Mercy and truth were met together there, and righteousness and peace flowed as a river. But it was not by virtue of the covenant that was made at Sinai, that mercy and peace were there. That covenant brought the people nothing, although everything was there for them to enjoy.

The comparative value of the two covenants which stand related to each other as "the first" and "the second," the "old" and the "new," is thus set forth in the book of Hebrews, which presents Christ as High Priest, and contrasts His priesthood with that of men. Here are some of the points of superiority of our great High Priest over earthly high priests: –

1. "Those priests were made without an oath; but this with an oath by Him that said unto Him, The Lord swore, and will not repent, Thou art a priest for ever after the order of Melchizedek." Hebrews 7:21.

2. They were priests but for a short time, because "they were not suffered to continue by reason of death;" therefore there was a continual change and succession. But Christ "ever liveth," and therefore He has "an unchangeable priesthood." Earthly priests continued to be priests as long as they lived, but they did not live long. Christ also continues to be priest as long as He lives, and He is "alive for evermore."

3. The Levitical priests were made priests "after the law of a carnal commandment." Their priesthood was only outward, in the flesh. They could deal with sin only in its outward manifestations, that is, actually not at all. But Christ is High Priest "after the power of an endless life" – a life that saves to the uttermost. He ministers the law in the Spirit.

4. They were ministers only of a worldly sanctuary, which man made. Christ "is set on the right hand of the throne of the Majesty in the heavens, a Minister of the sanctuary, and of the true tabernacle, which the Lord pitched, and not man."

5. They were mere sinful men, as was shown by their mortality. Christ is "declared to be the Son of God with power, according to the Spirit of holiness, by the resurrection from the dead" (Romans 1:4), and so He is "holy, harmless, undefiled, separate from sinners, and made higher than the heavens." Hebrews 7:26.

Now "by so much was Jesus made surety of a better covenant."[11] Hebrews 7:22. The covenant of which Christ is Minister is as much better than that of which the Levitical priests were ministers, whose priesthood dated only from the making of the covenant at Sinai, as Christ and His priesthood are better than they and their priesthood. That is to say, the covenant of which Christ as High Priest is Minister, is as much better than the covenant that dates from Sinai, as Christ is better than man; as heaven is higher than earth; as the sanctuary in heaven is greater than the sanctuary on earth; as the works of God are better than the works of the flesh; as "the law of the Spirit of life in Christ Jesus" is better than "the law of a carnal commandment;" as eternal life is better than a life that is but "a vapor that appeareth for a moment, and then vanisheth away;" as the oath of God is better than the word of man.

The Difference

And now we may read wherein this vast difference consists: "But now hath He obtained a more excellent ministry, by how much also He is the Mediator of a better covenant, which was established upon better promises. For if that first covenant had been faultless, then should no place have been sought for the second. For finding fault with them, He saith, Behold, the days come, saith the Lord, when I will make a new covenant with the house of Israel, and with the house of Judah; not according to the covenant that I made with their fathers, in the day when I took them by the hand to lead them out of the land of Egypt; because they continued not in My covenant, and I regarded them not, saith the Lord. For this is the covenant that I will make with the house of Israel after those days, saith the Lord; I will put My laws into their mind, and write them in their hearts; and I will be to them a God, and they shall be to me a people; and they shall not teach every man his neighbor, and every man his brother, saying, Know the Lord; for all shall know Me, from the least to the greatest. For I will be merciful to their unrighteousness and their sins and their iniquities will I remember no more." Hebrews 8:5-12

The following facts must stand out very prominently to the thoughtful reader of this text: –

1. Both covenants are only with Israel. Gentiles, as we have already seen, are "strangers from the covenants of promise." It is always admitted and even claimed that they have nothing to do with the old covenant; but they have even less connection with the new covenant.

---

[11] The reader will notice that the word "covenant" is used, as in the Revision, rather than "testament," as in the old version. The words "covenant" and "testament," as found in the common version of the Bible, are both from one and the same Greek word. Much confusion has resulted because the translators have arbitrarily rendered it "covenant" in some places, and "testament" in others. The rendering should be uniform; and since the reference is to that which in the translation from the Hebrew is always called "covenant," that word should always be used. Let it be remembered that wherever in any translation of the Bible the word "testament" is found, "covenant" is the word that should be used. The rendering "testament" is utterly indefensible and is misleading.

2. Both covenants are made with "the house of Israel;" not with a few individuals, nor with a divided nation, but "with the house of Israel and with the house of Judah," that is, with all the people of Israel. The first covenant was made with the whole house of Israel, before they were divided; the second covenant will be made when God shall have taken the children of Israel from among the heathen, and made them one nation, when "they shall be no more two nations, neither shall they be divided into two kingdoms any more at all." Ezekiel 37:22, 26. But concerning this we shall have more further on.

3. Both covenants contain promises, and are founded upon them.

4. The "new covenant" is better than the one made at Sinai.

5. It is better, because the promises upon which it is founded are better.

6. Yet it will be seen by comparing the terms of the new with those of the old, that the end contemplated by each is the same. The old said, "If ye will obey My voice;" the new says, "I will put My laws into their mind, and write them in their hearts." Each has reference to the law of God. Both have holiness, and all the rewards of holiness, as the object. In the covenant at Sinai it was said to Israel, "Ye shall be unto Me a kingdom of priests, and an holy nation." Exodus 19:6. That is just what God's own people really are, "a royal priesthood, an holy nation, a peculiar people." 1 Peter 2:5, 9.

But the promises of that covenant at Sinai were never realized, and for the very reason that they were faulty. The promises of that covenant all depended upon the people. They said, "All that the Lord hath spoken, we will do." Exodus 19:8; 24:7. They promised to keep His commandments, although they had already demonstrated their inability to do anything themselves. Their promises to keep the law, like the law itself, were "weak through the flesh." Romans 8:3. The strength of that covenant was therefore only the strength of the law, and that is death.

Why the Covenant at Sinai?

Why, then, was that covenant made? – For the very same reason that the law was spoken from Sinai; "because of transgression." The Lord says it was "because they continued not in My covenant." They had lightly esteemed the "everlasting covenant" which God had made with Abraham, and therefore He made this one with them, as a witness against them.

That "everlasting covenant" with Abraham was a covenant of faith. It was everlasting, and therefore the giving of the law could not disannul it. It was confirmed by the oath of God, and therefore the law could not add anything to it. Because the law added nothing to that covenant, and yet was not against its promises, it follows that the law was contained in its promises. The covenant of God with Abraham assured to him and his seed the righteousness of the law by faith. Not by works, but by faith.

The covenant with Abraham was so ample in its scope that it embraced all nations, even "all the families of the earth." It is that covenant, backed by the oath of God, by which we now have confidence and hope in coming to Jesus, in whom it was confirmed. It is by virtue of that covenant, and that alone, that any man receives the blessing of God, for the cross of Christ simply brings the blessing of Abraham upon us.

That covenant was wholly of faith, and that is why it assures salvation, since "by grace are ye saved, through faith; and that not of yourselves, it is the gift of God; not of works, lest any man should boast." The history of Abraham makes very emphatic the fact that salvation is wholly of God, and not by the power of man. "Power belongeth unto God" (Psalm 62:11); and the Gospel is "the power of God unto salvation to every one that believeth." Romans 1:16. From the case of Abraham, as well as that of Isaac and of Jacob, we are made to know that only God Himself can fulfill the promises of God. They got nothing by their own wisdom or skill or power; everything was a gift from God. He led them, and He protected them.

This is the truth that had been made most prominent in the deliverance of the children of Israel from Egypt. God introduced Himself to them as "The Lord God of your fathers, the God of Abraham, the God of Isaac, and the God of Jacob" (Exodus 3:15); and He charged Moses to let them know that He was about to deliver them in fulfillment of His covenant with Abraham. God spake unto Moses, and said unto him:

"I am JEHOVAH; and I appeared unto Abraham, unto Isaac, and unto Jacob as God Almighty, but by My name Jehovah I was not known to them. And I have also established My covenant with them, to give them, to give them the land of Canaan, the land of their sojourning, wherein they sojourned. And moreover I have heard the groanings of the children of Israel, whom the Egyptians keep in bondage, and I have remembered My covenant. Wherefore say unto the children of Israel, I am Jehovah, and I will bring you out from under the burdens of the Egyptians, and I will rid you out of their bondage, and I will redeem you with a stretched out arm, and with great judgments; and I will take you to Me for a people, and I will be to you a God; and ye shall know that I am Jehovah your God, which bringeth you out from under the burdens of the Egyptians. And I will bring you in unto the land, concerning which I lifted up My hand to give it to Abraham, to Isaac, and to Jacob; and I will give it you for an heritage; I am Jehovah." Exodus 6:2-8, R.V.

Read now again the words of God just before the making of the covenant at Sinai: –

"Thus shalt thou say to the house of Jacob, and tell the children of Israel: Ye have seen what I did unto the Egyptians, and how I bare you on eagle's wings, and brought you unto Myself. Now therefore, if ye will obey My voice indeed, and keep My covenant, then ye shall be a peculiar treasure unto Me above all people; for all the earth is Mine; and ye shall be unto Me a kingdom of priests, and an holy nation." Exodus 19:4-6.

Note how God dwelt upon the fact that He Himself had done all that had been done for them. He had delivered them from the Egyptians, and He had brought them to Himself. That was the thing, which they were continually forgetting, as indicated by their murmurings. They had even gone so far as to question whether the Lord was among them or not; and their murmurings always indicated the thought that they themselves could manage things better than God could. God had brought them by the mountain pass to the Red Sea, and into the desert where there was no food nor drink, and had miraculously supplied their wants in every instance, to make them understand that they could live only by His word." Deuteronomy 8:3.

The covenant, which God made with Abraham, was founded on faith and trust. "Abraham believed God, and it was counted unto Him for righteousness." So when God, in fulfillment of that covenant, was delivering Israel from bondage, all His dealing with them was calculated to teach them trust in Him, so that they might in truth be the children of the covenant.

The Lesson of Trust

Their response of Israel was self-confidence. Read the record of their distrust in God in Psalm 106. He had proved them at the Red Sea, in the giving of the manna, and at the waters of Meribah. In every place they had failed to trust Him perfectly. Now he comes to prove them once more, in the giving of the law. As we have already learned, God never intended that men should try to get righteousness by the law, or that they should think such a thing possible. In the giving of the law, as shown by all the attendant circumstances, He designed that the children of Israel, and we also, should learn that the law is infinitely above the reach of all human effort, and to make it plain that, since the keeping of the commandments is essential to the salvation which He has promised, He Himself will fulfill the law in us. These are the words of God: "Hear, O My people, and I will testify unto thee; O Israel, if thou wilt hearken unto Me, there shall no strange God be in thee, neither shalt thou worship any strange god." Psalm 81:8, 9. "Incline your ear, and come unto Me; hear, and your soul shall live." Isaiah 55:3. His word transforms the soul from the death of sin to the life of righteousness, even as it brought forth Lazarus from the tomb.

A careful reading of Exodus 19:1-6 will show that there is no intimation that another covenant was then to be made. Indeed, the evidence is to the contrary. The Lord referred to His covenant, – the covenant long before given to Abraham, – and exhorted them to keep it, and told what would be the result of their keeping it. The covenant with Abraham was, as we have seen, a covenant of faith, and they could keep it simply by keeping the faith. God did not ask them to enter into another covenant with Him, but only to accept His covenant of peace, which he had long before given to the fathers.

The proper response of the people therefore would have been, "Amen, even so, O Lord, let it be done unto us according to Thy will." On the contrary they said, "All that the Lord hath spoken we will do;" and they repeated their promise, with additional emphasis, even after they had heard the law spoken. It was the same self-confidence that led their descendants to say to Christ, "What shall we do, that we might work the works of God?" Think of mortal men presuming to be able to do God's work! Christ answered, "This is the work of God, that ye believe on Him whom He hath sent." Even so it was in the desert of Sinai, when the law was given and the covenant made.

They're assuming the responsibility of working the works of God, showed lack of appreciation of His greatness and holiness. It is only when men are ignorant of God's righteousness, that they go about to establish their own righteousness, and refuse to submit themselves to the righteousness of God. See Romans 10:3. Their promises were good for nothing, because they had not the power to fulfill them. The covenant, therefore, which was based on those promises was utterly worthless, so far as giving them life was concerned. All that they could get from that covenant was just what they could get from themselves, and that was death. To trust in it was to make a covenant with death, and to be in agreement with the grave. Their entering into that covenant was a virtual notification to the Lord that they could get along very well without Him; that they were able to fulfill any promise He could make.

But God did not give them up, "for He said, surely they are My people, children that will not lie; so He was their Saviour." Isaiah 63:8. He knew that they were moved by impulse in making that promise, and that they did not realize what it meant. They had zeal for God, but not according to knowledge. He had brought them out of the land of Egypt, that He might teach them to know Him, and He did not become angry with them because they were so slow to learn the lesson. He had borne with Abraham when he thought that he could work out God's plans, and He had been very patient with Jacob when he was so ignorant as to suppose that God's promised inheritance could be gained by sharp bargains and fraud. So now He bore with their children's ignorance and lack of faith, in order that He might afterwards bring them to the faith.

The Divine Compassion

God meets men just where they are. He has "compassion on the ignorant, and on them that are out of the way." Hebrews 5:2. He is always and everywhere seeking to draw all men to Himself, no matter how depraved they are; and therefore when He discerns even the faintest glimmer of a willingness or desire to serve Him, He at once nourishes it, making the most of it He can to lead the soul to greater love and more perfect knowledge. So although the children of Israel had failed in this supreme test of their trust in Him, He took advantage of their expressed willingness to serve Him, even though it was only in "their own weak way."

Because of their unbelief they could not have all that He wished them to have; but that which they did get through their lack of faith was a continual reminder of what they might have if they fully believed. Because of their ignorance of the greatness of His holiness, which ignorance was expressed by their promise to do the law, God proceeded, by the proclamation of the law, to show them the greatness of His righteousness, and the utter impossibility of their working it out.

Chapter 33

The Promises to Israel - The Veil and the Shadow

The Present Truth, December 17, 1896

"But, and if our Gospel is veiled, it is veiled in them that are perishing; in whom the god of this world hath blinded the minds of the unbelieving, that the light of the Gospel of the glory of Christ, who is the image of God, should not dawn upon them." 2 Corinthians 4:3, 4, R.V.

"And it came to pass, when Moses came down from Mount Sinai with the two tables of testimony in Moses' hand, when he came down from the mount, that Moses wist not that the skin of his face shone while he talked with Him." (Better, as in the margin of the Revision, "Because he talked with Him.") Exodus 34:29. Because Moses talked with God, his face shone even after he had left God's immediate presence. "And when Aaron and all the children of Israel saw Moses, behold the skin of his face shone; and they were afraid to come nigh him. And Moses called unto them; and Aaron and all the rulers of the congregation returned unto him; and Moses talked with them. And afterward all the children of Israel came nigh; and he gave them in commandment all that the Lord had spoken with him in Mount Sinai. And till Moses had done speaking with them, he put a veil on his face. But when Moses went in before the Lord, to speak with Him, he took the veil off, until he came out. And he came out, and spake unto the children of Israel that which he was commanded. And the children of Israel saw the face of Moses, that the skin of Moses' face shone; and Moses put the veil upon his face again, until he went in to speak with Him." Verses 30-35.

Unbelief blinds the mind. It acts as a veil, to shut out the light. It is only by faith that we understand, Moses had deep and abiding faith; therefore he "endured as seeing Him who is invisible." He needed no veil over his face even when he was in the immediate presence of the glory of God. The veil, which he put on his face when he came down to talk with the children of Israel, was solely on their account, because his face shone so that they could not look upon him. But when he went back to talk with the Lord, he took the veil off.

The veil over the face of Moses was a concession to the weakness of the people. If he had not put it on, then each of them would have been obliged to put a veil over his own face, in order to come near to listen to Moses. They were not able, as Moses was, to look upon the glory of the Lord with unveiled face. Practically, therefore, each one of them had a veil over his own face. The face of Moses was unveiled.

That veil over the face of the children of Israel represented the unbelief that was in their hearts. So the veil was really over their hearts. "Their minds were blinded;" and "even unto this day, when Moses is read, the veil is upon their heart." This is true not of the Jewish people alone, but of all who do not see Christ set forth in all the writings of Moses.

A veil interposed between people and the light, leaves them in the shadow. So when the children of Israel spread out the veil of unbelief between themselves and "the light of the Gospel of the glory of Christ," they naturally got only the shadow of it. They received only the shadow of the good things promised them, instead of the very substance. Let us note some of the shadows, as compared with the realities.

Shadow and Substance

1. God had said, "If ye will obey My voice indeed, and keep My covenant, then . . . ye shall be unto Me a kingdom of priests." But they never became a kingdom of priests. Only one tribe, the tribe of Levi, could have anything whatever to do with the sanctuary, and of that tribe only one family, that of Aaron, could be priests. It was certain death for any one not of the family of Aaron to presume to serve as priest in any way. Yet all who are really the children of God through faith in Christ Jesus are "a royal priesthood," even "an holy priesthood, to offer up spiritual sacrifices, acceptable to God by Jesus Christ." 1 Peter 2:5. This was what God promised to the nation of the Jews, at Sinai; but they never attained to it, because they did not keep His covenant of faith, but trusted in their own strength.

2. Instead of being brought to the heavenly sanctuary which God's hands established, and being planted in it, they had a worldly sanctuary made by man, and were not allowed to go into even that.

3. The throne of God, in the sanctuary above, is a living throne, self-moving, coming and going like a flash of lightning, in immediate response to the thought of the Spirit. Ezekiel 1. On the contrary, they had in the earthly sanctuary but a feeble representation of that throne in the shape of an ark of wood and gold, which had to be carried about on the shoulders of men.

4. The promise in the covenant with Abraham, which God's people were to keep, was that the law should be put into the heart. The children of Israel got it on tables of stone. Instead of by faith receiving "the law of the Spirit of life in Christ Jesus," (Romans 8:2), that is, upon "the living stone" in the midst of the throne of God (See I Peter 2:3, 4; Revelation 5:6), which would impart life to them, making them also

living stones, they received the law only on cold, lifeless stones, which could give them nothing but death.

5. In short, instead of the ministration of the righteousness of God in Christ, they got only the ministration of death; for the very same thing, which is a savor of life to them that believe, is a savor of death to them that do not believe.

But see the kindness and mercy of God even in this. He offered them the bright shining of His glorious Gospel, and they interposed a veil of unbelief, so that they could receive only the shadow. Yet that very shadow was an ever-present reminder of the substance. When a thick, passing cloud casts a shadow on the earth, we know, if we are not too dull to think, that it could not cast a shadow if it were not for the sun; so that even the cloud proclaims the presence of the sun. If therefore people nowadays, even professed Christians, were not as blind as the children of Israel ever were, they would be always rejoicing in the light of God's countenance, since even a cloud always proves the light to be present, and faith always causes the cloud to disappear, or else sees in it the bow of promise.

God's Witness in Unbelief

It was better for the Jews to have the law even as a witness against them, than not to have it at all. It was a great advantage to them in every way, to have committed unto them the oracles of God. Romans 3:2. It is better to have the law present to upbraid us for our sins, and to point out the way of righteousness, than to be left entirely without it. So the Jews, even in their unbelief, had an advantage over the heathen, because the Jews had "the form of righteousness and of the truth in the law." Romans 2:20. While that form could not save them, and only made their condemnation the greater if they rejected the instruction designed to be conveyed by it, yet it was an advantage in that it was a constant witness to them of God. God did not leave the heathen without witness, in that He spoke to them of Himself through the things that He had made, preaching the Gospel to them in creation; but the witness which He gave to the Jews, besides the other, was the very image of His own eternal realities.

And the very realities themselves were for His people. Only the veil of unbelief over their hearts kept them from having the substance of which they had the shadow; but "the veil is done away in Christ," (2 Corinthians 3:14), and Christ was even then present with them.

Whenever the heart shall turn to the Lord, the veil shall be taken away. Even the blindest could see that the sanctuary of the old covenant, and the ordinances of Divine service that were connected with it, were not the realities that God had sworn to give to Abraham and his seed. So they all might at once have turned to the Lord, even as individuals did throughout the whole history of Israel.

Moses talked with God with unveiled face. When the others "stood afar off," "Moses drew near." It is only by the blood of Christ that any can draw nigh. By the blood of Jesus we have boldness to enter even into the holiest, into the secret place of God. The fact that Moses did this shows his knowledge of the power of the precious blood and his confidence in it. But the blood that was able to give boldness and access to Moses, could have done the same to all the others, if they had believed as he did.

Do not forget that the presence of a shadow proves the present shining of the sun. If the glory of God's righteousness had not been present in its fullness, the people of Israel could not have had even the shadow. And since it was unbelief that caused the shadow, faith would have brought them at once into the full sunlight, and they could have been "to the praise of the glory of His grace."

Moses saw the glory with unveiled face, and was transformed by it. So if we believe, "we all, with unveiled face, reflecting as a mirror the glory of the Lord, are transformed into the same image from glory to glory, even as from the Lord the Spirit." 2 Corinthians 3:18. Even so it might have been with the children of Israel, if they had believed, for the Lord was never partial. That which Moses shared, all might have shared.

"That Which was Abolished"

"Christ is the end of the law for righteousness to every one that believeth." Romans 10:4. He "hath abolished death, and brought life and immortality to light through the Gospel;" (2 Timothy 1:10); and that Gospel was preached to Abraham, and to Israel in Egypt, and in the desert. But because of the unbelief of the people they "could not steadfastly look to the end of that which is abolished." 2 Corinthians 3:13. Because their faith did not lay hold on Christ, they got only the law as "the ministration of death," (Verse 7), instead of "the law of the Spirit of life in Christ Jesus."

People talk about "the Gospel age" and "the Gospel dispensation," as though the Gospel were an afterthought on the part of God, or at the most something, which God long delayed to give mankind. But the Scriptures teach us that "the Gospel dispensation" or "Gospel age" is from Eden lost to Eden restored. We know that "this Gospel of the kingdom shall be preached in all the world for a witness unto all nations; and then shall the end come." Matthew 24:14. That is the end of it, but the beginning was at the fall of man. The Apostle Paul directs our attention to man in the beginning, crowned with glory and honor, and set over the works of God's hands. Directing us to fix our gaze upon man in Eden, lord over all that he saw, the apostle continues, "But now we see not yet all things put under him." Hebrews 2:8. Why not? – Because he fell, and lost the kingdom and the glory. But we still look at the place where we first saw man in the glory and power of innocence, and where we saw him sin and come short of the glory, and "we see Jesus." Christ came to seek and to save that which was lost; and where should He seek except where it was lost? He came to save man from the fall, and so He necessarily went where man fell. Wherever sin abounds, there does grace much more abound. And so "the Gospel dispensation," with the cross of Christ shedding the light of the glory of God into the darkness of sin, dates from the fall of Adam. Where the first Adam fell, there the second Adam rises, for there the cross is erected.

"Since by man came death, by man came also the resurrection of the dead," because the second man Adam is a quickening Spirit, (1 Corinthians 15:21, 45), being "the resurrection and the life." Therefore in Christ death was abolished, and life and immortality were brought to light in the Gospel, the very day that Adam sinned. If it had not been so, Adam would have died that very day. Abraham and Sarah proved in their own bodies that Christ had abolished death, for they both experienced the power of the resurrection, rejoicing to see Christ's day. Long before their day, Enoch's translation without seeing death had proved that its power was broken; and his translation was due to his faith in Christ. Much more, then, was "the Gospel dispensation" in full glory as far down in the history of the world as Sinai. Whatever other dispensation than the Gospel dispensation any people have ever shared, has been solely because of their hardness and impenitent heart, which despised the riches of God's goodness and forbearance and long-suffering, and treasured up unto themselves wrath against the day of wrath.

So right there at Sinai the ministration of death was done away in Christ. The law was "in the hand of a Mediator," (Galatians 3:19), so that it was life to all who received it in Him. Death, which comes by sin, and the strength of which is the law, was abolished, and life put in its place to every one that believeth, no matter how many or how few they were. But let no one forget that as the Gospel was in full glory at Sinai, even so the law just as given at Sinai, is always present in the Gospel. If the law on the lifeless tables of stone was but a shadow, it was nevertheless an exact shadow, of the living law on the living stone, Christ Jesus. God would have all men know, wherever His voice is heard, that the righteousness, which Christ's obedience imparts to the believer, is the righteousness that is described in the law spoken from Sinai. Not one letter can be altered. It is an exact photograph of the character of God in Christ. A photograph is but a shadow, it is true; but if the light is clear it is an exact representation of some substance. In this case the light was "the light of the glorious Gospel of Christ, who is the image of God," (2 Corinthians 4:4), so that we may know the Ten Commandments to be the literal and exact form of God's righteousness. They describe to us just what the Holy Spirit will print in living letters of light upon the fleshy tables of our hearts if they are but sensitized by simple faith.

Chapter 34

The Promises to Israel - Two Laws

The Present Truth, December 24, 1896

From what has preceded, it will be evident that there are two laws just as there are two covenants, occupying the same relation to each other that the two covenants do to each other. One is the shadow of the other, the result of placing the veil of unbelief before the Light of life.

"For the commandment is a lamp, and the law is light; and reproofs of instruction are the way of life." Proverbs 6:23. But Christ is the only Light of the world, the Light of life; so that the true and living law is found only in Him. It is His life, because it is in His heart, and out of the heart are the issues of life. He is the Living Stone, where we find the law in Person, full of grace as well as of truth. Of this, the law on tables was but the shadow, albeit an exact and perfect shadow. It tells us exactly what we shall find in Christ.

Although the law on tables of stone describes the perfect righteousness of God, it has no power to make itself manifest in us, no matter how greatly we may desire it. It is "weak through the flesh." It is a faithful signpost, pointing out the way, but not carrying us in it. But Christ has "power over all flesh," and in Him we find the law so full of life that, if we but consent to the law that it is good, and confess that Christ is come in the flesh, it will manifest itself in the thoughts and words and acts of our lives, in spite of the weakness of the flesh.

To those who know the law only as it stands in a book, and who consequently think that it rests wholly on them to do it, it is a law of works, and as such it does nothing but pronounce a curse upon them. But to those who know the law in Christ, it is a law of faith, which proclaims the blessing of pardon and peace.

As known only on tables of stone or in a book, it is a "law of sin and death," (Romans 8:2), since "the sting of death is sin, and the strength of sin is the law." 1 Corinthians 15:56. But as known in Christ, it is "the law of the Spirit of life," "because of righteousness."

As "written and engraven in stones," it can never be anything else than "the ministration of death." He who preaches simply the written law, telling people of their duty to keep it, and inciting them to do the best they can to keep it, is but ministering condemnation. But the same law written in fleshy tablets of the heart, "with the Spirit of the living God" (2 Corinthians 3:3), is "life and peace;" and he who preaches that Christ "is come in the flesh," (1 John 4:2), and that when He dwells in a man today He is as obedient to the law as He was eighteen hundred years ago, is a minister of righteousness.

Known only as a code of rules to which we must make our lives conform – a "law of commandments contained in ordinances" – it is but a "yoke of bondage," because one's best efforts to keep it are themselves only sin; "for the Scripture hath concluded [shut up] all under sin;" and with each work "done in righteousness which we did ourselves," the law but tightens its death grip on us, and strengthens the bars of our prison. But "the Lord is the Spirit; and where the Spirit of the Lord is, there is liberty." 2 Corinthians 3:17. Therefore in Christ the law is the "perfect law of liberty." James 1:25.

When the Jews at Sinai volunteered to work God's works for Him, they undertook their own salvation. They ignored the history of Abraham, and God's covenant with him, to which their attention had been specially called. But God is long-suffering, not willing that any should perish, but that all should come to repentance; and so, in harmony with His covenant with Abraham, He did not cast off the people, but endeavored to teach them of Himself and His salvation, even out of their unbelief. He gave them a system of sacrifices and offerings, and a daily and yearly round of ceremonies that were exactly in keeping with the law, which they had elected to keep, namely, the law of works.

Of course this sacrificial system could not save them any more than could the broken law of works out of which it grew. Any man who had understanding enough to know the nature of sin and the necessity for atonement, had sense enough to know that pardon and righteousness could never be obtained by the ceremonies connected with the tabernacle. The very offering of a sacrifice indicated that death is the wages and fruit of sin. But anyone could see that the life of a lamb, a goat, or a bullock, was not worth as much as a man's own life. Therefore none of those animals, or all of them together, could answer for the life of a single man. Thousands of rams, or even a human sacrifice, could not atone for a single sin. Micah 4:6, 7.

The faithful among the people understood this well. David said, after he had committed a great sin, "Thou desirest not sacrifice, else would I give it: Thou delightest not in burnt offering." Psalm 51:6. And God, through the prophets, taught the people: "To what purpose is the multitude of your sacrifices unto me?" "I delight not in the blood of bullocks, or of lambs, or of he goats." Isaiah 1:11. "Your burnt offerings are not acceptable, nor your sacrifices sweet unto Me." Jeremiah 6:20. There was no virtue in them, for the law had only "a shadow of good things to come, and not the very image of the things," and could "never with those sacrifices which they offered year by year continually make the comers thereunto perfect." Hebrews 10:1.

It would of course have been better, nay, the very best thing, if the people of Israel had preserved the simple and strong faith of Abraham and Moses, in which case they would have had no tabernacle but the one "which the Lord pitched, and not man;" no High Priest except Christ Himself, "made an High Priest for ever, after the order of Melchizedek;" no limit to the priesthood, but every one of them a priest "to offer up spiritual sacrifices acceptable to God by Jesus Christ;" no law but "the law of the Spirit of life in Christ;" in short, only the reality, and not the mere shadow. But since the people did not believe, it was a wonderful exhibition of God's kindness and love and forbearance that He gave them what must have served as a continual object lesson. The very "weakness and unprofitableness" (Hebrews 7:18) of the law of works was always apparent to every thoughtful person; and when the soul became awakened, that law whose only profit was conviction, and whose only power was death, directed them to Christ, to whom it shut them up for freedom and life. It made evident to them that in Christ, and in Him alone, they could find salvation. The truth as it is in Jesus, is the truth that sanctifies.

How Forgiveness Come

Another point that it is necessary to notice particularly, although it has already been fully covered, is that nobody ever received salvation or the pardon of any sin by virtue of the law of works or the sacrifices connected with it. Moreover, God never caused the people to expect that the law could save, and nobody who truly believed Him ever thought that it could. Samuel said to Saul, "To obey is better than sacrifice, and to hearken than the fat of rams." 1 Samuel 15:22.

The prophet king, from a heart melted to contrition by the mercy of God, wrote: "Thou desirest not sacrifice, else would I give it; thou delightest not in burnt offering. The sacrifices of God are a broken spirit; a broken and a contrite heart, O God, Thou wilt not despise." Psalm 51:16, 17. Through Hosea the Lord, said: "I desired mercy and not sacrifice; and the knowledge of God more than burnt offerings." Hosea 6:6. Instead of the offering of fat beasts, the Lord desired that the people should "let judgment run down as waters, and righteousness as a mighty stream." Amos 5:24. Recall the chapter on drinking in the righteousness of God.

"By faith Abel offered unto God a more excellent sacrifice than Cain, by which he obtained witness that he was righteous." Hebrews 11:4. He did not obtain righteousness by the sacrifice of the firstlings of the flock, but by the faith, which prompted the offering. "Being justified by faith, we have peace with God through our Lord Jesus Christ." Romans 5:1. "By grace are ye saved through faith; and that not of yourselves; it is the gift of God." Ephesians 2:8. And so it was from the beginning; for "Abraham believed God, and it was counted unto him for righteousness," and the same is affirmed of Enoch and Noah and all the patriarchs and prophets.

After the building of the tabernacle, sacrifices could not be offered in any other place; yet many of the people would necessarily be far away from it. Three times a year they were to assemble to it to worship. But they did not have to wait for those seasons to come, in order to receive forgiveness of the sins that they might have committed in the meantime. Wherever a man might be when he sinned, and became conscious of the plague of his own heart, he could acknowledge the sin to the Lord, who was always at hand, and experience, as well as we can, that "if we confess our sins, He is faithful and just to forgive us our sins, and to cleanse us from all unrighteousness." 1 John 1:9. This is demonstrated in the case of David, when the prophet of God reproved him. David said, "I have sinned against the Lord;" and immediately came the assurance, "The Lord also hath put away thy sin." 2 Samuel 12:13.

When this had taken place, then the repentant and forgiven soul could "offer the sacrifices of righteousness" (Psalm 4:5; 51:19), which would be acceptable to God. Then would the Lord be pleased with burnt offerings and whole burnt offerings upon His altar. And why? – Because they showed the gratitude of the heart, and because they were a recognition of the fact that all belonged to God, and that everything came from Him. In all true sacrifice there is the underlying principle that He who saves the soul is abundantly able to supply all physical needs, even though every vestige of worldly goods should be consumed. It is not the thought that we are giving to God, but that God gives to us, that makes the true sacrifice, since the only real sacrifice is the sacrifice of Christ. This was plainly manifest in every sacrifice that was offered. The people could see that they were not enriching the Lord, for the sacrifice was consumed. Every one who offered intelligently – everyone who worshipped in spirit and in truth – simply indicated that he depended solely on God both for the life that now is and for that which is to come.

The Old Covenant Valueless

The old covenant, therefore, together with the law, which pertained to it, was never for one moment of any value whatever for pardon and salvation from sin. It was "made void" even from the beginning. (See Psalm 89:30) A demonstration of this is furnished by the pleading of Moses with God, when the children of Israel had made and worshipped the golden calf. When God said, "Let Me alone, that My wrath may wax hot against them, and that I may consume them," Moses besought the Lord and said: –

"Lord, why doth Thy wrath wax hot against Thy people, which Thou hath brought forth out of the land of Egypt with great power, and with a mighty hand? Wherefore should the Egyptians speak, and say, for mischief did He bring them out, to slay them in the mountains, and to consume them from the face of the earth? Turn from Thy fierce wrath, and repent of this evil against Thy people. Remember Abraham, Isaac, and Israel, Thy servants, to whom Thou swarest by Thine own self, and saidst unto them, I will multiply your seed as the stars of heaven, and all this land that I have spoken of will I give unto your seed, and they shall inherit it for ever." Exodus 32:10-13.

Not a word was there about the covenant that had just been made, but only the covenant with Abraham. No particle of dependence was placed in the promises that the people had made, but only in the promise and the oath of God. If that covenant from Sinai had ever been of any value, it would surely have been when it was first made; but we see that even then it sunk entirely out of sight. It had no more power to save the people than had the parchment on which it was written.

Jeremiah in later years prayed:

"O Lord though our iniquities testify against us, do Thou it for Thy name's sake; for our backslidings are many; we have sinned against Thee." "We acknowledge, O Lord, our wickedness, and the iniquity of our fathers; for we have sinned against Thee. Do not abhor us, for Thy name's sake, do not disgrace the throne of Thy glory; remember, break not Thy covenant with us. Are there any among the vanities of the Gentiles that can cause rain? Or can the heavens give showers? Art not Thou He, O Lord our God? Therefore we will wait upon Thee; for Thou hast made all these things." Jeremiah 14:7, 20-22.

That was all the plea God desired then, as well as now, for He said, "Return, thou backsliding Israel, saith the Lord; and I will not cause Mine anger to fall upon you; for I am merciful, saith the Lord, and I will not keep anger for ever. Only acknowledge thine iniquity, that thou hast transgressed against the Lord thy God." Jeremiah 3:12, 13. It was as true then as now, that "if we confess our sins, He is faithful and just to forgive us our sins."

God's power as Creator and Redeemer, and His promise and oath, are all that any really repentant Jew ever depended on for salvation. None of them ever thought of depending upon their own works or promises, as the means of salvation. In short, from the days of Abel until now, there has been but one way of life and salvation; only one way of approaching to God; only one Name under heaven by which men could be saved. Since the day when salvation through the Seed of the woman was made known to Adam and Eve, before they were driven from Eden, there has been no more change in the plan of salvation, nor in God's requirements for salvation, nor in the number to whom salvation was offered, than there has been in God Himself and His throne in heaven.

Men have changed, but God has not.

There have always been men who have trusted in their own words and promises, and in ceremonies; but that does not prove that God wished them to do so. In the days of Moses and of Christ the majority of men trusted mostly in form and ceremony; and so they do today. Men have always been more ready to grasp the shadow than the substance. But that does not prove that in the ancient days God expected men to be saved by the law of works, any more than it proves that justification is not by faith now.

Works of Supererogation

There has always been a tendency among men to multiply rites and ceremonies. This is the inevitable result of trusting to works for salvation. So it was in the days of Christ, and so it is now. When men get the idea that their works must save them, or that they themselves must do God's works, they cannot be content with attempting to do no more than God's commandments. So they teach for doctrines "the commandments of men," adding to them continually until no man could even enumerate the "good works" that are required, much less could he do them. The yoke which even at first is galling and insupportable, becomes heavier and heavier, until at last religion becomes a matter of merchandise, and men for money or some other consideration buy themselves off from the necessity of doing the works that have been imposed upon them. And since it is even more impossible for men to do the commandments of God by their own efforts than it is to do the commandments of men, God's law soon sinks in their estimation, even below the precepts of men.

All this is the natural and inevitable tendency of a failure to see Christ in the writings of Moses, and to understand that whatever ceremonies God ever gave were intended by their very emptiness to impress upon the people the absolute necessity of depending only on Christ, in whom alone is the substance.

The Use of a Likeness

One word further as to the shadow and the substance. As we have seen, the law delivered to the people in the wilderness of Sinai was but the shadow of the real law, which is the life of God. This is often urged in depreciation of the law; many people seem to think that since the law is but the shadow of good things, therefore we should choose that which is as opposite to it as possible. Not so do men argue in temporal matters. If we have a photograph – a shadow – of a man whom we wish to find, we do not light on a man whose features bear no resemblance to the likeness, and say, "This is the man." No; we find a man of whom the photograph is the exact likeness, and then we know that we have the one we seek. Now the real law is the life of God, and the law delivered to the children of Israel – the shadow of good things – is the photograph of God's character.

The one man in the entire world who in every particular meets the specifications of that photograph, is, "the Man Christ Jesus," in whose heart is the law. He is the image of the invisible God, but the living image – the Living Stone. Coming to Him in faith, we also become living stones, having the same law written in us that was in Him, for His Spirit transforms us into the same living image; and the law on the tables of stone from Sinai will be the witness that the resemblance is perfect. But if there is in any particular a deviation from the perfect photograph, lack of resemblance will show that we are not of the true family of God.

Chapter 35

The Promises to Israel - Entering the Promised Land

The Present Truth, December 31, 1896

"And about the time of forty years suffered He their manners in the wilderness." Acts 13:18. In these few words the Apostle Paul in his discourse in the synagogue at Antioch disposed of the forty years' wandering of the Israelites in the wilderness; and for the purpose of our present study we may pass it by nearly as hastily. Their manners were such that God literally "suffered" them. The record is one of murmurings and rebellion. "They believed not in God, and trusted not in His salvation." Psalm 78:22. "How oft did they provoke Him in the wilderness, and grieve Him in the desert! Yea, they turned back and tempted God, and limited the Holy One of Israel. They remembered not His hand, nor the day when He delivered them from the enemy; how He had wrought His signs in Egypt, and His wonders in the field of Zoan." Verses 40-43. Although for forty years they daily saw the works of God, they did not learn His ways; wherefore, says the Lord, "I was grieved with that generation, and said, They do alway err in their heart; and they have not known My ways. So I swore in My wrath, they shall not enter into My rest." Hebrews 3:10, 11.

An Inheritance of Faith

"So we see that they could not enter in because of unbelief." What does that teach us as to the nature of the inheritance to which God was leading His people? – Simply this, that it was an inheritance that could be possessed only by those who had faith – that faith alone could win it. Worldly, temporal possessions may be, and are, gained and held by men who disbelieve, and who even despise and blaspheme God. Indeed, unbelieving men have the most of this world's goods. Many besides the writer of the seventy-third Psalm have been envious at the prosperity of the wicked; but such feeling of envy arises only when one looks at the things that are temporal, instead of at the things that are eternal. "The prosperity of fools shall destroy them." God has chosen the poor of this world, "rich in faith, and heirs of the kingdom which He hath promised to them that love Him." James 2:5. That kingdom is "not of this world" (John 18:36), but is "a better country, that is, an heavenly," for which the patriarchs looked. It was to this country that God promised to lead His people when He delivered them from Egypt. But only those who are "rich in faith" can possess it.

The time had come when God could carry out His purpose with His people. The faithless ones who had said that their little ones would die in the desert had perished, and now those same children, grown to manhood, and trusting the Lord, were about to enter the Promised Land. After the death of Moses, God said to Joshua: "Arise, go over this Jordan, thou, and all this people, unto the land which I do give to them, even to the children of Israel. Every place that the sole of your foot shall tread upon, that have I given unto you, as I said unto Moses." Joshua 1:2, 3.

Crossing the Jordan

But the Jordan rolled between the Israelites and the land to which they were to go with all their flocks and little ones. The river was at its height, overflowing all its banks, and there were no bridges; but the same God who had brought His people through the Red Sea was still leading them, and He was as able as ever to do wonders. All the people took their places according to the Lord's directions, the priests bearing the ark being about a thousand paces in advance of the host. Onward they marched toward the river, whose flood still kept on its way. To the very brink of the stream they came, yet the waters receded not an inch. But this people had learned to trust the Lord, and, as He had told them to go on, they hesitated not for an instant. Into the water they went, although they knew that it was so deep that it could not possibly be forded, and swift enough to carry them away. They had nothing to do with considering difficulties; their part was to obey the Lord and go forward, and His to make the way.

"And it came to pass, . . . as they that bare the ark were come unto Jordan, and the feet of the priests that bare the ark were dipped in the brim of the water, that the waters which came down from above stood and rose up upon an heap very far from the city Adam, that is beside Zaretan; and those that came down toward the sea of the plain, even the salt sea, failed, and were cut off; and the people passed over right against Jericho. And the priests that bare the ark of the covenant of the Lord stood firm on dry ground in the midst of Jordan, and all the Israelites passed over on dry ground, until all the people were passed clean over Jordan." Joshua 3:14-17.

What a display of faith and trust in God!

The bed of the Jordan was dry, it is true, for the people to pass over, but on the right hand was a wall of water, piling still higher and higher, with no visible support. Picture to yourself that mighty heap of water, apparently threatening to overwhelm the people, and you can better appreciate the faith of those who calmly passed over before it. All the time of the passage the priests stood calm and unmoved in the midst of the riverbed, and the people marched over without breaking ranks. There was no unseemly scramble to get over quickly, lest the waters should come down upon them; for "he that believeth shall not make haste."

Free at Last

"At that time the Lord said unto Joshua, Make thee sharp knives, and circumcise again the children of Israel the second time." "For the children of Israel walked forty years in the wilderness, till all the people that were men of war, which came out of Egypt, were consumed, because they obeyed not the voice of the Lord; unto whom the Lord swore that He would not show them the land, which the Lord swore unto their fathers that He would give us, a land that flows with milk and honey. And their children, whom He raised up in their stead, them Joshua circumcised; because they had not circumcised them by the way. And it came to pass, when they had done circumcising all the people, that they abode in their places in the camp, till they were whole. And the Lord said unto Joshua, This day have I rolled away the reproach of Egypt from off you." Joshua 5:2-9.

In order to see the full force of this ceremony at this time we must recall the significance of circumcision, and must also know what is meant by "the reproach of Egypt." Circumcision signified righteousness by faith (Romans 4:11); true circumcision, whose praise is not of men, but of God, is obedience to the law, through the Spirit (Romans 2:25-29); it is complete distrust of self, and confidence and rejoicing in Christ Jesus. Philippians 3:3. In the instance before us we see that God Himself commanded the people to be circumcised, a positive proof that He Himself accepted them as righteous. As with Abraham, so with them, their faith was counted to them for righteousness.

"Righteousness exalteth a nation; but sin is a reproach to any people." Proverbs 14:34. Sin was "the reproach of Egypt," and it was this that was rolled away from the children of Israel; for the true circumcision of the heart, which alone is all that God counts as circumcision, is "the putting off the body of the sins of the flesh by the circumcision of Christ." Colossians 2:11. "Thus saith the Lord God: In the day when I chose Israel, and lifted up Mine hand unto the seed of the house of Jacob, and made Myself known unto them in the land of Egypt, when I lifted up Mine hand unto them, saying, I am the Lord your God; . . . then said I unto them, Cast ye away every man the abominations of his eyes, and defile not yourselves with the idols of Egypt; I am the Lord your God. But they rebelled against Me, and would not hearken unto Me; they did not every man cast away the abominations of their eyes, neither did they forsake the idols of Egypt." Ezekiel 20:58.

It was because they would not forsake the idols of Egypt, that the men who left that country with Moses did not enter into the Promised Land. A people cannot at one and the same time be both free and in bondage. The bondage of Egypt – "the reproach of Egypt" – was not merely the physical labor which the people were forced to do without reward, but was the abominable idolatry of Egypt, into which they had fallen. It was from this that God would deliver His people, when He said to Pharaoh, "Let My people go, that they may serve Me."

This freedom the people had at last obtained. God Himself declared that the bondage, the sin, the reproach of Egypt was rolled away from them. Then could it be sung, "Open ye the gates, that the righteous nation which keepeth the truth may enter in." Isaiah 26:2.

The Victory of Faith

"By faith the walls of Jericho fell down, after they were compassed about seven days." Hebrews 11:30.

"Now faith is the substance of things hoped for, the evidence of things not seen." Hebrews 11:1.

"For the weapons of our warfare are not carnal, but mighty through God to the pulling down of strongholds." 2 Corinthians 10:4.

The children of Israel were in the Promised Land, but yet to all appearances they were no more in possession than they were before. They still dwelt in tents, while the inhabitants of the land were entrenched in their cities, which were "walled up to heaven," fully as strong as when the mere report of them caused the children of Israel to lose heart and turn back forty years before. But stonewalls and multitudes of armed men avail nothing when the battle is the Lord's.

"Now the city of Jericho was straightly shut up because of the children of Israel; none went out, and none came in." Joshua 6:1. Jericho was the first city to be taken and the mode of operation which the Lord directed, was one calculated to test to the utmost the faith of the Israelites. All the people were to march round the city in perfect silence, with the exception that the priests who went ahead with the ark were to blow on their trumpets. "Joshua had commanded the people, saying, Ye shall not shout, nor make any noise with your voice, neither shall any noise proceed out of your mouth, until the day I bid you shout; then shall ye shout." Joshua 6:10. As soon as they had completed this silent circuit of the city, they were to go into camp. The same thing was to be done for six successive days, and on the seventh day the circuit was to be made seven times.

Picture to yourself the situation. Tramp, tramp, the whole multitude went round the city, and then went into camp. Again and again they repeated this, with no apparent result. The walls stood as high and as grim as before; not a stone had fallen, not a bit of mortar had been loosened. Yet not one word of complaint was heard from one of the people.

We can well believe that for the first day or two the sight of that great host marching silently about the city filled the inhabitants with dread, more especially as they had previously been terrified by the reports of what God had done for those people. But as the march was repeated day after day, seemingly to no purpose, it would be most natural for the beleaguered ones to pick up courage, and regard the whole affair as a farce. Many would begin to mock, and to taunt the Israelites with their senseless methods. The history of warfare furnished no precedent for such a mode of proceeding to capture a city, and it would have been contrary to human nature if some of the people of the city had not openly ridiculed the marchers outside.

But not a single word of retort came from those ranks. Patiently the children of Israel bore whatever taunts may have been hurled at them. Not a voice was heard saying, "What is the use of all this?" "What kind of general is this man Joshua?" "Does he suppose that by our measured tread we can set the walls to vibrating so that they will fall down?" "What's the use of tiring our legs and wearing out our shoes in this child's parade?" "Well, I am tired of this fooling, and shall stay in my tent until we can do something worth the while." Anyone who knows anything of human nature knows that these and similar expressions would freely be uttered under such circumstances by the most of people; and it would be remarkable if there were not open revolt against the proceedings. This would have been the case with the children of Israel forty years before; and the fact that they patiently and quietly marched around the city thirteen times, seemingly with no object, is proof of the most remarkable faith that the world has ever known. Think of an entire nation among which there was not one fault-finder, not one to utter a word of complaint when put to inconvenience which he could not understand, and which was apparently useless.

The seventh day was nearly gone, and the thirteenth round of the city was completed. Everything remained just as at the beginning of their march. Now came the last, the crowning test of faith. "And it came to pass at the seventh time, when the priests blew with the trumpets, Joshua said unto the people, Shout; for the Lord hath given you the city." Joshua 6:16.

Why should they shout? – Because the Lord had given them the city; they were to shout the victory. But what evidence was there that the victory was won? they could see no gain. Oh, faith is "the evidence of things not seen." The victory was theirs, because God had granted it to them, and their faith claimed it at His word. Not a moment did they hesitate; their faith was perfect, and at the word of command a triumphant shout rose from that vast assembly. "And it came to pass, when the people heard the sound of the trumpet, and the people shouted with a great shout, that the wall fell down flat." Joshua 6:20.

The promise to those people was the very same that God now extends to us; and all things recorded of them are for our learning. "They got not the land in possession by their own sword, neither did their own arm save them" (Psalm 44), but the Lord's right hand saved them. Even so will He grant unto us that we shall "be saved from our enemies, and from the hand of all that hate us," that we being delivered out of the hand of our enemies might serve Him without fear, in holiness and righteousness all the days of our life. Luke 1:68-75. This deliverance is through Christ, who is now, as well as in the days of Joshua, the "Captain of the Lord's host." He says, "In the word ye shall have tribulation; but be of good cheer; I have overcome the world." John 16:33. "And ye are complete in Him, which is the Head of all principality and power." Colossians 2:10. Therefore "this is the victory that hath overcome the world, even our faith." 1 John 5:4.

Chapter 36

The Promises to Israel - Vainglory and Defeat

The Present Truth, January 7, 1897

"Thou standest by faith; be not high-minded, but fear." Romans 11:20.

"Wherefore let him that thinketh he standeth, take heed lest he fall." 1 Corinthians 10:12.

A man is never in greater danger than when he has just achieved some great success, or gained a great victory. If he is not very much on his guard, his joyous song of thanksgiving will have a chorus of vainglorious self-congratulation. Beginning with recognition of God's power, and praise and thanksgiving for it, man insensibly puts himself in the place of God, and assumes that his own wisdom and strength brought him the success and the victory. Thus he exposes himself to attack when he is sure to be overcome, since he has separated from the source of power. Only in the Lord Jehovah is there everlasting strength.

"And Joshua sent men from Jericho to Ai, which is beside Bethaven, on the east side of Bethel, and spake unto them, saying, Go up, and view the country. And the men went up and viewed Ai. And they returned to Joshua, and said unto him, Let not all the people go up; but let about two or three thousand men go up and smite Ai; and make not all the people to labour thither; for they are but few. So there went up thither of the people about three thousand men; and they fled before the men of Ai. And the men of Ai smote of them about thirty-six men; . . . wherefore the hearts of the people melted, and became as water." Joshua 7:2-5.

No One Beyond Danger

The story of Jericho and Ai is sufficient answer to those who repeat with as much assurance as though it were Scripture, the saying, "Once in grace always in grace," the meaning being that if a person is once really walking in the fear of God he can never fall. There can be no question but that the children of Israel did really and fully trust the Lord when they crossed the Jordan and marched round Jericho. God Himself witnessed that they had the righteousness of faith, and His word declares that they gained a glorious victory through faith. Nevertheless it was but a few days afterward that they suffered a serious defeat. It was the beginning of apostasy. Although God afterwards wrought many wonders for them, and showed Himself always ready to do all that their faith would grasp, the whole people of Israel were never again perfectly united to "fight the good fight of faith." Only for a little season, after the outpouring of the Spirit on the day of Pentecost, were the multitude of them that believed "of one heart and of one soul." But that the same union and strength in perfect faith will be witnessed again among God's people on earth, is as sure as the promise of God.

The Cause of the Defeat

There was sin in the camp when Israel went up against Ai, and this was the cause of their defeat. The whole people suffered, not simply because of Achan's sin, but because all had sinned. "Behold, his soul which is lifted up is not upright in him; but the just shall live by his faith." Habakkuk 2:4. Whether they were blinded by "the deceitfulness of sin," and then became exalted in their minds, or whether their self-exaltation led to their sin, is not material; certain it is that the people had given place to sin, and had become self-confident, which is in itself sin. Because of sin they suffered defeat; so long as sin was given a place in their hearts, they could not go on with the conquest of the land; and this again proves that the promised inheritance, into which God was leading them, was such as could be possessed only by righteous people – those who had the righteousness of faith.

The men who went up to view the country made the people believe that but few men were needed to capture Ai, because it was a small city. But they had no ground for such an assumption. True, Ai was not nearly as large as Jericho, but numbers had nothing to do with the taking of that city. "By faith the walls of Jericho fell down;" and if the Israelites had been only half or even one-tenth as numerous as they were, the result would have been the same. It required the same power to take Ai that it did to take Jericho, namely, the power of God, laid hold of by faith. When the men said that but few of the people were needed for the capture of Ai, they assumed that it was their military skill that was to secure the land for them. But that was a grievous error. God had promised to give them the land, and it could not be obtained except as a gift. The mightiest army that the world has ever seen, armed with the most approved weapons of war, could not take it; while a few unarmed men, strong in faith and giving glory to God, could have possessed it with ease. The force that takes the kingdom of heaven is not the force of arms.

Defeat Not in God's Plan

Another thing that we learn from the story of Ai is that God did not intend that His people should ever suffer defeat, or that in the occupation of the land a single man should lose his life. In ordinary warfare the loss of thirty-six men in an assault upon a strongly fortified city would not be counted great, even if the assault were successful;

but in taking possession of the land of Canaan it was a terrible reverse. The promise was, "Every place that the sole of your foot shall tread upon, that have I given unto you," and "there shall not any man be able to stand before thee," (Joshua 1:3, 5), and now they themselves had been obliged to flee, with the loss of men. The influence that the passage of the Jordan and the capture of Jericho would have had to impress and overawe the heathen, was now broken. Trusting to their strength, the Israelites had lost the power of God's presence, and had demonstrated their own weakness.

The Means of Defense

The fact that it was altogether contrary to God's plan that any of the Israelites should lose their lives in taking possession of the Promised Land, is further shown by the fact, which may well be noted here, that it was not His design that they should have to fight for the possession of the promised inheritance. We have already seen that numbers and arms had nothing to do with the taking of Jericho, and that when they depended on their weapons, force that in ordinary warfare would have been amply sufficient was of no avail. Recall also the wonderful deliverance from Egypt, and the overthrow of the entire army of Pharaoh, without the lifting of a single weapon or the use of any human power, and that God led the people by the longest and most difficult route in order that they might not see war (Exodus 13.18), and then read the following promise: –

"If thou shalt say in thine heart, these nations are more than I, how can I dispossess them? thou shalt not be afraid of them; but shalt well remember what the Lord thy God did unto Pharaoh and to all Egypt; the great temptations which thine eyes saw, and the signs, and the wonders, and the mighty hand, and the stretched out arm, whereby the Lord thy God brought thee out; so shall the Lord thy God do unto all the people of whom thou art afraid. Moreover, the Lord thy God will send the hornet among them, until they that are left, and hide themselves from thee, be destroyed. Thou shalt not be affrighted at them; for the Lord thy God is among you, a mighty God and terrible." Deuteronomy 7:17-21.

Just as the Lord did to Pharaoh and to all Egypt, so did he promise to do to all the enemies that should set themselves against the progress of the Israelites to the Promised Land. But the children of Israel did not strike a single blow to effect their deliverance from Egypt and the overthrow of all its armies. When Moses, forty years before, had attempted to deliver Israel by physical force, he most signally failed, and was obliged to flee in disgrace. It was only when he knew the Gospel as the power of God unto salvation, that he was able to lead the people forth without any fear of the wrath of the king. This is conclusive proof that God did not design that they should fight for the possession of the land; and if they did not fight, of course they could not lose any of their number in battle. Read further as to the manner in which God proposed to give them the land: –

"I will send My fear before thee, and will destroy all the people to whom thou shalt come, and I will make all thine enemies turn their backs unto thee. And I will send hornets before thee, which shall drive out the Hivite, the Canaanite, and the Hittite, from before thee. I will not drive them out from before thee in one year; lest the land become desolate, and the beast of the field multiply against thee. By little and little I will drive them out from before thee, until thou be increased, and inherit the land." Exodus 23:27-30.

When Jacob, years before, sojourned in the same land, with his family, the "terror of God was upon the cities that were round about them, and they did not pursue after the sons of Jacob." Genesis 35:5. "When they were but a few men in number; yea, very few, and strangers in it. When they went from one nation to another, from one kingdom to another people; He suffered no man to do them wrong; yea, He reproved kings for their sakes; saying, Touch not Mine anointed, and do my prophets no harm." Psalm 105:12-15. That same power was to bring them into the land, and speedily give them an eternal inheritance in it, for afterward, the Lord, bewailing their unfaithfulness, said: –

"Oh that My people had hearkened unto Me, and Israel had walked in My ways! I should soon have subdued their enemies, and turned My hand against their adversaries. The haters of the Lord should have submitted themselves unto Him; but their time should have endured for ever." Psalm 81:13-15.

Why They Fought

"But the children of Israel did fight throughout all their natural existence, and under God's direction, too," it will be urged. That is very true, but it does not at all prove that it was God's purpose that they should fight.

We must not forget that "their minds were blinded" by unbelief, so that they could not perceive the purpose of God for them. They did not grasp the spiritual realities of the kingdom of God, but were content with shadows instead; and the same God who bore with their hardness of heart in the beginning, and strove to teach them by shadows, when they would not have the substance, still remained with them, compassionately considerate of their infirmities. God Himself suffered them, because of the hardness of their hearts, to have a plurality of wives, and even laid down rules regulating polygamy, in order to diminish as far as possible the resulting evils, but that does not prove that He designed it for them. We well know that "from the beginning it was not so." So when Jesus forbade His followers to fight in any cause whatever, He introduced nothing new, any more than when He taught that a man should have but one wife, and should cleave to her as long as he lived He was simply enunciating first principles – preaching a thorough reformation.

Executing the Judgment Written

One thing, however, which should never be lost sight of by people who are disposed to cite God's commands to the Israelites as sanctioning wars either of defense or conquest, is the fact that God never told them to destroy any whose cup of iniquity was not filled to the full, and who had not irrevocably rejected the way of righteousness. In the end of this world, when the time comes that the saints possess the kingdom, judgment will be given to the saints of the Most High (Daniel 7:22), and the saints will judge not only the world, but also angels. 1 Corinthians 6:2, 5. They will also, as joint-heirs with Christ, have a share in the execution of the judgment, for we read: –

"Let the saints be joyful in glory: let them sing aloud upon their beds. Let the high praises of God be in their mouth, and a two-edged sword in their hand; to execute vengeance upon the heathen, and punishments upon the people; to bind their kings with chains, and their nobles with fetters of iron; to execute upon them the judgment written; this honor have all His saints." Psalm 149:5-9.

Since Christ associates His people with Himself in the kingdom, making them all kings and priests, it is no more incongruous for His saints, in connection with Him, and by His direct authority, to execute just judgment upon the incorrigibly wicked, than it is for Him to do it. And so, when we remember that the deliverance from Egypt was the beginning of the end, and that God was then purposing to give His people the very same kingdom which He now promises to us, and to which Christ will call the blessed when He comes, we can well understand that a righteous people might then, as well as in the future, be the agents of God's justice. But that would not be a war of conquest, even for the possession of the Promised Land, but the execution of judgment. But it must not be forgotten that God Himself personally gives directions when such judgment is to be executed, and does not leave men to guess at His will in such a case. Moreover, only those who are themselves without sin can execute judgment upon sinners.

War Not a Success

Yet one more thing must be remembered in connection with this question of fighting and the possession of the land of Canaan, the promised inheritance, and that is that the children of Israel did not get it after all, with all their fighting. The same promise that was given them, remains for us; "but if Joshua had given them rest, then would He not afterwards have spoken of another day" in which to seek and find it. Hebrews 4:1, 8. The reason why they did not get it was their unbelief, and that was why they fought. If they had believed the Lord, they would have allowed Him to clear the land of its totally depraved inhabitants, in the way that He proposed. They in the meantime would not have been idle, but would have performed the work of faith which God set them, and which must next claim our attention.

Chapter 37

Israel: A Missionary People

The Present Truth, January 14, 1897

WHEN God sent Moses to lead Israel from Egypt, His message to Pharaoh was, "Israel is My son, even My firstborn; and I say unto thee, Let My son go, that he may serve Me" (Exodus 4:22, 23); and He brought them forth, and gave them the lands of the heathen, "that they might observe His statutes and keep His laws." Psalm 105:44, 45. The great advantage of the Jews over other people was that "unto them were committed the oracles of God." Romans 3:1, 2. To be sure they did not receive those "lively oracles" in all their living power, and thus make their advantage infinitely greater; but that was not the fault of God, and we are not now considering what Israel actually had and were, but what they might have possessed, and what they ought to have been.

Two things have always been true namely, that "no man liveth unto himself," and that "God is no respecter of persons;" and these two truths combined form a third, which is, that whenever God bestows any gift or advantage upon any person, it is in order that he may use it for the benefit of others. God does not bestow blessings upon one person or people that He does not wish all to have. When He promised a blessing to Abraham, it was in order that he might be a blessing – that in him all the people of the earth might be blessed. It was in the line of the promise to Abraham that God delivered Israel. Therefore, in giving them the advantage of possessing His law, it was that they might make known to other people that inestimable advantage, so that the other people also might share it.

God's purpose was that His name should be made known in all the earth. Exodus 9:15. His desire that all people should know Him was as great as that the children of Israel should know Him. To know the only true God, is life eternal (John 17:3); therefore in revealing Himself to Israel, God was showing them the way of Eternal life, or the Gospel, in order that they might proclaim the same Gospel to others. The reason why God made Himself known to Israel in so marked a manner, was that they were, so to speak, nearer at hand than other people. The memory of God's dealing with Abraham, Isaac, Jacob, and Joseph, and of their faith, was preserved among the Jews, thus making them more accessible. God chose them, not because He loved them more than He did others, but because He loved all men, and would make Himself known to them by means of the agents that were nearest at hand. The idea that God ever was exclusive, and that He ever confined His mercies and truth to one special people, is most dishonoring to His character. Never did He leave the heathen without witness of Himself, and wherever He could find a man or people that would consent to be used, them He straightway enlisted in His service, to make a more full revelation of Himself.

Effect of the Proclamation of the Gospel in Egypt

The Gospel is the power of God to salvation, and since God's mighty power was exhibited in the salvation of Israel from Egypt, it is evident that the Gospel was at that time proclaimed, as it has never been since. The effect of that proclamation is shown by the words of a heathen woman, the harlot Rahab. When the two spies came to her house in Jericho, she concealed them, and said to them: –

"I know that the Lord hath given you the land, and that your terror is fallen upon us, and that all the inhabitants of the land faint because of you. For we have heard how the Lord dried up the waters of the Red Sea for you, when ye came out of Egypt; and what ye did unto the two kings of the Amorites, that were on the other side of Jordan, Sihon and Og, whom ye utterly destroyed. And as soon as we had heard these things our hearts did melt, neither did there remain any more courage in any man, because of you; for the Lord your God; He is God in Heaven above, and in earth beneath." Joshua 2:9-11. And then she begged for and received the promise of deliverance.

"By faith the harlot Rahab perished not with them that believed not, when she had received the spies in peace." Hebrews 11:31. That which happened to her might have been the lot of every other resident of Jericho, provided they had exercised the same faith that she did. They had heard the same things that she had, and knew as a matter of fact, as well as she did, that "Jehovah your God, He is God in heaven above, and in earth beneath." But knowledge is not faith. The devils know that there is one God, but they have no faith. Faith is trust – submission. Rahab was willing to submit to the requirements of God, and to live as one of His people, while her fellow-countrymen were not. In her case we see the evidence that God saves people, not because they are good, but because they are willing to be made good. Jesus is sent to bless us, in turning us away from our iniquities. That poor heathen woman of disreputable life, who could utter a lie with a composed countenance, and with no consciousness of guilt, had a most meager idea of the difference between right and wrong; yet God acknowledged her as one of His people, because she did not turn away from light, but walked in it as it came to her. She believed to the saving of her soul. Her faith lifted her out of her sinful surroundings, and set her in the way of knowledge; and no stronger evidence can be found that Christ is not ashamed to acknowledge even the heathen as His brethren, than the fact that He is not ashamed to have one of them, a harlot, to boot, recorded in the roll of His ancestry after the flesh.

God's Solicitude for all Men

But the special point in this reference to Rahab is that God had not shut Himself up to the Jewish people. Wherever there was an idolatrous inhabitant of Canaan, who was willing to acknowledge God, that moment he was enrolled among God's people. This lesson is not merely theoretical, the point being that the promise to Abraham included all the world, and not merely the offspring of Jacob, but it is practically consoling and uplifting. It shows us how longsuffering the Lord is, "not willing that any should perish, but that all should come to repentance." 2 Peter 3:9. It shows us how quickly God seizes upon the slightest inclination to seek Him, and uses it as a means of drawing the erring soul still nearer. He gently breathes upon the tiniest spark, if possibly it may be enlarged to a flame. His ear is continually turned to earth, alert to catch the faintest whisper, so that the feeblest cry, yea, the first impulse to call, from the lowest depths, is instantly heard and responded to.

Priests of God

That God's design for Israel was that they should proclaim the Gospel to all the world, is seen in the fact that if they abode in His covenant they were to be a kingdom of priests. All were to be priests of God. Now the work of a priest is thus set forth in Malachi 2:5-7, where God says of Levi: –

"My covenant was with him of life and peace; and I gave them to him for the fear wherewith He feared Me, and was afraid before My name. The law of truth was in his mouth, and iniquity was not found in his lips; he walked with Me in peace and equity, and did turn many away from iniquity. For the priest's lips should keep knowledge, and they should seek the law at his mouth; for he is the messenger of the Lord of hosts."

To turn men away from iniquity, is the work of Christ through His resurrection; therefore, the work of the true Priest is simply to preach the Gospel; – to proclaim the living Saviour, in whom is the living law that is perfect, converting the soul. But since all the children of Israel were to be priests, and therefore all familiar with the law, it is evident that they were to be priests in behalf of others, and not merely to be settled teachers among themselves. If they had accepted God's proposition, and been content to abide in His covenant instead of insisting on one of their own, there would have been no need of any priesthood to make the law of truth and peace known to them; they would all have known the truth, and consequently all have been free; but the office of a priest is to teach the law, and therefore it is positive that God's purpose in bringing Israel out of Egypt was to send them all over the world preaching the Gospel.

What an easy and speedy task this would have been for them, backed by the power of God! The fame of what God had done in Egypt had preceded them, and as they went forth with the same power, they could preach the Gospel in its fullness to people already prepared to accept or reject. Leaving their wives and little ones safe in the land of Canaan, and going out two by two, as Jesus afterward sent forth His disciples, it would have taken them but a short time to carry the Gospel to the remotest parts of the earth. Suppose enemies attempted to oppose their progress? One could chase a thousand, and two put ten thousand to flight. That is, the power of the presence of God with any two of them would render them in the eyes of their enemies equal to ten thousand men, and none would dare attack them. So they could go about their appointed work of preaching the Gospel, without fear of molestation. The terror which their presence would inspire in opposers, shows the power which the message they proclaimed would have on hearts open to receive truth.

As they should go forth thus clothed with the full power of God, the ground would not need to be gone over the second time. All who heard would at once take their position either for or against the truth; and this decision would be final, since when one rejects the Gospel proclaimed in its fullness, that is with the mighty power of God, there is nothing more that can be done for him, for there is no greater power than that of God. So a very few years, or possibly months, after the crossing of the Jordan, would have sufficed for the preaching of the Gospel of the kingdom in all the world as a witness to all nations.

Evidences of God's Impartiality

But Israel did not fulfill its high calling. Unbelief and self-trust deprived them of the prestige with which they entered the Promised Land. They did not let their light shine, and so in time they themselves lost it. They were content to colonize in Canaan, instead of possessing the whole earth. They assumed that the light, which God had given them, was due to the fact that He loved them better than He did others, and so they became haughty, and despised others. Nevertheless, God ceased not to indicate to them that they were to be the light of the world. The history of the Jews, instead of showing that God was shut up to them, shows that He was continually trying to use them to make His name known to others. Witness the account of Naaman the Syrian, who was sent to the king of Israel to be healed of his leprosy. See the case of the widow of Sarepta, to whom Elijah was sent. The Queen of Sheba came from far to hear the wisdom of Solomon. Jonah was sent, much against his will, to warn the Ninevites, who repented at his preaching. Read the prophecies of Isaiah, Jeremiah, and Ezekiel, and see how often the various nations are directly appealed to. All of these things show that God was not then, any more than now, the God of the Jews only, but of the Gentiles also. At last, when Israel had utterly refused to fulfill the mission to which God had called them, He sent them into captivity, that thus the heathen might receive some of the knowledge of God, which they would not impart voluntarily. There a few faithful souls were the means of bringing the truth clearly before the heathen king Nebuchadnezzar, who in time humbly acknowledged God, and published his confession of faith throughout the whole earth. King Cyrus, also, and other Persian kings, in royal proclamations made known the name of the one true God in all the world.

Gathering into One Fold

Thus we see that there was nothing God so much desired as the salvation of the heathen round about the Jews, and not only of those near at hand, but those who were most distant, for the promises were not only to the Jews and their children, but to all that were "far off." See Acts 2:39; Isaiah 47:19. That God made no difference between Jews and Gentiles is seen in the fact that Abraham, the head of the Jewish race, was himself a Gentile, and received the assurance of acceptance with God while he was yet uncircumcised, "that he might be the father of all them that believe, though they be not circumcised; that righteousness might be imputed unto them also." Romans 4:11, 12. God was always as ready to accept people from among the heathen, as He was when He called Abraham out from among them. When Christ came, He declared that He was sent only to the lost sheep of the house of Israel, and even while He said that, He showed who were the lost sheep of the house of Israel, by sending healing to a believing heathen woman. Matthew 15.

What Christ did for that Canaanitish woman, He was equally ready and anxious to do for every believing inhabitant of Canaan and of the whole world, in the days of Joshua. All who did not stubbornly cling to their idols, were to be gathered into the fold of Israel, till there should be but one fold, under the One Shepherd. There was salvation for all who would accept it, but they must become Israelites indeed.

Israel to be Separate

It was for this reason that the Israelites were forbidden to make any league with the inhabitants of the land. A league implies likeness, equality, the union of two similar powers. But Israel, when true to its calling, had nothing in common with the inhabitants of the land. They were to be a separate people, separate solely because of the sanctifying presence of the Lord. When God said to Moses, "My presence shall go with thee, and I will give thee rest," Moses replied, "If Thy presence go not with me, carry us not up hence. For wherein shall it be known here that I and Thy people have found grace in Thy sight? is it not in that Thou goest with us? so shall we be separated, I and Thy people, from all the people that are upon the face of the earth." Exodus 33:14-16. To make a league with the nations round them, was to be joined to them, and that meant separation from the presence of God. The presence of God was the one thing that would make and keep the people of Israel separate from the nations, and His presence could have no other effect than that very thing. The presence of God will do the same thing in these days, for He changes not. Therefore if one should say that it is not necessary for the people of God to be separate from the nations, he would really be saying that it is not necessary for them to have God's presence.

The same principle was involved when the people wanted a king. Read the account in 1 Samuel 8. The people said to Samuel, "Give us a king to judge us like all the nations." The thing displeased Samuel, and doubtless hurt his feelings, but the people insisted, saying, "Give us a king to judge us." Then the Lord said to Samuel, "Hearken unto the voice of the people in all that they say unto thee; for they have not rejected thee, but they have rejected Me, that I should not reign over them. According to all the works which they have done since the day that I brought them up out of Egypt even unto this day, wherewith they have forsaken Me, and served other gods, so do they also unto thee." Then Samuel, at the command of the Lord, set before the people some of the evils that would result if they had a king; but they refused to be persuaded, saying, "Nay, but we will have a king over us, that we may be like all the nations."

In the Bible the "nations" are the heathen. The Hebrew word, which is often rendered "nations", is the identical word from which the word "heathen" always comes. Perhaps Psalm 96:5 makes the case as clear as may be to the English reader. "For all the gods of the nations are idols; but the Lord made the heavens." Here it is very evident that the "nations" are heathen. In Psalm 2. where we read, "Why do the heathen rage, and the people imagine a vain thing?" The Revision has it. "Why do the nations rage, and the people imagine a vain thing?" Such an idea as a "Christian nation" is as much a contradiction of terms as a "Christian heathen," or a "Christian sinner." A "nation" in God's use of the term, when speaking of earthly nations, is a collection of heathen. So what the Jews really said was this: "We will have a king over us, that we also may be like all the heathen." That was what they wanted, because all other people acknowledged other gods than Jehovah, and all the people on earth, with the exception of Israel, had kings over them. The Danish Bible renders 1 Samuel 8:20 plainly, "We will also be like all the heathen."

God's plan for Israel was that it should not be a nation. We are apt to look at what was, as though it was what ought to have been, forgetting that from first to last the people refused, to a greater or less extent, to walk in the counsel of God. We see the Jewish people with judges, and officers, and all the paraphernalia of civil government; but we must remember that God's covenant provided something far different, which, on account of unbelief, they never fully realized.

Israel the Church of Christ

The word "church" is in very common use, yet perhaps comparatively few of those who use it realize that it is from a Greek word which means "called out," and that it applies to Israel more than to any other people. They constituted God's church; they had been called out of Egypt. In the Old Testament they are referred to as "the congregation," that is, those who were assembled or had flocked together; for they formed the Lord's flock, of which He was Shepherd. God is known as the "Shepherd of Israel." Psalm 80:1;

see also 23:1. So the church in later times is called God's flock. Acts 20:28. Stephen, in his talk before the Sanhedrim, spoke of Israel as "the church in the wilderness."

There is but one church, for the church is Christ's body (Ephesians 1:19-23), and there is but one body. Ephesians 4:4. That one church is composed of those who hear and follow the voice of Christ, for Christ says: "My sheep hear My voice," "and they follow Me." John 10:27. That church in the wilderness is therefore identical with the true church of Christ in every age. This is most clearly shown by Hebrews 3:2-6. As you read the passage; remember, "The house of God" is "the church of the living God." 1 Timothy 3:15. Now the text says that Christ was faithful in the house of God, even as Moses was. Moses was faithful in the house of God as a servant, and Christ as a Son over the same house, "whose house are we, if we hold fast the confidence and the rejoicing of the hope firm unto the end." Jesus was called out of Egypt, as it is written, "Out of Egypt have I called my Son." Matthew 2:15. He was the Head and Leader of the host that came out with Moses. 1 Corinthians 10:1-10. Christ and Moses therefore, are in the same fellowship and communion, and whoever is a partaker of Christ, must acknowledge Moses as a brother in the Lord.

These facts are most important, since as we learn God's plan for Israel, we learn the true model for the church of God in all ages, even unto the end. We may not indiscriminately quote what Israel did, as authority for what we should do, since they often rebelled against God, and their history is more often a record of apostasy than of faith; but we may and should study God's promises and reproofs to them, for what He had for them He has also for us.

The Church the Kingdom

The people of Israel constituted a kingdom from the beginning, centuries before Saul was set over them; for the church of God is His kingdom, and His subjects are all His children. The "household of God" is "the commonwealth of Israel." Ephesians 2:19. Christ, with the Father, sits upon "the throne of grace," and the true church acknowledges Him, and Him only, as Lord. The Apostle John, in writing to the church, subscribes himself, "your brother, and companion in tribulation, and in the kingdom and patience of Jesus Christ." Revelation 1:2. Christ declared Himself to be a King, even the King of the Jews (Matthew 27:11), and received homage as "the King of Israel." John 1:49. But even while claiming to be king, Jesus declared, "My kingdom is not of this world; if My kingdom were of this world, then would My servants fight, that I should not be delivered to the Jews; but now is My kingdom not from thence." John 18:36. As Christ's kingdom is not of this world, so His church, His body, the people whom He has chosen and called out of the world, are to form no part of the world, although in it. It is to make no sort of alliance with the world, for any purpose whatever. Its sole use in the world is to be the light of the world, the salt by which as much of the world as possible is to be preserved. It is to be no more a part of the world than the light is of the darkness in which it shines. "What communion hath light with darkness?" 2 Corinthians 6:14. There are two distinct classes on earth – the church and the world; but when the church forms an alliance with the world, whether formally, or by adopting the world's methods or principles, then there is really only one class – the world. By the grace of God, however, there have always been a faithful few, even in the time of greatest apostasy.

Not a Theocracy

It is quite common to speak of Israel as a theocracy. This is indeed what God designed it to be, and what it should have been, but what in the truest sense it never was. Least of all was Israel a theocracy when the people demanded an earthly king, "that we also may be like all the heathen," for in so doing they rejected God as their King. It is passing strange the people will refer to what Israel did in direct opposition to the wishes of God, as a warrant for similar action on the part of the church now, and to their rejection of God as evidence that they were ruled by His power.

The word "theocracy" is a combination of two Greek words, and means literally, "the rule of God." A true theocracy, therefore, is a body in which God is sole and absolute ruler. Such a government has rarely been seen on this earth, and never to any great extent. A true theocracy existed when Adam was first formed and placed in Eden, when "God saw everything that He had made, and, behold, it was very good." Genesis 1:31. God formed Adam of the dust of the ground, and set him over the works of His hands. He was made ruler "over the fish of the sea, and over the fowl of the air, and over the cattle, and over all the earth, and over every creeping thing that creepeth upon the earth." Genesis 1:26. He therefore had all power given to him. But at his best state, when crowned with glory and honor, Adam was but dust, with no more power in himself than the dust on which he walked. Therefore the mighty power that was manifested in him was not his own power at all, but the power of God working in him. God was absolute Ruler, but it pleased Him, so far as this earth was concerned, to reveal His power through man. During Adam's loyalty to God there was therefore a perfect theocracy on this earth.

Such a theocracy has never existed since, for man's fall was the acknowledging of Satan as the god of this world. But individually it existed in its perfection in Christ, the second Adam, in whose heart was God's law, and in whom dwelt all the fullness of the Godhead bodily. When Christ shall have renewed the earth and restored all things as in the beginning, and there is but one fold and one Shepherd, one king in all the earth, that will be a perfect theocracy. The will of God will be done in all the earth as it now is in heaven. Christ is now gathering out a people in whom His character will be reproduced, in whose hearts He will dwell by faith, so that each one of them, like Himself, may "be filled with all the fullness of God." Ephesians 3:17-19.

These gathered ones constitute the church of Christ, which, as a whole, is "the fullness of Him that filleth all in all." Ephesians 1:22, 23. So while the true theocracy is first of all in the heart of individuals who day by day sincerely say to their heavenly Father, "Thine is the kingdom," the multitude of them that believe – the church – when perfectly joined together in the same mind by the Holy Spirit, constitutes the only true theocracy that has ever existed in this earth. When the church is apostate, it seeks by alliances with the world, by assuming kingly power, to exhibit a theocratic form of government, but it is only a counterfeit form, with no Divine power, whereas God's true followers, few in number, scattered throughout the world, and unknown to the nations, furnish an example of a real theocracy.

Through the prophet who opened his mouth to curse, but who instead uttered blessings, God said of His people Israel, "The people shall dwell alone, and shall not be reckoned among the nations." Numbers 23:9. The people of God are in the world, not of it, for the purpose of showing forth the excellency of Him who has called them out of darkness. But this they can do only as they acknowledge God to be supreme. The church is the kingdom in which God rules alone, and its only law is God's law of love. It is God's voice alone that it hears and follows, and it is God's voice alone that speaks through it.

No Earthly Model

Nothing among earthly kingdoms or associations of whatever kind can serve as a model for the true theocracy, God's church and kingdom; nor can the acts of human organizations be taken as precedents. It is unique in every particular, depending on none of the things upon which human governments depend for the maintenance of unity, and yet so marvelous an exhibition of order and harmony and power, that it astonishes all.

But although the true people of God are to dwell alone, not reckoned among the nations, and consequently having no part in the direction or management of civil governments, they are by no means indifferent to the welfare of mankind. Like their Divine Head, their mission is to do good. As Adam was the son of God (Luke 3:38), the whole human facility, although fallen, are His children, – prodigal sons, – and therefore God's true children will regard all men as their brethren, for whose welfare and salvation they are to labor. Their work is to reveal God to the world as a kind and loving Father, and this they can do only by allowing His love to shine forth in their lives.

Christ's kingdom on earth has as its sole work to show by practical likeness to Christ, its allegiance to Him as rightful Lord of all, and by thus showing forth His excellencies, to induce as many as possible to accept Him as King, so that they may be prepared to receive Him when He comes on the throne of His glory. Matthew 25:31. Christ, the King, came into the world for no other purpose than to bear witness to the truth

(John 18:37), and so His loyal subjects have no other object in life; and the power by which they witness is that of the Holy Ghost abiding in them, and dwelling in them (Acts 1:8), and not by their mingling in political or social strife. For a little while after Christ's ascension to heaven, the church was content with this power, and wonderful progress was made in the work of preaching the Gospel of the kingdom; but soon the church began to adopt worldly methods, and its members to interest themselves in the affairs of State, instead of Christ's kingdom, and the power was lost. But let it be remembered that in those days of the church's loyalty, the very same power was present that was given to Israel for the same purpose hundreds of years before; and remember further that the people through whom the power of God was thus manifested were in both instances the very same, "for salvation is of the Jews." John 4:22.

"As for God, His way is perfect," and we know that "whatsoever God doeth, it shall be for ever; nothing can be put to it, nor anything taken from it; and God doeth it, that men should fear before Him." Ecclesiastes 3:14. Therefore although Israel in the days of the judges and the prophets proved unfaithful to their trust, and the same church from the days of the apostles has been to a large extent unmindful of its privileges and duty, the time must come when the church – the Israel of God – shall come out from the world and be separate, and so, free from all earthly entanglements, and depending alone upon Christ, will shine forth as the morning, "fair as the moon, clear as the sun, and terrible as an army with banners."

Chapter 38

The Promises to Israel - The Promised Rest (Part 1 of 2)

The Present Truth, January 21, 1897

"My presence shall go with thee, and I will give thee rest." Exodus 33:14.

It was with these words that God encouraged Moses to lead the people of Israel forward after they had so grievously sinned in making and worshipping the golden calf.

The Rest of Christ

In our study of the rest that God promised His people, it will be well to remember that the promise here recorded is identical with that in Matthew 11:28. Rest was promised, and could be found, only in God's presence, which was to go with His people. So Christ, who is "God with us" (Matthew 1:23), and who is with us "all the days, even to the end of the world" (Matthew 28:20), says, "Come unto Me, all ye that labor, and are heavy laden, and I will give you rest." The rest that was offered to the children of Israel in the desert is the very same rest that Christ offers to all mankind, rest in God, in the everlasting arms – for the only begotten Son "is in the bosom of the Father." John 1:19. "As one whom his mother comforteth, so will I comfort you." Isaiah 66:13.

But God always was and is everywhere present; why then do not all people have rest? – For the simple reason that as a general thing men do not recognize His presence, nor even His existence. Instead of taking God into account in all the affairs of life, most people live as though He did not exist. "Without faith it is impossible to please Him; for He that cometh to God must believe that He is." Hebrews 11:6. This shows that the general inability to please God, and so to find rest, arises from practical unbelief that He exists.

How can we know that God exists? – Ever since the creation of the world, the invisible things of God, namely, His eternal power and Divinity, have been clearly revealed in the things that He has made (See Romans 1:20), so that those who do not know Him are without excuse. It is as Creator that God reveals Himself, for the fact that He creates marks Him as the self-existent God, and distinguishes Him from all false gods. "The Lord is great, and greatly to be praised; He is to be feared above all gods. For all the gods of the nations are idols; but the Lord made the heavens." Psalm 96:4, 5. "The Lord is the true God, He is the living God, and an everlasting King. . . . The gods that have not made the heavens and the earth, even they shall perish from the earth, and from under these heavens. He hath made the earth by His power, He hath established the world by His wisdom." Jeremiah 10:10-12. "My help cometh from the Lord, which made heaven and earth." Psalm 121:2. "Our help is in the name of the Lord, who made heaven and earth." Psalm 124:8. Now since rest is found only in God's presence, and His presence is truly known and appreciated only through His works, it is evident that the promised rest must be very closely connected with creation.

The Rest and the Inheritance Inseparable

This we find is the case, for the rest and the inheritance were always associated together in the promise. When the children of Israel were being instructed in the wilderness, they were told: "Ye shall not do after all the things that we do here this day, every man whatsoever is right in his own eyes. For ye are not as yet come to the rest and to the inheritance, which the Lord your God giveth you. But when ye go over Jordan, and dwell in the land which the Lord your God giveth you to inherit, and when He giveth you rest from all your enemies round about, so that ye dwell in safety; then there shall be a place which the Lord your God shall choose to cause His name to dwell there." Deuteronomy 12:8-16. So also Moses said to the tribes that had their lot on the east side of Jordan: "The Lord your God hath given you this land to possess it; ye shall pass over armed before your brethren the children of Israel, all that are sons of power. But your wives, and your little ones, and your cattle . . . shall abide in your cities which I have given you; until the Lord have given rest unto your brethren, as well as unto you, and until they also possess the land which the Lord your God hath given them beyond Jordan." Deuteronomy 3:18-20. The rest and the inheritance are really one. Our inheritance is rest, in the place of the weariness that sin brings. In Christ, who is "God with us," we find rest, "in whom also we have obtained an inheritance, being predestinated according to the purpose of Him that worketh all things after the counsel of His own will." The Holy Spirit is the first fruits of this inheritance, until the purchased possession is redeemed. "The Lord is the portion of mine inheritance." Psalm 16:5.

He is both our rest and our inheritance; having Him, we have all.

We have already seen the children of Israel in the land of promise; the land, and therefore the rest, was theirs, for we read this statement of what was true in the days of Joshua: –

"And the Lord gave unto Israel all the land which He swore to give unto their fathers; and they possessed it, and dwelt therein. And the Lord gave them rest round about, according to all that He swore unto their fathers; and there stood not a man of all their enemies before them; the Lord delivered all their enemies into their hand. There failed not aught of any good thing which the Lord had spoken unto the house of Israel; all came to pass." Joshua 21:3-48.

Joshua Rehearses God's Faithfulness

But if we should stop here, we should fall into grave error. Passing by one chapter, we come to the record of what Joshua told "all Israel" and their elders, their judges, etc., "a long time after that the Lord had given rest unto Israel from all their enemies round about." Joshua 23:1, 2.

After reminding them of what the Lord had done for them, he said: –

"Behold, I have divided unto you by lot these nations that remain, to be an inheritance for your tribes, with all the nations that I have cut off, even unto the great sea westward. And the Lord your God, He shall expel them from before you, and drive them from out of your sight; and ye shall possess their land, as the Lord your God hath promised unto you. Be ye therefore very courageous to keep and to do all that is written in the book of the law of Moses, that ye turn not aside there from to the right hand or to the left; that ye come not among these nations, these that remain among you; neither make mention of the name of their gods, nor cause to swear by them, neither serve them, nor bow yourselves unto them; but cleave unto the Lord your God, as ye have done unto this day. For the Lord hath driven out from before you great nations and strong; but as for you, no man hath been able to stand before you unto this day. One man of you shall chase a thousand; for the Lord your God, He it is that fighteth for you, as He hath promised you. Take good heed therefore unto yourselves, that ye love the Lord your God. Else if ye do in anywise go back, and cleave unto the remnant of these nations, even these that remain among you, and shall make marriages with them, and go in unto them, and they to you; know for a certainty that the Lord your God will no more drive out any of these nations from before you; but they shall be snares and traps unto you, and scourges in your sides, and thorns in your eyes, until ye perish from off this good land which the Lord your God hath given you. And, behold, this day I am going the way of all the earth; and ye know in all your hearts and in all your souls, that not one thing had failed of all the good things which the Lord your God spake concerning you; all are come to pass unto you, and not one thing hath failed thereof. Therefore it shall come to pass, that as all good things are come upon you, which the Lord your God promised you; so shall the Lord bring upon you all evil things, until He have destroyed you from off this good land which the Lord your God hath given you. When ye have transgressed the covenant of the Lord your God, which

He commanded you, and have gone and served other gods, and bowed yourselves to them; then shall the anger of the Lord be kindled against you, and ye shall perish quickly from off the good land which He hath given you." Joshua 23:4-15.

The Rest Assured Only to Faith

In this portion of Scripture we have further evidence that the inheritance is the promised rest. We are plainly told that God had given Israel rest, and that this talk occurred a long time after that; yet in that very talk they were told the conditions upon which they might surely have the rest, and upon which the enemies that were still in the land would be driven out. It all depended on Israel's faithfulness to God. If they should go back from serving the Lord, and go after other gods, then they were to know for a certainty that God would no more drive out the remaining nations from before them, but those nations should continually harass them, and the Lord would utterly destroy them from off the face of the land which He had given them.

Now how could the children of Israel be said to have rest from all their enemies, and to have the land in possession, when those enemies were still in the land, and there was a possibility that the enemies might drive them out, instead of being driven out? The Scriptures themselves afford the answer. For instance, when all the kings of the Amorites threatened the Gibeonites, who were in league with the Israelites, the Lord said to Joshua, "Fear them not; for I have delivered them into thy hand." Joshua 10:8. What did Joshua then do? –He went and took them. He did not doubtingly say, "I don't see any evidence that the Lord has delivered them into my hands, for I haven't them;" neither did he foolishly say. "Since the Lord has given them into my hand I can disband my forces and take my ease."

In either case he would have been overcome, even after God had given him the victory. By his activity, Joshua showed that he really believed what the Lord said. Faith works, and continues to work.

In like manner the people were told that God had given them the victory, while at the same time they stood outside the high walls and barred gates of Jericho. It was true that God had given them the victory, and yet it all depended on them. If they had refused to shout, they would never have seen the victory.

In Christ we have the rest and the inheritance; but in order to be made partakers of Christ we must "hold fast the beginning of our confidence steadfast unto the end." Hebrews 3:14. Jesus says, "In the world ye shall have tribulation; but be of good cheer; I have overcome the world." John 16:33. Yet in the very same talk He said, "Peace I leave with you, My peace I give unto you." John 16:27. What! peace in the midst of tribulation? Yes; for take notice that He says, "Not as the world giveth, give I unto you. Let not your heart be troubled, neither let it be afraid." To have tribulation, and yet not be troubled; to be in the midst of danger, and yet have no fear; to be in the heat of battle, and yet enjoy perfect peace, – truly this is giving in a far different way from what the world gives.

The Warfare Already Accomplished

Listen to the message which the prophet Isaiah was commissioned to give to Israel when they were passing through the most trying experiences, a message that is for us even more than for the men who lived when it was spoken: "Comfort ye, comfort ye My people, saith your God. Speak ye to the heart of Jerusalem, and cry unto her, that her warfare is accomplished, that her iniquity is pardoned." Isaiah 40:1, 2. Glorious assurance! The warfare is accomplished, the battle ended, the victory won! Shall we conclude therefore that we may safely go to sleep? By no means; we must be awake, and make use of the victory, which the Lord has won, for us. The conflict is against principalities and powers (Ephesians 6:12), but Jesus has "spoiled principalities and powers," and made a triumphant show of them (Colossians 2:15), and has been raised to sit in heavenly places, "far above all principality, and power, and might, and dominion, and every name that is named, not only in this world, but also in that which is to come" (Ephesians 1:20, 21), and God has also raised us up with Him, to sit with Him in the same heavenly places (Ephesians 2:1-6), equally high above all principality, and power, and might, and dominion, and every name that is named, not only in this world, but also in that which is to come. We may, therefore, and certainly ought to say, from the heart, "Thanks be to God, which giveth us the victory through our Lord Jesus Christ."

Lessons From the Psalms

David understood and rejoiced in this victory when he was hunted like a partridge on the mountains. Yet one time he was hiding in a cave in the wilderness of Ziph, and the Ziphites came to Saul and treacherously revealed his hiding-place, and said, "Now, therefore, O king, come down according to all the desire of thy soul to come down; and our part shall be to deliver him into the king's hand." 1 Samuel 23:15-20. Yet David, knowing all this, took his harp and composed a psalm of praise, saying, "I will freely sacrifice unto Thee; I will praise Thy name, O Lord, for it is good. For He hath delivered me out of all trouble." Psalm 54:6, 7. Read the entire Psalm, including the introduction. So he could sing, "Though an host should encamp against me, my heart shall not fear." Psalm 28:3. The third Psalm, with its expressions of confident trust in God, and its note of victory, was composed while he was exiled from his throne, fleeing before Absalom. We need so to learn the twenty-third Psalm, that it will not be mere empty words when we say, "Thou preparest a table before me in the presence of mine enemies; Thou anointest my head with oil; my cup runneth over."

The Strong Man Overcome

The victory that hath overcome the world is our faith. Oh, that we could realize and ever bear in mind the fact that the victory is already won, that Christ, the Mighty One, has come upon the strong man, our adversary and oppressor, and has overcome him, and taken from him all his armor wherein he trusted, so that we have to fight only with a conquered and disarmed foe. The reason why we are overcome is that we do not believe and know this fact. If we know it, and remember it, we shall never fall; for who would be so foolish as to allow himself to be taken captive by an enemy without armor and without strength?

How many of the blessings that God has given are lost because our faith does not grasp them? How many blessings has He given us? –"Blessed be the God and Father of our Lord Jesus Christ, who hath blessed us with every spiritual blessing in the heavenly places in Christ." "His Divine power hath given unto us all things that pertain unto life and godliness, through the knowledge of Him that hath called us to glory and virtue." 2 Peter 1:3. And yet, notwithstanding the fact that all things are ours (1 Corinthians 3:21), we often act as though we had nothing. A man, a professor of religion and a leader in the church, once said when these texts were repeated to him for his encouragement, "If God has given me all these things, why don't I have them?" There are doubtless many who will read their own experience in this question. The answer was easy; it was because he did not believe that God had given them to him. He couldn't feel that he had them, and therefore he didn't believe that he had them; whereas it is faith that must grasp them, and a man cannot hope to be able to feel a thing that he does not touch. The victory is not doubt, not sight, not feeling, but faith.

Chapter 39

The Promises to Israel - The Promised Rest
(Part 2 of 2)

The Present Truth, January 28, 1897

THE Israelites were in possession of the land; not one word of God had failed; He had with Himself given them all things; but they did not appreciate the wondrous gift, and so received the grace of God in vain.

They were at least nominally faithful to God during the life of Joshua, but after his death "the children of Israel did evil in the sight of the Lord, and served Baalim; and they forsook the Lord God of their fathers, which brought them out of the land of Egypt, and followed other gods, of the gods of the people that were round about them, and bowed themselves unto them, and provoked the Lord to anger. And they forsook the Lord, and served Baal and Ashtaroth. And the anger of the Lord was hot against Israel, and He delivered them into the hands of spoilers that spoiled them, and He sold them into the hands of their enemies round about, so that they could not any longer stand before their enemies. Whithersoever they went out, the hand of the Lord was against them for evil, as the Lord had said, and as the Lord had sworn unto them; and they were greatly distressed." God told them that because of their disobedience He would not drive the nations out from before them, but that their enemies should remain and be as thorns in their sides. Judges 2:1-15. Thus we see that although God gave them rest, they did not enter into it. It was therefore as true of them as of those who fell in the wilderness that "they could not enter in because of unbelief."

What About Our Position?

"Let us therefore fear, lest, a promise being left us of entering into His rest, any of you should seem to come short of it. For unto us was the Gospel preached, as well as unto them; but the word preached did not profit them, not being mixed with faith in them that heard it." Hebrews 4:1, 2. We are in the world in precisely the same situation that ancient Israel was, with the same promises, the same prospects, the same enemies, the same dangers.

There are no foes upon whom we may use ordinary weapons of warfare, although the followers of the Lord are assured that they shall suffer persecution (2 Timothy 3:12), and that they shall be hated by the world, with a hatred that will not stop short of death (John 15:18, 19; 16:1-3); nevertheless "the weapons of our warfare are not carnal." In this, however, our case is in no wise different from that of Israel of old.

Their victory was to be had only by faith, and, as we have already seen, if they had been truly faithful, there would have been no more need of their using the sword to drive out the Canaanites than there was to use it for the overthrow of Pharaoh and his hosts. Indeed, the reason why they did not gain full possession of the land was because of that unbelief which made the sword necessary; for it is absolutely impossible that the heavenly country which God promised Abraham can ever be gained by men with swords or guns in their hands. There was no more need for Israel to fight in the days of old than there is for us; for "when a man's ways please the Lord, He maketh even his enemies to be at peace with him" (Proverbs 16:7), and we are absolutely forbidden to fight.

When Christ commands His followers not to fight, and warns them that if they do they shall perish, He is not introducing a new order of things, but simply leading His people back to first principles. Ancient Israel affords an illustration of the fact that they who use the sword shall perish with the sword; and, although the Lord bore long with them, and made many concessions to their weakness, and has borne still longer with us, He wishes us to avoid their errors. All the things concerning them "are written for our admonition, upon whom the ends of the world are come." 1 Corinthians 10:11.

The Promise of Canaan

But we must go a little further, and see that our situation is precisely that of ancient Israel, and that the same rest and inheritance which God gave them, and which they foolishly allowed to slip from their hands, is ours, provided we "hold fast the confidence and the rejoicing of the hope firm unto the end." Fortunately, the evidence is very simple and plain, and we have already considered the most of it at some length. Let us refresh our minds with the following facts.

Canaan is a land, which God gave to Abraham and to his seed "for an everlasting possession." Genesis 17:7, 8.

It was to be an everlasting possession for both Abraham and his seed. But Abraham himself had not so much as a foot-breadth of the land in his actual possession (Acts 7:5), and none of his seed had it either, for even the righteous ones among them (and only the righteous are Abraham's seed) "all died in faith, not having received the promise." Hebrews 9:13, 39.

Therefore, as previously shown, the possession of the land involved the resurrection of the dead at the coming of Christ to restore all things. By the resurrection of Christ, God has begotten us unto a lively hope, "to an inheritance incorruptible, and undefiled, and that fadeth not away, reserved in heaven for you, who are kept by the power of God through faith unto salvation ready to be revealed in the last time." 1 Peter 1:3-6.

A World-Wide Kingdom

But the possession of the land of Canaan meant nothing less than the possession of the whole world, as we learn by comparing Genesis 17:7, 8, 11, and Romans 4:1-13. Thus: circumcision was the seal of the covenant to give Abraham and his seed the land of Canaan for an everlasting possession. But circumcision was at the same time a sign or seal of righteousness by faith; and "the promise that he should be the heir of the world, was not to Abraham or his seed, through the law, but through the righteousness of faith." That is to say, that which sealed to Abraham his right to the possession of the land of Canaan, was the seal of his right to the whole world.

In giving to him and his seed the land of Canaan, God gave to them the whole world. Not of course "this present evil world," for "the world passeth away;" and Christ gave Himself for us that He might deliver us from it and its destruction; but "we, according to His promise, look for new heavens and a new earth, wherein dwelleth righteousness." 2 Peter 3:13. It was not the temporal possession of a few thousand square miles of land tainted by the curse that God promised to Abraham and to his seed, but the eternal possession of the entire earth freed from every vestige of the curse. Even though it were true that the little territory of Canaan constituted the whole of the promised inheritance, still it would be true that the Israelites never had it; for the promise which God confirmed was to give Abraham and his seed the land of Canaan for an everlasting possession, that is, Abraham must have it for an everlasting possession, and his seed must also have it for an everlasting possession. But they all died, and in time even the country itself passed into the hands of other people. No temporal dwelling in Palestine could possibly fulfill the promise. The promise still remains to be fulfilled to Abraham and to all the seed.

The New Earth

The rest is the inheritance; the inheritance is the land of Canaan; but the possession of the land of Canaan means the possession of the whole earth, not in its present state, but restored as in the days of Eden. Therefore the rest which God gives is inseparable from the new earth: it is rest which the new earth state alone can give, rest found only in God; and when all things are restored, then God in Christ will absolutely and without hindrance fill all things, so that everywhere will there be complete rest. Since rest is found only in God, it is most evident that the children of Israel did not enjoy the rest and the inheritance, even while in Palestine, for although "He cast out the heathen also before them, and divided them an inheritance by line, and made the tribes of Israel to dwell in their tents, yet they tempted and provoked the Most High God, and kept not His testimonies; but turned back, and dealt unfaithfully like their fathers; they were turned aside like a deceitful bow. For they provoked Him to anger with their high places, and moved Him to jealousy with their graven images," so that "God greatly abhorred Israel." Psalm 78:55-59.

Remember that it was an heavenly country that Abraham looked for. Nevertheless, the promise of God to give him and his seed (including us, if we are Christ's, Galatians 3:16, 29) the land of Canaan for an everlasting possession will be fulfilled to the very letter.

When the Lord comes for His people to take them to Himself, to the place which He has prepared for them (see John 14:3), the righteous dead will be raised incorruptible, and the righteous living ones will likewise be changed to immortality, and both together will be caught up "in the clouds, to meet the Lord in the air; and so shall we ever be with the Lord." 1 Thessalonians 4:16, 17; 1 Corinthians 15:51-54. The place to which they will be taken is the free Jerusalem above, "which is the mother of us all" (Galatians 4:26); for that is where Christ now is, and where He is preparing a place for us. A few texts may be quoted to show this fact more clearly. That the heavenly Jerusalem is the place where Christ is now "in the presence of God for us," is evident from Hebrews 12:22-24, where we are told that those who believe are now come to Mount Zion, unto "the city of the living God, the heavenly Jerusalem," "to God the Judge of all," and to Jesus the Mediator of the new covenant." Christ "is set on the right hand of the throne of the Majesty in the heavens," (Hebrews 8:1), and from this throne, it will be well to remember, proceeds "the river of water of life." Revelation 22:1.

The City for Which Abraham Looked

This city, the New Jerusalem, the city that God has prepared for those of whom He is not ashamed, because they seek an heavenly country (Hebrews 11:16), is the capital of His dominions. It is the "city which hath foundations, whose builder and maker is God" (verse 10), for which Abraham looked. In the twenty-first first chapter of Revelation we find a description of those foundations, where we also find that the city will not always remain in heaven, but will descend to this earth with the saints who have reigned in it with Christ for a thousand years after the resurrection. Revelation 20. Of the descent of the city we read: –

"And I John saw the holy city, New Jerusalem, coming down from God out of heaven, prepared as a bride adorned for her husband. And I heard a great voice out of heaven saying, Behold, the tabernacle of God is with men, and He will dwell with them, and they shall be His people, and God Himself shall be with them, and be their God. And God shall wipe away all tears from their eyes; and there shall be no more death, neither sorrow, nor crying, neither shall there be any more pain; for the former things are passed away. And He that sat upon the throne said, Behold I make all things new. And He said unto me, Write; for these things are true and faithful. And He said unto me, It is done. I am Alpha and Omega, the beginning and the end. I will give unto him that is athirst of the fountain of the water of life freely. He that overcometh shall inherit all things; and I will be his God, and he shall be My son. But the fearful, and unbelieving, and the abominable, and murderers, and whoremongers, and sorcerers, and idolaters, and all liars, shall have their part in the lake which burneth with fire and brimstone; which is the second death."

From Isaiah 49:17-21 we learn that the believing, righteous ones, the children of the New Jerusalem, constitute the adornment, which the city has when it comes down prepared as a bride adorned for her husband. So we see that the saints of God go at once to the New Jerusalem, when Christ comes for them, and then return with it to this earth, when the time has come for the cleansing of the earth from all things that offend, and them that do iniquity, and for the renewing of all things as at first.

The Place Where the City Will Come Down

But to what spot on this earth will the city descend? Speaking of the time of the destruction of the wicked, the prophet Zechariah says: –

"Then shall the Lord go forth, and fight against those nations, as when He fought in the day of battle. And His feet shall stand in that day upon the mount of Olives, which is before Jerusalem on the east, and the mount of Olives shall cleave in the midst thereof toward the east and toward the west, and there shall be a very great valley; and half of the mountain shall remove toward the north, and half of it toward the south. And ye shall flee by the valley of My mountains; for the valley of the mountains shall reach unto Azel; yea, ye shall flee like as ye fled from before the earthquake in the days of Uzziah king of Judah; and the Lord my God shall come, and all the holy ones with thee. And it shall come to pass in that day that the light shall not be with brightness and with gloom; but it shall be one day which is known unto the Lord; not day, and not night; but it shall come to pass that at evening time there shall be light. And it shall come to pass in that day, that living waters shall go out from Jerusalem; half of them toward the eastern sea, and half of them toward the western sea; in summer and in winter shall it be. And the Lord shall be King over all the earth; in that day shall the Lord be One, and His name One." Zechariah 14:3-9.

Thus we see that when God brings back the captivity of His people, He brings them to the very spot of earth that He promised to Abraham for an everlasting possession – the land of Canaan. But the possession of that land is the possession of the whole earth, not for a few years, but for eternity. "There shall be no more death." It was this glorious inheritance that the children of Israel had in their grasp when they crossed the Jordan, and which they faithlessly allowed to slip. If they had been faithful, a very short time would have sufficed to make the name and the saving power of God known in every part of the earth, and then the end would have come. But they failed, and so the time was lengthened, until our day; but the same hope has been the one thing ever before the people of God. So we may look forward to the possession of the land of Canaan with as much earnestness as did Abraham, Isaac, Jacob, Joseph, and Moses, yea, and David also, and all the prophets, and with the same confident hope.

The Restoration of the Israel of God

With these few outlines well fixed in mind, the reading of the prophecies both of the Old and the New Testament will be a delight, for we shall be spared much confusion, and many seeming contradictions will be seen to be plain. When we read of the restoration of Jerusalem, so that it will be the joy and praise of the whole earth, we shall know that the New Jerusalem comes down from heaven, to take the place of the old. If a city on this earth is burnt entirely to the ground, and men build a new city on the same site, the city is said to be rebuilt, and it is called by the same name. So with Jerusalem, only the city is rebuilt in heaven, so that there is no interval between the destruction of the old and the appearance of the new. It is as though the new city sprang at once from the ruins of the old, only infinitely more glorious.

So also when we read of the return of Israel to Jerusalem, we know that it is not the return of a few thousand mortals to a mass of ruins, but the coming of the innumerable, immortal host of the redeemed to the ever new city where their citizenship has long been recorded. Mortal men will not rebuild the city with brick and stone and mortar, but God Himself will rebuild it with gold and pearls and all manner of precious stones. "When the Lord shall build up Zion, He shall appear in His glory." Psalm 102:16.

He says to Jerusalem, "O thou afflicted, tossed with tempest, and not comforted, behold I will lay thy stones with fair colors, and lay thy foundations with sapphires. And I will make thy windows of agates, and thy gates of carbuncles, and all thy borders of pleasant stones. And all thy children shall be taught of the Lord; and great shall be the peace of thy children." Isaiah 54:11-13. These are the stones in which her children take pleasure. Psalm 102:14.

Here will be rest, perfect eternal peace.

The promise is, "in righteousness shalt thou be established; thou shalt be far from oppression; for thou shalt not fear; and from terror; for it shall not come near thee." "In that day shall this song be sung in the land of Judah: We have a strong city; salvation will God appoint for walls and bulwarks."

God Himself will be with His people for evermore, "and they shall see His face," and therefore they will have rest, for He said, "My presence," literally, My face, "shall go with thee, and I will give thee rest."

Why will men nullify all these glorious promises, by reading them as though they taught merely the temporal possession of a ruined city on this old sin-cursed earth? It is because they limit the Gospel, not realizing that all the promises of God are in Christ, to be enjoyed by none except those who are in Christ, and in whom He dwells by faith. Would that God's professed people might speedily receive "the Spirit of wisdom and revelation" in the knowledge of God, that the eyes of their understanding might be enlightened, that they might "know what is the hope of His calling, and what the riches of the glory of His inheritance in the saints," and that it is to be gained only by "the exceeding greatness of His power to usward who believe, according to the working of His mighty power which He wrought in Christ when He raised Him from the dead, and set Him at His own right hand in the heavenly places." Ephesians 1:17-20.

Now that we have taken this hasty glance ahead, and have seen the consummation of God's promise to give His people rest in the land of Canaan, we may return and fill in a few of the details, which will be more easily understood by reason of this outline, and which in turn will bring out in still bolder relief the view we have already had.

The paper in this series, which appears next week, will consider – under the title "Another Day" – the rest that now remaineth for the people of God. Hebrews 4.

Chapter 40

The Promises to Israel - Another Day
(Part 1 of 2)

The Present Truth, February 4, 1897

"For if Joshua had given them rest, then would He not afterward have spoken of another day. There remaineth therefore a rest to the people of God." Hebrews 4:8, 9.

We have seen that although not one word of God's promises to Israel failed, "the word preached did not profit them, not being mixed with faith in them that heard it," (Hebrews 4:2), and that a long time after the Lord had given them rest, He set before them, through Joshua, the conditions on which they might enjoy the inheritance.

The Kingdom the Lord's

Passing over a period of more than four hundred years, during which time the history of the children of Israel is a record of apostasy and repentance and apostasy again, we come to the time of David, when the kingdom of Israel was at the height of its power. Although, in demanding a king, the children of Israel rejected God, He did not reject them. It was not God's design that Israel should ever have any other king than Himself, but they were not content to walk by faith, having a King whom they could not see. Nevertheless, the kingdom still remained the Lord's, and therefore He exercised His right to appoint rulers.

Even so it is in all the world. "The earth is the Lord's, and the fullness thereof." "His kingdom ruleth over all." The people of the world do not recognize Him as King, and boast in the pride of their own Governments; yet "the Most High ruleth in the kingdom of men, and giveth it to whomsoever He will." "He removeth kings, and setteth up kings." Daniel 4:32; 2:21. "There is no power but of God; the powers that be are ordained of God." Romans 13:1. This is why every soul ought to be subject unto "the higher powers," and is an evidence that the Lord's kingdom includes the whole earth, even though the rulers who for a season are allowed to imagine that they are holding the reins, set themselves up against Him.

Strangers and Sojourners in David's Time

So when in the providence of God David came to the throne of Israel, "and the Lord had given him rest round about from all his enemies" (2 Samuel 7:1), it was in his heart to build a temple to the Lord. At first the prophet Nathan, speaking his own words, said to him, "Go, do all that is in thine heart," but afterwards he spoke the word of the Lord, and said that David should not build it. At that time the Lord said to David: –

"I will appoint a place for My people Israel, and will plant them, that they may dwell in their own place, and be moved no more; neither shall the children of wickedness afflict them any source as at the first, and as from the day that I commanded judges to be over My people Israel. Moreover the Lord telleth thee that He will make thee an house." 2 Samuel 7:10, 11.

The people of Israel therefore had not yet obtained the rest and the inheritance. David was a powerful king, and had "a great name, like unto the name of the great men that are in the earth," yet when he bequeathed the kingdom, with all the material for the building of the temple, to his son Solomon, he said in his prayer to God, "We are strangers before Thee, and sojourners, as were all our fathers; our days on the earth are as a shadow, and there is none abiding." 1 Chronicles 29:15.

At the time when the kingdom of Israel was as great and powerful as it ever was on this earth, the king declared himself to be as much a stranger and sojourner in the land as was Abraham, who had "none inheritance in it, no, not so much as to set his foot on." David in his house of cedar, as well as Abraham, Isaac, and Jacob, who dwelt in tents, "sojourned in the land of promise as in a strange country." Not only Abraham, Isaac, and Jacob, but Gideon, Samson, Jephthae, David, Samuel, and the prophets, with many others, "having obtained a good report through faith, received not the promise." Hebrews 11:32-39. What stronger evidence could there be that the inheritance, which God promised to Abraham and his seed, was never a temporal possession in "this present evil world"?

The Temporal Jerusalem Signifies Slavery

Since the great king David, at the height of his power, had not received the promise, what utter folly it is to suppose that the promise to restore Israel to their own land can ever be fulfilled by any return of the Jews to old Jerusalem. Those who are building their hopes on "Jerusalem, which now is," are losing all the blessedness of the Gospel. "We have not received the spirit of bondage again to fear," therefore we will put no confidence in anything connected with old Jerusalem; for "Jerusalem which now is," "is in bondage with her children; but Jerusalem which is above is free, which is the mother of us all." Galatians 4:25, 26. When the promise is fulfilled, and the people of Israel really possess the land, and are no more strangers and sojourners in it, their days will no more be as a shadow, but they will abide forever.

But "the Lord is not slack concerning His promise, as some men count slackness; but is longsuffering to usward, not willing that any should perish, but that all should come to repentance." 2 Peter 3:9. "The longsuffering of our God is salvation." Verse 15. Even in the days of Moses, the time of the promise was at hand (Acts 7:19), but the people would not have it. They chose this present evil world, rather than the world to come. But God had sworn by Himself that the seed of faithful Abraham should enter in, and "seeing therefore it remaineth that some must enter therein, and they to whom it was first preached entered not in because of unbelief; again, He limiteth a certain day, saying in David, To-day, after so long a time; as it is said, To-day, if ye will hear His voice, harden not your hearts." Hebrews 4:6, 7.

The unbelief of man cannot make the promise of God of none effect. Romans 3:3. "If we believe not, yet He abideth faithful; He cannot deny Himself." 2 Timothy 2:13. If not a single soul of the natural descendants of Abraham and Jacob proved themselves children of Abraham, but were all children of the devil (John 8:39-44), God's promise to the seed of Abraham, Isaac, and Jacob would be fulfilled to the letter, for God is able even of the stones of the ground to "raise up children unto Abraham." Matthew 3:19. That would simply be a repetition of what He did in the beginning, when He made man of the dust of the ground. If Joshua had given them rest, then of course there would have been no need of any further day of salvation; but the unfaithfulness of professed followers of God delays the fulfillment, and so God in His mercy grants another day, and that is "To-day." "Behold, now is the accepted time; behold, now is the day of salvation." 2 Corinthians 6:2. "To-day if ye will hear His voice, harden not your hearts."

"Today"

Just think of it! Even when David lived, it is called "after so long a time." It was indeed a "long time," fully five hundred years after the promise might have been fulfilled; and yet, after so much longer a time the Lord still offers "another day." That other day is today; we have not a year given us in which to accept the offer of salvation, not next month, not next week, not even to-morrow, but only today. That is all the time that God has given us – probation is but one day long. With how much greater force, therefore, the words come to us after so long a time, "To-day, if ye will hear His voice, harden not your hearts." What a glorious treasure God has given us in today, – the opportunity of entering into the gate of righteousness. Christ is the door, and by Him all may enter in "while it is called to-day." Shall we not accept it as "the day, which the Lord hath made" and "be glad and rejoice in it?" "The voice of rejoicing and salvation is in the tabernacles of the righteous;" "for we are made partakers of Christ, if we hold the beginning of our confidence steadfast unto the end." "For thus saith the Lord God, the Holy One of Israel; In returning and rest shall ye be saved; in quietness and in confidence shall be your strength." Isaiah 30:15.

This rest is announced in the Gospel, for Christ says, "Come unto Me, all ye that labor, and are heavy laden, and I will give you rest. Take My yoke upon you, and learn of Me; for I am meek and lowly in heart; and ye shall find rest unto your souls. For My yoke is easy, and My burden is light." Matthew 11:28-30. The people of Israel in old time failed of this rest, not because it was not offered them, but because when the Gospel was preached to them they did not believe; the Gospel that is now preached to us is the very same that was preached to them. Hebrews 4:2.

The rest is all prepared, for "we which have believed do enter into rest, as He said, As I have sworn in My wrath, If[12] they shall enter into My rest." God has sworn by Himself that the seed of Abraham – those who have his faith – should enter into rest; and that was equivalent to an oath that they who did not believe should not enter in, and therefore God did indeed swore that the faithless ones should not enter in. This was not an arbitrary decree, but a statement of fact, for it is as impossible for an unbelieving person to enter into rest as it would be for a man to live and grow strong without eating, drinking, or breathing.

The fact that "they could not enter in because of unbelief" shows that they would have entered in if they had believed; and the fact that perfect rest was all ready for them, is still further shown by the statement, "the works were finished from the foundation of the world." Hebrews 4:3. When works are finished, rest must ensue; accordingly we read, "God did rest the seventh day from all His works." Verse 4. That is what God said in one place of the seventh day; but in another place He said, "They shall not enter into My rest." Verse 5. We see, therefore, that the rest which was ready, and which the children of Israel did not enter into because of unbelief, was the rest connected with the seventh day. For it was God's rest that was offered them, and it was His rest that they failed to secure, and the seventh day is the Sabbath – rest – of the Lord; it is the only rest of which we read in connection with God – God rested on the seventh day from all His work – and that rest was ready as soon as the work of creation was completed.

God's Work and God's Rest

The rest that is promised is God's rest. Rest follows labor, but not until the labor is completed. A man cannot rest from a given work until that work is finished. God's work is creation, a complete, perfect work; "God saw everything that He had made, and, behold, it was very good. And the evening and the morning were the sixth day.

---

[12] In an oath there are two parts –the condition, and the consequence if that condition is unfulfilled. For instance, a man swears, "I will forfeit one thousand pounds, if I do not save that man from prison;" or, "I pledge myself that I will not allow the prisoner to escape." The Hebrew is very concise, and gives us the condition, without naming the consequence in connection with the oath. Each one can fill in all the dire results that his imagination can picture, if God should break His word. When God swears by Himself, He really pledges His very existence to be forfeited, –if the thing turns out contrary to His word; but that awful alternative is not stated, because it is beyond the range of possibility. Therefore we should always read this expression, wherever it occurs, as it is in the Revised Version: "As I swore in My wrath, They shall not enter into My rest."

Thus the heavens and the earth were finished, and all the host of them. And on the seventh day God ended His work, which He had made; and He rested on the seventh day from all His work, which He had made. And God blessed the seventh day, and sanctified it; because that in it He had rested from all His work which God created and made." Genesis 1:31; 2:1-3.

The work was perfect, – it was as good as God Himself could make it, as perfect as He is, – and it was all done; therefore the rest was also perfect. There was no taint of the curse; it was absolute, pure, unalloyed rest. God looked upon His work, and there was nothing to cause Him regret; there was nothing to induce Him to say, "If I had it to do over again–;" there was no room for alteration or amendment; He was perfectly satisfied and delighted with what He had wrought. Ah, what tongue or pen can describe, or what mind imagine, the sense of boundless satisfaction, the delicious peace and content that must necessarily follow work all done and well done? This earth affords no such enjoyment, for–

> *"Labor with what zeal we will,*
> *Something still remains undone;*
> *Something uncompleted still*
> *Waits the rising of the sun;"*

but all that sweet satisfaction and delicious rest God enjoyed in as much greater degree than human mind can imagine it, as God is greater than man, on that seventh day when God rested from all His work.

The Rest Into Which Adam Entered

This incomparable rest is what God gave man in the beginning. "The Lord God took the man and put him in the Garden of Eden to dress it and to keep it." Genesis 2:15. "Eden" means delight, pleasure; the garden of Eden is the garden of delight; the Hebrew word which in this place is rendered "put" is a word meaning rest; it is the word from which the proper name Noah comes (for the signification, see Genesis 5:29, and margin); therefore Genesis 2:15 may be rendered thus: "And the Lord God took the man, and caused him to rest in the garden of delight to dress it and to keep it."

Man entered into rest, because he entered into God's perfect, finished work. He was God's workmanship, created in Christ Jesus unto good works, which God had before prepared, that he should walk in them. "This is the work of God, that ye believe," (John 6:29), and it was solely by faith that Adam could enjoy God's work and share His rest; for as soon as he disbelieved God, taking the word of Satan instead, he lost everything. He had no power in himself, for he was but dust of the ground, and he could retain his rest and his inheritance only as long as he allowed God to work in him "both to will and to do of His good pleasure."

"We which believe do enter into rest," because "this is the work of God, that ye believe." The two statements are not contradictory, but are identical in meaning, because the work of God, which is ours by faith, is completed work, and therefore to enter upon that work is to enter upon rest. God's rest, therefore, is not idleness, not laziness. Christ said, "My Father worketh hitherto, and I work," (John 5:17), yet "the everlasting God, the Lord, the Creator of the ends of the earth, fainteth not, neither is weary." Isaiah 40:28. He works by His word to uphold that which He created in the beginning; so those who have believed God, and have therefore entered into rest, are exhorted to "be careful to maintain good works;" (Titus 3:8); but as those good works were obtained by faith, and "not by works done in righteousness, which we did ourselves," (verse 5), so they are to be maintained by faith; but faith gives rest, and therefore the rest of God is compatible with and necessarily accompanied by, the greatest activity.

Chapter 41

The Promises to Israel – Another Day (Part 2 of 2)

The Present Truth, February 11, 1897

In studying this subject last week we saw that the rest promised is God's rest – the rest into which Adam entered when the Lord "caused him to rest in the garden of delight."

It is sin that brings weariness. Adam in the Garden of Eden had work to perform; yet he had absolutely perfect rest all the time he was there, till he sinned. If he had never sinned, such a thing as weariness would never have been known on this earth. Work is not part of the curse, but fatigue is. "Because . . . thou hast eaten of the tree, of which I commanded thee, saying, Thou shalt not eat of it; cursed is the ground for thy sake; in sorrow shalt thou eat of it all the days of thy life; thorns also and thistles shall it bring forth to thee; and thou shalt eat the herb of the field; in the sweat of thy face shalt thou eat bread, till thou return unto the ground." Genesis 3:17-19.

Keeping the Rest

Up to this time he had enjoyed perfect rest while laboring. Why? – Because his work was simply to "keep" that perfect work which God had prepared for him and committed to him. Adam did not have to create anything. If he had been asked to create no more than one flower or a single blade of grass, he could have wearied himself to death over the task, and died leaving it unfinished; but God did the work, and placed Adam in possession of it, with directions to keep it, and this he did so long as he "kept the faith."

Note that this perfect rest was rest in the new earth, and note further that if sin had never entered, the earth would have remained new forever. It was sin that brought blight upon the earth, and has caused it to wax old. God's perfect rest is found only in a heavenly state, and the new earth was most decidedly "a better country, even an heavenly." That which was given to man in the beginning, when he was "crowned with glory and honor," which he lost when he "sinned, and came short of the glory of God," but which the Second Adam has in His own right, being crowned with glory and honor, because of the suffering of death, is what God has promised to Abraham and his seed, and will be given to them when the Messiah comes at "the times of restitution of all things."

A Bit of Eden Still Remains

That perfect, new creation has disappeared – but the rest still remains. The proof that the works were finished and the rest prepared from the foundation of the world is that "God did rest the seventh day from all His works." The Sabbath of the Lord – the seventh day – is a portion of Eden that remains amid the curse; it is a portion of the new-earth rest spanning the abyss from Eden lost till Eden restored. For as the Sabbath rounded out the creation week, and was the proof that the work was finished, it was the seal of a perfect new creation. Now a new creation is necessary, and it must be brought about by the same power as in the beginning. In Christ all things were created, and "if any man be in Christ he is a new creation;" and the seal of perfection is the same in both cases. The Sabbath therefore is the seal of perfection, of perfect righteousness.

What the Sign Signifies

But it must be understood that Sabbath rest does not consist merely in abstaining from manual labor from sunset on Friday evening till sunset on Saturday; – that is but a sign of the rest, and like all other signs is a fraud if the thing signified is not present. The true Sabbath rest consists in complete and continuous recognition of God as the Creator and Upholder of all things, the One in whom we live, and move, and have our being, our life and our righteousness. Keeping the Sabbath is not a duty to be discharged in order to obtain the favor of God, but the keeping of the faith by which righteousness is accounted to us.

There is no room for the objection that we ought not to keep the seventh-day Sabbath because we are not saved by works; for the Sabbath is not a work, it is a rest – God's rest. "He that is entered into his rest, he also hath ceased from his own works, as God did from His." Hebrews 4:10. True Sabbath-keeping is not justification by works, and is utterly disconnected from any idea of such a thing; it is, on the contrary, justification by faith, – it is the absolute rest that comes from perfect faith in the power of God to create a new man and to keep the soul from falling into sin.

But "faith cometh by hearing, and hearing by the word of God," (Romans 10:17), so that it is idle for anybody to profess faith in God while ignoring or rejecting any word of God. Man is to live by every word that proceedeth out of the mouth of God. In every word of God there is life. If a man knew no more than one word of God, and accepted that word as God's word indeed, he would be saved by it. God has compassion on the ignorant, and does not require that men should know a certain amount before they can be saved; but willful ignorance is a different thing. A person's ignorance may be the result of deliberately rejecting knowledge, and he who does that, rejects life. For as there is life in every word of God, and the life is one and the same in every word, whoever rejects but one word that clearly comes to him, thereby rejects the whole. Faith takes the Lord for all that He is, – for all that we see of Him, and for all the infinite unknown.

A Gift to Man

Let it not be forgotten that the Sabbath is not a burden which God lays upon people (whoever heard of perfect rest being a burden?) but a blessing which He offers them; it is the removal of burdens. "Come unto Me all ye that labor, and are heavy laden, and I will give you rest." Instead of forcing it upon people, God says that it is impossible for anybody to share the Sabbath rest, if he does not believe. To the man who says, "I don't believe that it is necessary for me to keep the Sabbath," the Lord replies, "You cannot keep it; you shall not enter into My rest; you have no part nor lot in it." It is impossible for a man to keep the Sabbath of the Lord without faith, because "the just shall live by faith." The Sabbath is God's rest, God's rest is perfection, and perfection cannot be obtained except by perfect faith.

"God is a Spirit; and they that worship Him must worship Him in Spirit and in truth." John 4:24. His rest therefore is spiritual rest, so that mere physical rest without spiritual rest is not Sabbath keeping at all. Only those who are spiritual can truly keep the Sabbath of the Lord. So long as the Spirit led Adam, he enjoyed perfect rest, both of body and soul; but as soon as he sinned, he lost the rest. But although the curse upon the earth causes weariness of body, the Sabbath still remains from Eden, the pledge and seal of spiritual rest. The abstaining from all our own work and pleasure on the seventh day, – from everything by which we could personally profit, – is simply in recognition of God as Creator and Upholder of all things, – the one by whose power we live; but this apparent rest is but a farce if we do not really and wholly recognize Him as such, and commit ourselves fully to His keeping.

The Sabbath, therefore, is especially the poor man's friend; it appeals above all to the laboring man, for it is to the poor that the Gospel is preached. The rich will hardly listen to the Lord's call, for they are likely to feel content with their lot; they trust in their riches, and feel able to take care of themselves in the present, and as for the future, "their inward thought is that their houses shall continue for ever;" but to the poor man, who knows not how he is to get a living, the Sabbath comes bringing hope and joy, in that it directs his mind to God, the Creator, who is our life. It says, "Seek first the kingdom of God, and His righteousness, and all these things shall be added unto you." Instead of being obliged to say, "How can I get a living if I keep the Sabbath?" the poor man may see in the Sabbath the solution of the problem of life. "Godliness is profitable unto all things, having promise of the life that now is, and of that which is to come." 1 Timothy 4:8.

The Blessed Day and the Blessed Man

Bear in mind that while the Sabbath day is the seventh day of the week, the rest, which the Sabbath day brings to view, is continuous. Just as a day is not a man, so there is a difference between blessing a day and blessing a man. God blessed the seventh day (Genesis 2:3), but He blesses men every day. Only those who rest in the Lord all the time keep the Sabbath. While nobody can be a Sabbath-keeper and ignore the day upon which God has placed his blessing, it is equally true that the man who does not continually rest in the Lord does not keep the Sabbath.

Thus, rest in the Lord is found only by faith in Him; but faith saves from sin, and living faith is as continuous as the breath, for "the just shall live by faith." If now a man distrusts the Lord during the week, is doubting and fearing as to how he shall get along, perhaps fretting and worrying, is impatient, or harsh, or in any way unjust to his fellow-men, he is certainly not resting in the Lord, – he is not remembering the Sabbath day, to keep it holy; for if he really remembered the Sabbath day, he would know God's power to provide for him, and he would commit the keeping of his soul to Him in well-doing, "as unto a faithful Creator."

The Cross of Christ

The Sabbath comes revealing Christ the Creator as the burden bearer.

He bears the burdens of the whole world, with all its toil and sin and sorrow, and He bears it easily; – His burden is light. "His own self bare our sins in His own body on the tree, that we, being dead to sins, should live unto righteousness; by whose stripes we are healed." 1 Peter 2:24. It is in the cross of Christ that we receive life, and are made new creatures. The power of the cross, therefore, is creative power. So when on the cross Jesus cried, "It is finished," He was simply announcing that in Him, through His cross, could be obtained the perfect works of God, which were finished from the foundation of the world. Thus the Sabbath – the seventh day rest that commemorates creation completed in the beginning – is a blessed reminder of the fact that in the cross of Christ that same creative power is freely offered to deliver us from the curse, and make us in Him as complete as was everything when God saw it and pronounced it "very good." The word of life, which is proclaimed to us in the Gospel, is "that which was from the beginning."

He does not fail nor become impatient or discouraged; therefore we may confidently cast all our care on Him. Thus the Sabbath is indeed a delight. In the Psalm for the Sabbath day, David sang, "For You, Lord, have made me glad through Your work; I will triumph in the works of Your hands." Psalm 92:4. The Sabbath means triumphing in the works of God's hands, not in our own works. It means victory over sin and death – everything connected with the curse – through our Lord Jesus Christ, by whom the worlds were made. It is a remnant of Eden before the curse came, and therefore he who keeps it indeed really begins his eternal rest, – he has the rest, the perfect rest, which the new earth alone can give.

God's Invitation to Sabbath-Keeping

Now we can understand why the Sabbath occupies so prominent a place in the record of God's dealings with Israel. It is not because the Sabbath was for them exclusively, any more than salvation was exclusively for them; but it is because Sabbath-keeping is the beginning of that rest which God promised His people in the land of Canaan. It is sometimes said that the Sabbath was not given to the Gentiles, but it must also be remembered that the land was not promised to the Gentiles. The Gentiles are "strangers from the covenants of promise." But it is true that the Gentiles – all the world – were called to come to Christ, the living water. "Ho, every one that thirsteth, come ye to the waters." The promise to Israel was, and is, that "nations that knew not thee shall run unto thee because of the Lord thy God, and for the Holy One of Israel." Still further in the call, the Lord says: –

"Keep ye judgment, and do justice; for My salvation is near to come, and My righteousness to be revealed. Blessed is the man that doeth this, and the son of man that layeth hold on it; that keepeth the Sabbath from polluting it, and keepeth his hands from doing any evil. Neither let the son of the stranger, that hath joined himself to the Lord, speak, saying, "The Lord hath utterly separated me from His people. . . . Also the sons of the stranger, that join themselves to the Lord, to serve Him, and to love the name of the Lord, to be His servants, every one that keepeth the Sabbath from polluting it, and taketh hold of My covenant; even them will I bring to My holy mountain; and make them joyful in My house of prayer; their burnt-offerings and their sacrifices shall be accepted upon Mine altar; for Mine house shall be called an house of prayer for all people. The Lord God which gathereth the outcasts of Israel saith, Yet will I gather others to him beside those that are gathered to him." Isaiah 56:1-8.

And to both these and those, – to all to whom He proclaims peace, both near and far (Isaiah 57:19), – the Lord declares: –

A Glorious Promise

"If thou turn away thy foot from the Sabbath, from doing thy pleasure on My holy day; and call the Sabbath a delight, the holy of the Lord, honorable; and shalt honor Him, not doing thine own ways, nor finding thine own pleasure, nor speaking thine own words; then shalt thou delight thyself in the Lord; and I will cause thee to ride upon the high places of the earth, and feed thee with the heritage of Jacob thy father; for the mouth of the Lord hath spoken it." Isaiah 58:13, 14.

Those who call the Sabbath a delight – not a burden – shall delight themselves in the Lord. Why? –Because the Sabbath of the Lord is the Lord's rest – rest that is found only in His presence, where there is "fullness of joy" and everlasting pleasure. It is the rest of Eden, for Eden is delight, pleasure; it is the rest of the new earth, for Eden belongs to the new earth. We have read that those who come to the Lord to keep His Sabbath, shall be made joyful in the house of the Lord, and of them it is said, "They shall be abundantly satisfied with the fatness of Thy house; and Thou shalt make them drink of the river of Thy pleasures," literally, "Thy Eden." Psalm 36:8. This is the heritage of the Lord, now is the time, today is the day in which we may enter upon it, for He is the portion of our inheritance, and in Him we have all things.

Chapter 42

The Promises to Israel - Again in Captivity (Part 1 of 3)

The Present Truth, February 18, 1897

Although the children of Israel sang the song of deliverance by the Red Sea, and with good reason, too, it was not until they had crossed the Jordan that they were really free from Egypt. They did not hold the beginning of their confidence steadfast unto the end, but "in their hearts turned back again into Egypt, saying unto Aaron, Make us gods to go before us." Acts 7:39, 40. When they crossed the Jordan, however, and came into the land of Canaan, they had the testimony from God that the reproach of Egypt was rolled away from them. Then they had rest, and were free in the Lord.

But this freedom was not long retained; murmuring, distrust, and apostasy soon appeared among God's people. They desired a king, that they might be like the heathen about them, and their desire was granted to the full. They "mingled among the heathen, and learned their works. And they served their idols, which were a snare unto them, Yea, they sacrificed their sons and their daughters unto devils, and shed innocent blood, even the blood of their sons and of their daughters, whom they sacrificed unto the idols of Canaan; and the land was polluted with blood." Psalm 106:35-38. Thus they became literally like the heathen round them.

A little glance at the history of some of the kings of Israel and Judah will show how completely the children of Israel, in getting a king, had the fulfillment of their wish to be like the heathen. To Saul, the first king, the prophet of God said, "To obey is better than sacrifice, and to hearken than the fat of rams. For rebellion is as the sin of witchcraft, and stubbornness is as iniquity and idolatry. Because thou hast rejected the word of the Lord, He hath also rejected thee from being king." 1 Samuel 15:22, 23.

Solomon took many strange wives from among the heathen and "it came to pass, when Solomon was old, that his wives turned away his heart after other gods; and his heart was not perfect with the Lord his God, as was the heart of David his father. For Solomon went after Ashtoreth, the goddess of the Zidonians, and after Milcom the abomination of the Ammonites." 1 Kings 11:4, 5.

Under Rehoboam, Solomon's son, "Judah did evil in the sight of the Lord, and they provoked Him to jealousy with their sins which they had committed, above all that their fathers had done. For they also built them high places, and images, and groves,[13] on every high hill, and under every green tree. And there were also Sodomites in the land; and they did according to all the abominations of the nations which the Lord cast out before the children of Israel." 1 Kings 14:22-24.

The same thing is recorded of Ahaz (2 Kings 16:1-4), and although "the Lord brought Judah low because of Ahaz king of Israel; for he made Judah naked, and transgressed sore against the Lord," yet "in the time of his distress did he trespass yet more against the Lord; this is that king Ahaz. For he sacrificed unto the gods of Damascus, which smote him; and he said, Because the gods of the kings of Syria help them, therefore will I sacrifice to them, that they may help me. But they were the ruin of him, and of all Israel." 2 Chronicles 28:19-23.

"Worse Than the Heathen"

Manasseh, son of Hezekiah, "did that which was evil in the sight of the Lord, after the abominations of the heathen, whom the Lord cast out before the children of Israel. For he built up again the high places which Hezekiah his father had destroyed; and he reared up altars for Baal, and made a grove, as did Ahab king of Israel; and worshipped all the host of heaven, and served them. . . . And he built altars for all the host of heaven in the two courts of the house of the Lord. And he made his son pass through the fire, and observed times, and used enchantments, and dealt with familiar spirits and wizards: he wrought much wickedness in the sight of the Lord, to provoke Him to anger. And he set a graven image of the grove that he had made in the house, of which the Lord said to David, and to Solomon his son, in this house, and in Jerusalem, which I have chosen out of all the tribes of Israel, will I put My name for ever; neither will I make the feet of Israel move any more out of the land which I gave their fathers; only if they will observe to do according to all that I have commanded them, and according to all the law that My servant Moses commanded them. But they hearkened not; and Manasseh seduced them to do more evil than did the nations whom the Lord destroyed before the children of Israel." "Moreover Manasseh shed innocent blood very much, till he had filled Jerusalem from one end to another; beside his sin wherewith he made Judah to sin, in doing that which was evil in the sight of the Lord." 2 Kings 21:1-9; 16.

Amon succeeded Manasseh, "but he did that which was evil in the sight of the Lord, as did Manasseh his father; for Amon sacrificed unto all the carved images which Manasseh his father had made, and served them." 2 Chronicles 33:22.

---

[13] The word "groves" in this and the following texts, is a very unfortunate, misleading rendering of the original. The Revision has "Asherah." As we can see by carefully noting the use of the term, it cannot mean a grove of trees, since we read of groves being set up "under every green tree, and in the house of the Lord." The thing itself was an obscene image pertaining to the lascivious rites of one form of sun worship.

In The Northern Kingdom

If we take the kings that reigned over the northern portion of Israel after the kingdom was divided upon the death of Solomon, we find a worse record still. There were some righteous kings in Jerusalem; but beginning with Jeroboam, "who did sin, and who made Israel to sin" (1 Kings 14:16), each successive king over the rest of Israel was worse than the one before him. Nadab, the son of Jeroboam, "did evil in the sight of the Lord, and walked in the way of his father, and in his sin wherewith he made Israel to sin." 1 Kings 15:26. Baasha "did evil in the sight of the Lord, and walked in the way of Jeroboam, and in his sin wherewith he made Israel to sin." Verse 34. Omri, who built Samaria, "wrought evil in the eyes of the Lord, and did worse than all that were before him. For he walked in all the way of Jeroboam the son of Nebat, and in his sin wherewith he made Israel to sin, to provoke the Lord God of Israel to anger with their vanities." 1 Kings 16:25, 26. Yet bad as Omri was, "Ahab the son of Omri did evil in the sight of the Lord above all that were before him;" "and Ahab did more to provoke the Lord to anger than all the kings of Israel that were before him." Verses 30, 33.

These matters went on until the Lord could say by the prophet Jeremiah, "Run ye to and fro through the streets of Jerusalem, and see now, and know, and seek in the broad places thereof, if ye can find a man, if there be any that executes judgment, that seeketh truth." Jeremiah 5:1. Such a man was hard to find; "For among My people are found wicked men; they lay wait, as he that setteth snares; they set a trap, they catch men. As a cage is full of birds, so are their houses full of deceit; therefore are they become great, and waxen rich. They are waxen fat, they shine; yea, they overpass the deeds of the heathen." Verses 26-28.

Inasmuch as God drove the heathen out of the land, because of their abominable idolatry, it is very evident that the children of Israel could have no real inheritance in it when they were just like the heathen, and even worse. The fact that those who call themselves by the name of the Lord adopt heathen customs and manners does not make these customs one bit more acceptable to God. The fact that heathenism is in the church, does not recommend it. On the contrary, a high profession only makes the evil practice more heinous. The children of Israel were therefore not really in possession of the land of Canaan while they were following the ways of the heathen; nay, since the reproach of the bondage in Egypt was the sin into which they had fallen, it is evident that even while boasting of their freedom in the land of Canaan they were actually in the worst kind of bondage. When at a later date the Jews boastingly said, "We be Abraham's seed, and have never yet been in bondage to any man," Jesus repeated, "Verily, verily, I say unto you, every one that committeth sin is the bondservant of sin. And the bondservant abideth not in the house for ever; the Son abideth ever." John 8:33-35.

God's Faithfulness

Yet there were wondrous possibilities all the time within reach of the people. At any time they might have repented and turned to the Lord, and they would have found Him ready to fulfill His promise to them to the uttermost. Although "all the chief of the priests and the people transgressed very much after all the abominations of the heathen," still "the Lord God of their fathers sent to them by His messengers, rising up betimes, and sending; because He had compassion on His people, and on His dwelling-place." 2 Chronicles 36:14, 15. Many wonderful deliverances, when the Israelites were oppressed by their enemies, and humbly sought the Lord, showed that the same God who delivered their fathers from Egypt, was ready and waiting to exert the same power in their behalf, in order to perfect that for which He had brought them into the promised land.

One remarkable instance of the working of God for those who trust Him, and of the victory of faith, is found in the history of Jehoshapat. (2 Chronicles 20) It is specially valuable to us, for it shows us how to gain victories; and it also shows us again, what we have so many times noted, that the real victories of Israel were gained by faith in God, and not by the use of the sword. The story in brief is this: –

The Moabites and the Ammonites, together with other people, came against Jehoshaphat to battle. Their numbers were vastly in excess of those of the Israelites, and in their "Jehoshaphat feared, and set himself to seek the Lord, and proclaimed a fast throughout all Judah. And Judah gathered themselves together, to ask help of the Lord; even out of all the cities of Judah they came to seek the Lord."

Jehoshaphat's prayer on that occasion is a model. He said, "O Lord God of our fathers, art not Thou God in Heaven? And rulest not Thou over all the kingdoms of the heathen? and in Thine hand is there not power and might, so that none is able to withstand Thee? Art Thou not our God, who didst drive out the inhabitants of this land before Thy people Israel, and gavest it to the seed of Abraham Thy friend forever? . . . And now, behold the children of Ammon and Moab and Mount Seir, . . . how they reward us, to come to cast us out of Thy possession, which Thou hast given us to inherit. O Lord our God, wilt Thou not judge them? for we have no might against this great company that cometh against us; neither know we what to do; but our eyes are upon Thee."

First he recognized God as God in heaven, and therefore having all power. Next he claimed all this power as his own by claiming God as his own God. Then he was ready to make known his need, and to prefer his request, with full assurance of faith. To one who prays in that way, all things are possible. Too many offer prayer to God, without any just sense of His existence, as though they were praying to an abstract name, and not to a living, personal Saviour, and of course they receive nothing, for they do not really expect anything. Every one who prays should first contemplate God, before thinking of himself and his own needs. It is doubtless the case that most people when they pray think more about themselves than they do of God; instead of that, they should become lost in contemplation of God's greatness and His kindness; then it is not difficult to believe that God is a rewarder of them that diligently seek Him. As the Psalmist said, "They that know Thy name will put their trust in Thee; for Thou, Lord, hast not forsaken them that seek Thee." Psalm 9:10.

While the people were still gathered to pray, the prophet of God came, and said, "Hearken ye, all Judah, and ye inhabitants of Jerusalem, and thou King Jehoshaphat, Thus saith the Lord unto you, Be not afraid nor dismayed, for the battle is not yours, but God's." "Ye shall not need to fight in this battle; set yourselves, stand ye still, and see the salvation of the Lord with you, O Judah and Jerusalem; fear not, nor be dismayed; to-morrow go out against them; for the Lord will be with you."

The people believed this message, "and they rose early in the morning and went forth into the wilderness of Tekoa; and as they went forth, Jehoshaphat stood, and said, Hear me, O Judah, and ye inhabitants of Jerusalem; Believe in the Lord your God, so shall ye be established; believe His prophets, so shall ye prosper. And when he had consulted with the people, he appointed singers unto the Lord, and that should praise the beauty of holiness, as they went out before the army, and to say, Praise the Lord: for His mercy endureth for ever."

"When They Began to Sing"

A strange way that, to go out to battle. It reminds us somewhat of the march round Jericho, and the shout of victory. As a general thing, people getting such a promise as they did at that time, that God would fight for them, would think that they showed great faith in going out at all against the enemy. They would say, "God has promised to help us, but we must do our part;" and so they would make every preparation for fighting. But these people at that time were just simple enough to take the Lord at His word; they knew that they must indeed do their part, but they knew that their part was to believe, and to go forward as though they did really believe. And they did believe. So strong was their faith that they sang. It was no forced song that was heard, weakly issuing from trembling lips, but a full, deep, spontaneous, hearty song of joy and victory, and all this while the enemy was before them in overwhelming numbers. And what was the result?

"And when they began to sing and to praise, the Lord set ambushments against the children of Ammon, Moab, and Mount Seir, which were come against Judah; and they were smitten. For the children of Ammon and Moab stood up against the inhabitants of Mount Seir, utterly to slay and destroy them; and when they had made an end of the inhabitants of Seir, every one helped to destroy another. And when Judah came toward the watch tower in the wilderness, they looked unto the multitude, and, behold, they were dead bodies fallen to the earth, and none escaped."

As soon as they began to sing, the enemy was overthrown. A panic seized the host of Ammonites and Moabites, and they beat down one another. It may well be that, when they heard the songs and shouts of joy, they thought that Israel had received reinforcements, and such was the case. The people of Israel had such reinforcements that they did not need to do any fighting themselves. Their faith was their victory, and their singing was the evidence of their faith.

This is a lesson for us in our conflicts with our adversaries – principalities and powers and wicked spirits. "Resist the devil, and he will flee from you;" but we are to "resist steadfast in the faith." Only such resistance will cause him to flee, for he knows that he is stronger than we; but when he is resisted in the faith of Jesus, he must flee, for he knows that he has no strength at all against Christ. And so we learn again that "the redeemed of the Lord shall return, and come with singing unto Zion." In such experiences as that just considered, the Lord was showing Israel how they should overcome, and that He was always waiting and anxious to complete the promise made to the fathers.

Chapter 43

The Promises to Israel - Again in Captivity (Part 2 of 3)

The Present Truth, February 25, 1897

We know that at any time within a period of several hundred years the children of Israel might have enjoyed the fullness of the promise to Abraham, – eternal rest in the earth made new, with Christ and all the glorified saints victorious over the last enemy, – because when Moses was born the time of the promise had drawn near, and Joshua did not die until "a long time after that the Lord had given rest unto Israel." Joshua 23:1. The time when God through David offered them "another day," – to day, – is spoken of as "after so long a time." God was anxiously waiting for the people to take all that He had given them. How true this is may be seen by His words to them by the prophet Jeremiah.

If They Had Obeyed God

Even though the people were so firmly fixed in their idolatry, that the sin of Judah was written with a pen of iron and with the point of a diamond, the gracious Lord made the following promise: –

"Thus saith the Lord unto Me; Go and stand in the gate of the children of the people, whereby the kings of Judah come in, and by which they go out, and in all the gates of Jerusalem: and say unto them, Hear ye the word of the Lord, ye kings of Judah, and all Judah, and all the inhabitants of Jerusalem, that enter in by these gates, thus saith the Lord: Take heed to yourselves, and bear no burden on the Sabbath day, nor bring it in by the gates of Jerusalem; neither carry forth a burden out of your houses on the Sabbath day, neither do ye any work, but hallow ye the Sabbath day, as I commanded your fathers. But they obeyed not, neither inclined their ear, but made their neck stiff, that they might not hear, nor receive instruction. And it shall come to pass, if ye diligently hearken unto Me, saith the Lord, to bring in no burden through the gates of this city on the Sabbath day, but hallow the Sabbath day, to do no work therein; then shall there enter into the gates of this city kings and princess sitting upon the throne of

David, riding in chariots and on horses, they, and their princes, the men of Judah, and the inhabitants of Jerusalem: and this city shall remain for ever. And they shall come from the cities of Judah, and from the places about Jerusalem, and from the land of Benjamin, and from the plain, and from the mountains, and from the south, bringing burnt offerings, and sacrifice, and meat offerings, and incense, and bringing sacrifices of praise, unto the house of the Lord." Jeremiah 17:19-26.

It is not for us to speculate as to how this promise would have been fulfilled; it is enough for us to know that God said it, and He is able to make every promise good. To build up the old city, and make it new would certainly have been as easy as to "change our vile body, that it may be fashioned like unto His glorious body" (Philippians 3:21), or to make an entirely new city to take the place of the old one.

Promises of Restoration Which Were Rejected

Bear in mind that this promise by Jeremiah was in the very last days of the kingdom of Judah, for Jeremiah did not begin to prophesy till "the days of Josiah the son of Amon" (Jeremiah 1:2), in the thirteenth year of his reign, only twenty-one years before the beginning of the Babylonian captivity. Before Jeremiah began to prophesy, nearly all the prophets had finished their labors, and passed away. The prophecies of Isaiah, Hosea, Amos, Micah, and others, – all the principal prophets – were in the hands of the people before Jeremiah was born. This is a fact that should by no means be overlooked, for it is most important. In those prophecies are many promises of the restoration of Jerusalem, all of which might have been fulfilled if the people had given heed. But like all God's promises, they were in Christ; they pertained, like the one before us, to eternity, and not simply to time. But since the people of those days did not accept them they remain equally fresh for us. Only the coming of the Lord, for whom we are now looking, could fulfill them. Those prophecies contain the Gospel for this time, just as surely as do the books of Matthew and John and the Epistles.

Always the Test

Notice further that the keeping of the Sabbath is made the test; to all to whom that truth is revealed. If they kept the Sabbath, then they and their city would endure forever. Why was this? – Recall what we have studied about God's rest, and you have the answer. The Sabbath is the seal of creation finished and perfect. As such it reveals God as Creator and Sanctifier (Ezekiel 20:12, 20), as Sanctifier by His creative power. The Sabbath is not a work, by which we may vainly try to win the favor of God, but it is rest, – rest in the everlasting arms. It is the sign and memorial of God's eternal power; and the keeping of it is the seal of that perfection which God alone can work out, and which He freely bestows upon all who trust Him. It means full and perfect trust in the Lord, that He can and will save us by the same power by which He made all things in the beginning. Therefore we see that since the same promise is left us, that was given to ancient Israel, it must necessarily be that the Sabbath also should be made specially prominent in our day, more especially as the day of Christ's coming approaches.

The Judgment Pronounced

But there was an alternative, in case the people refused to rest in the Lord. The prophet was commissioned to say still further: –

"But if ye will not hearken unto Me, to hallow the Sabbath day, and not to bear a burden, even entering into the gates of Jerusalem on the Sabbath day; then will I kindle a fire in the gates thereof, and it shall devour the palaces of Jerusalem, and it shall not be quenched." Jeremiah 17:27.

And so it was; although God was faithful and longsuffering in sending messages of warning to His people, "they mocked the messengers of God, and despised His words, and misused His prophets, until the wrath of the Lord arose against His people, till there was no remedy. Therefore He brought upon them the king of the Chaldees, who slew their young men with the sword in the house of their sanctuary, and had no compassion upon young man or maiden, old man, or him that stooped for age; He gave them all into his hand. And all the vessels of the house of God, great and small, and the treasures of the house of the Lord, and the treasures of the king, and of his princes; all these he brought to Babylon. And they burnt the house of God, and brake down the wall of Jerusalem, and burnt all the palaces thereof with fire, and destroyed all the goodly vessels thereof. And them that had escaped from the sword carried he away to Babylon; where they were servants to him and his sons until the reign of the kingdom of Persia; to fulfill the word of the Lord by the mouth of Jeremiah, until the land had enjoyed her Sabbaths; for as long as she lay desolate she kept Sabbath, to fulfill threescore and ten years." 2 Chronicles 36:16-21.

The King of Babylon Ruler in Jerusalem

The last king in Jerusalem was Zedekiah, but he was not an independent king. Several years before he came to the throne, Nebuchadnezzar had besieged Jerusalem, and the Lord had given the city to him. Daniel 1:1, 2. Although Jehoiakim was overcome, he was allowed to reign in Jerusalem as a tributary prince, which he did for eight years. At his death his son Jehoiachin succeeded him, but he reigned only three months before Nebuchadnezzar besieged Jerusalem again, and conquered it, and carried the king and his family and all the craftsmen and smiths away to Babylon; "none remained save the poorest sort of the people of the land." 2 Kings 24:8-16.

Still there was a king left in Jerusalem, for Nebuchadnezzar made Mattaniah king, changing his name to Zedekiah. Verse 17. The word Zedekiah means "the righteousness of Jehovah," and was given to the new-made king because Nebuchadnezzar "made him swear by God" (2 Chronicles 36:13) that he would not rebel against his authority. The following shows that Nebuchadnezzar had a right to demand this: –

"In the beginning of the reign of Jehoiakim the son of Josiah king of Judah, came this word unto Jeremiah from the Lord, saying, Thus saith the Lord to me; Make thee bonds and yokes, and put them upon thy neck, and send them to the king of Edom, and to the king of Moab, and to the king of the Ammonites, and to the king of Tyrus, and to the king of Zidon, by the hand of the messengers which come to Jerusalem unto Zedekiah king of Judah: And command them to say unto their masters, Thus saith the Lord of hosts, the God of Israel; Thus shall ye say unto your masters: I have made the earth, the man and the beast that are upon the ground, by My great power and by My outstretched arm, and have given it unto whom it seemed meet unto Me. And now have I given all these lands into the hand of Nebuchadnezzar the king of Babylon, My servant; and the beasts of the field have I given him also to serve him. And all nations shall serve him, and his son, and his son's son, until the very time of his land come: and then many nations and great kings shall serve themselves of him. And it shall come to pass that the nation and kingdom which will not serve the same Nebuchadnezzar the king of Babylon, and that will not put their neck under the yoke of the king of Babylon, that nation will I punish, saith the Lord, with the sword, and with the famine, and with the pestilence, until I have consumed them by his hand. Therefore hearken not ye to your prophets, nor to your diviners, nor to your dreamers, nor to your enchanters, nor to your sorcerers, which speak unto you, saying, Ye shall not serve the king of Babylon: for they prophesy a lie unto you, to remove you far from your land; and that I should drive you out, and ye should perish. But the nations that bring their neck under the yoke of the king of Babylon, and serve him, those will I let remain still in their own land, saith the Lord; and they shall till it, and dwell therein." Jeremiah 27:1-11.

Nebuchadnezzar, therefore, had as much right to rule in Jerusalem as any of the kings of Israel had ever had. His kingdom, moreover, was more extensive than that over which any king of Israel had ruled; and, more than all, after much instruction from the Lord, he used his opportunity to spread throughout all the world the knowledge of the true God. See Daniel 4. Therefore when Zedekiah rebelled against Nebuchadnezzar, he was wickedly setting himself against the Lord, who had given Israel into the power of Nebuchadnezzar, as a punishment for their sins. In the following words we have a graphic description of the movement of Nebuchadnezzar against Jerusalem, and how God guided the action of the heathen king even while he was using divination: –

"Also, thou son of man, appoint thee two ways, that the sword of the king of Babylon may come: both twain shall come forth out of one land: and choose thou a place, choose it at the head of the way to the city. Appoint a way that the sword may come to Rabbath of the Ammonites, and to Judah in Jerusalem the defenced. For the king of Babylon stood at the parting of the way, at the head of the two ways, to use divination; he made his arrows bright, he consulted with images, he looked in the liver. At his right hand was the divination for Jerusalem, to appoint captains, to open the mouth in the slaughter, to lift up the voice with shouting, to appoint battering rams against the gates, to cast a mount, and to build a fort. And it shall be unto them as a false divination in their sight, to them that have sworn oaths: but he will call to remembrance the iniquity that they may be taken. Therefore thus saith the Lord God: Because you have made your iniquity to be remembered, in that your transgressions are discovered, so that in all your doings your sins do appear: because, I say, that ye are come to remembrance, ye shall be taken with the hand."

The End of Israel's Independent, Temporal Dominion

Then follow the fateful words addressed to Zedekiah: –

"And thou, profane wicked prince of Israel, whose day is come, when iniquity shall have an end, Thus saith the Lord God: Remove the diadem, and take off the crown: this shall not be the same: exalt him that is low, and abase him that is high. I will overturn, overturn, overturn it: and it shall be no more, until He come whose right it is: and I will give it Him." Ezekiel 21:19-27.

Zedekiah was profane and wicked, because to all his abominable idolatry he added the sin of perjury, breaking a solemn oath. Therefore the kingdom was utterly removed. The diadem passed from the descendants of David, and was placed on the head of a Chaldean, and the kingdom of Babylon is before us. Of its extent we have already read, and we have further the words of the prophet Daniel in explanation of the great image that Nebuchadnezzar saw in a dream given him by the God of heaven: –

"Thou, O king, art a king of kings; for the God of heaven hath given thee a kingdom, power, and strength, and glory. And wheresoever the children of men dwell, the beasts of the field and the fowls of the heaven hath He given into thine hand, and hath made thee ruler over them all. Thou art this head of gold." Daniel 2:37, 38.

In this we trace the dominion, which in the beginning was given to man (see Genesis 1:26), although the glory and power were greatly diminished. But we see that God still had His eye upon it, and was working towards its restoration, according to the promise to Abraham.

From Babylon to the Setting Up of the Everlasting Kingdom

Very little time is devoted in the Bible to descriptions of human grandeur, and the prophet hastens to the end. Three overturnings or revolutions are foretold in Ezekiel 21:27, following the passing of the dominion of the whole earth into the hands of

Nebuchadnezzar. As his kingdom was world-wide, the revolutions foretold must also be the overthrow and establishment of universal empire. So the prophet Daniel, continuing his explanation of Nebuchadnezzar's dream, said: –

"And after thee shall arise another kingdom inferior to thee, and another third kingdom of brass, which shall bear rule over all the earth." Daniel 2:39.

The kingdom that succeeded the Babylonian is shown in Daniel v. to have been that of Medo-Persia; and in Daniel 8:1-8, 20, 21 we learn that the third kingdom, the successor of Medo-Persia in universal worldly dominion, was that of Grecia. Thus briefly have we outlined before us the history of the world for several hundred years. The first two overturnings of Ezekiel 21:29 are made clear; Babylon was followed by Medo-Persia, and that in turn by the Grecian empire.

The last of this earth's universal kingdoms, following the third great revolution, is not directly named, but it is clearly enough indicated. The birth of Christ took place in the days of Cæsar Augustus, who issued a decree that all the world should be taxed or enrolled. Luke 2:1. Therefore we are warranted in naming Rome as the product of the third great world revolution. In fact, we are shut up to that empire, for there is none other known to history that could take its place. Thus Babylon ruled the world; in its days three revolutions were foretold, bringing three successive empires in its stead; Medo-Persia and Greece are expressly named in the line of succession, and then we have the emperor of Rome named as ruling the world. This is strictly Scriptural evidence; corroborative evidence, or rather, evidence testifying to the exactness of the sacred record, may be found without limit in secular history.

But the revolution that resulted in giving the rulership of the world to Rome, was the last general revolution that shall take place in this world "until He come whose right it is." Many men since Rome fell have dreamed of world-wide dominion, but their dreams have come to naught.

Christ was on earth, it is true, but it was as a stranger, like Abraham, with no place of His own where He could lay His head. He came, however, "to proclaim liberty to the captives," and announced that whoever would abide in His word should know the truth, and be made free by it. Day by day and year after year as the centuries have rolled by, the proclamation of freedom has been sounding, and weary captives have been set free from the power of darkness. It is not for us to know the times and the seasons which the Father has put in His own power; but we know that when all the professed church of Christ shall consent to be filled with His Spirit, the whole world will soon hear the Gospel message in the fullness of its power, and the end will come, when the groaning creation itself will be delivered from the bondage of corruption into the glory of the liberty of the children of God.

Chapter 44

The Promises to Israel - Again in Captivity
(Part 3 of 3)

The Present Truth, August 27, 1896

Boast as they will of their freedom and independence, men in love slavery, and would rather be in bondage than be free. This is demonstrated by facts.

Rejecting Liberty

The God of the universe has made a proclamation of freedom to all mankind; He has even given liberty to all; yet but few will take advantage of it.

The experience of ancient Israel is but the experience of the human heart.

Twice the Lord made it very plain to Abraham that his seed should be free, – once when He said that his servant Eliezer should not be his heir, and again when He told him that the son of a bondwoman could not be heir.

Later He delivered Israel from the bondage of Egypt, that they might enjoy freedom, even the freedom of obedience to the perfect law of liberty, but they murmured, and "in their hearts turned back again into Egypt, saying unto Aaron, Make us gods to go before us." Acts 7:39, 40.

Forty years later God rolled away from them the reproach of Egypt, yet they afterward desired to be like the heathen round them, by having a king, who, as they were assured, would make them slaves. And so it proved; for they not only learned the ways of the heathen, but "overpassed" them.

"The Lord God of their fathers sent to them by His messengers, rising up betimes, and sending; because He had compassion on His people, and on His dwelling-place; but mocked the messengers of God, and despised His words, and misused His prophets, until the wrath of the Lord arose against His people till there was no remedy" (2 Chronicles 36:15, 16), and He fulfilled His threat to carry them away beyond Babylon. Amos 5:25-27; Acts 7:43.

Slaves of Sin

This Babylonian captivity was only the visible expression of the bondage in which the people had already voluntarily placed themselves. They had flattered themselves that they were free, while they were "the servants of corruption; for of whom a man is overcome of the same is he brought in bondage." 2 Peter 2:19. "Whosoever comitteth sin is the bondservant of sin." John 8:34. Physical slavery is a small matter compared with soul-bondage, and but for the latter, the former never could have been known.

The carrying of Israel to the city of Babylon was strikingly fitting. It was not an accident that they were taken there rather than anywhere else. Babylon – Babel – means confusion, but confusion because of self-exaltation and pride; "for where envying and strife is, them is confusion and every evil work." James 3:16. The origin of the name Babylon was on this wise: –

The Builders of Babel

"And the whole earth was of one language, and of one language and of one speech. And it came to pass, as they journeyed from the east, that they found a plain in the land of Shinar, and they dwelt there. And they said to another, Go to, let us make brick, and burn them thoroughly. And they had brick for stone, and slime had they for mortar. And they said, Go to, let us build us a city and a tower, whose top may reach unto heaven; and let us make us a name, lest we be scattered abroad upon the face of the whole earth. And the Lord came down to see the city and the tower, which the children of men builded. And the Lord said, Behold, the people is one, and they have all one language; and this they begin to do; and now nothing will be restrained from them, which they have imagined to do. Go to, let us go down, and there confound their language, that they may not understand one another's speech. So the Lord scattered them abroad from thence upon the face of all the earth; and they left off to build the city. Therefore is the name of it called Babel, because the Lord did there confound the language of all the earth." Genesis 11:1-9.

Defying God

Those people had the idea that they could build a city so great and a tower so high that they could defy the judgments of God. They really thought themselves greater than God. The same idea possessed Lucifer, of whom we read: –

"How art thou fallen from heaven, O Lucifer, son of the morning! how art thou cut down to the ground which didst weaken the nations! Or thou hast said in thine heart, I will ascend into heaven, I will exalt my throne above the stars of God; I will sit also upon the mount of the congregation, in the sides of the north; I will ascend above the heights of he clouds; I will be like the Most High." Isaiah 14:12-14.

It will be clearly seen that the spirit that was in Lucifer was identical with that which was in the builders of Babel, and the reason or this is that it was Satan himself – Lucifer fallen – who prompted that work. He is "the prince of this world" (John 14:30), "the spirit hat now worketh in the children of disobedience." Ephesians 2:2. Now let us go back to the beginning of the chapter from which the preceding paragraph was quoted, and see the relation of fallen Lucifer to Babylon, noting in passing that the thirteenth chapter of Isaiah tells of the destruction to come upon Babylon.

The Prince of This World

That proud city shall be utterly destroyed, –

"For the Lord will have mercy on Jacob, and will yet choose Israel and set them in their own land; and the strangers shall be joined them, and they shall cleave to the house of Jacob. And the people shall take them, and bring them to their place; and the house of Israel shall possess them in the land of the Lord for servants and handmaids; and they shall take them captive whose captives they were; and they shall rule over their oppressors. And it shall come to pass in the day that the Lord shall give thee rest from thy sorrow, and from thy fear, and from thy hard bondage wherein thou wast made to serve, that thou shalt take up this proverb against the king of Babylon, and say, How hath the oppressor ceased! The golden city ceased! The Lord hath broken the staff of the wicked, and the sceptre of the rulers. He who smote the people in wrath with a continual stroke, he that ruled the nations in anger persecuted, and none hindereth. The whole earth is at rest, and is quiet, they break forth into singing. Yea, the fir trees rejoice at thee, and the cedars of Lebanon, saying, Since thou art laid down, no feller is come up against us. Hell from beneath is moved for thee to meet thee at they coming; it stirreth up the dead for thee, even all the chief ones of the earth; it has raised up from their thrones all the kings of the nations they shall speak and say unto thee, Art thou also become weak as we? Art thou become like unto us? Thy pomp is brought down to the grave, and the noise of thy viols; the worm is spread under thee, and the worms cover thee." Isaiah 1-11.

Then follows the direct address by the Lord, "How art thou fallen from heaven, O Lucifer, son of the morning," etc., as previously quoted, stating that his fall is because of his self-exaltation, continuing thus: –

"Yet thou shalt be brought down to hell, to the sides of the pit: They that see thee shall narrowly look upon thee, and consider the saying, Is this the man that made the earth to tremble, that did shake kingdoms; that made the world as a wilderness, and destroyed the cities thereof; that opened not the house of his prisoners? All the kings of the nations, even all of them, lay in glory every one in his own house. But thou art cast out of thy grave like an abominable branch, and as the raiment of those that are slain, thrust through with a sword, that go down to the stones of the pit; as a carcass trodden under feet. Thou shalt not be joined with them in burial, because thou hast destroyed thy land, and slain thy people; the seed of evil-doers shall never be renowned." Verses 15-20.

The Divine Purpose – The Destruction of the Oppressor

So much of direct address to this wonderful tyrant. Then follows he continuation of the narrative concerning him: –

"Prepare slaughter for his children for the iniquity of their fathers; that they do not rise, nor possess the land, nor fill the face of the world with cities. For I will rise up against them, saith the Lord of hosts, and cut off from Babylon the name, and remnant, and son, and nephew, saith the Lord. I will also make it a possession for the bittern, and pools of water; and I will sweep it with the besom of destruction, saith the Lord of hosts. The Lord of hosts hath sworn, saying, Surely, as I have thought, so shall it come to pass; and as I have purposed, so shall it stand; that I will break the Assyrians in My land, and upon My mountains tread him under foot; then shall his yoke depart from off them, and his burden depart from off their shoulders." Verses 21-25.

And now come the striking words, summing up the whole matter: –

"THIS IS THE PURPOSE UPON THE WHOLE EARTH; AND THIS IS THE HAND THAT STRETCHED OUT UPON ALL THE NATIONS. For the Lord of hosts hath purposed, and who shall disannul it? and His hand is stretched out, and who shall turn it back?" Verses 26, 27.

The Pride of Earthly Dominion

The reader cannot have failed to notice that the complete and final deliverance of all Israel is coincident with the utter destruction of the king of Babylon; and further that this king of Babylon is on, who rules over all the earth; his destruction gives the whole earth rest. It must also have been noted that this king of Babylon is also addressed as Lucifer, the one who thought to dispute the dominion of the world with God. The fact is, therefore, that whoever was that nominal, visible ruler of Babylon; Satan was its real king. This is evident also from the fact that Babylon was a heathen kingdom and "the things which the Gentiles sacrifice, they sacrifice to devils and not to God." 1 Corinthians 10:20. He is "the god of this world." That spirit of self-exaltation is radically opposed to the Spirit of God whose meekness and gentleness constitute His greatness; it is that spirit of antichrist "who opposeth and exalteth himself above all: that is called God, or that is worshipped, so that he as God sitteth in the temple of God, showing himself that he is God." 2 Thessalonians 2:4 This spirit was pre-eminently characteristic of Babylon, except in the brief space when Nebuchadnezzar came to his senses.

In his pride he said, "Is not this great Babylon, that I have built for that house of the kingdom by the might of my power, and for the honor of my majesty?" Daniel 4:30. Belshazzar used the vessels of the house of God, and drank wine out of them, together with his wives and his concubines, "and praised the gods of gold, and of silver, of brass of iron, of wood, and of stone" (Daniel 5:3, 4), thus boasting that the gods which he had made were greater than the God of Israel. Of Babylon it was said, "Thou hast trusted in thy wickedness; thou hast said, None seeth me. Thy wisdom and thy knowledge it hath perverted thee; and thou hast said in thine heart, I am, and none else beside me." Isaiah 47:10.

What Deliverance from Babylon Is

It was this same spirit that actuated the Jewish people. When they insisted on having a king, that they might be like the heathen round them, they rejected God, because they thought they could manage things better themselves. "Hath a nation changed their gods which are yet no gods? But My people have changed their glory for that which doth not profit. Be astonished, O ye heavens, at this, and be horribly afraid, be ye very desolate, saith the Lord. For My people have committed two evils; they have forsaken Me, the Fountain of living waters, and hewed them out cisterns, broken cisterns, that can hold no water." Jeremiah 2:11-13. "Have I been a wilderness unto Israel? a land of darkness? Wherefore say My people, We are lords; we will come no more unto Thee?" Verse 31.

Therefore when the children of Israel were taken to Babylon, that city of pride and boasting, it was but a striking and visible manifestation of the condition in which they had long been. They were carried to Babylon because they did not keep the Sabbath, as we read in Jeremiah 7:27, and 2 Chronicles 36:20, 21. We have already learned that Sabbath-keeping is resting in God; it means the perfect recognition of Him as supreme and rightful ruler. Therefore we must understand that the complete deliverance from Babylon is the deliverance from the bondage of self, to absolute trust in God, and obedience to Him.

The Seventy Years Fulfilled

Just as God had named a definite time when He would deliver His people from Egypt, so He named the exact time of the captivity of Israel in the city of Babylon. "For thus saith the Lord, That after seventy years be accomplished at Babylon, I will visit you, and perform My good word toward you, in causing you to return to this place. For I know the thoughts that I think toward you, saith the Lord, thoughts of peace, and not of evil, to give you an expected end. Then shall ye call upon Me, and ye shall go and pray unto Me, and I will hearken m to you. And ye shall seek Me, and find Me, when ye shall search for Me with all your heart. And I will be found of you, saith the Lord; and

I will turn away your captivity, and I will gather you from all the nations, and from all the places whither I have driven you, saith the Lord; and I will bring you again into the place whence I caused you to be carried away captive." Jeremiah 29:10-14.

Exactly as in the first instance, so in the second, everything came to pass according to the Word of God.

The captivity began in B.C. 606, and sixty-eight years later, in B.C. 538 the city of Babylon fell into the hands of the Medes and Persians. See Daniel 5. Of that time we read, "In the first year of Darius the son of Ahasuerus, of the seed of the Medes, which was made king over the realm of the Chaldeans; in the first year of his reign I Daniel understood by books the number of the years, whereof the word of the Lord came to Jeremiah the prophet, that He would accomplish seventy years in the desolations of Jerusalem. And I set my face unto the Lord God, to seek by prayer and supplications, with fasting, and sackcloth, and ashes." Daniel 9:1-3. Here was at least one man seeking God with his whole heart. We do not know if there were others who sought the Lord as Daniel did, there were certainly not many, but God nevertheless fulfilled His part to the letter.

Two years after Daniel's prayer, in the year B.C. 536 just seventy years after the beginning of Israel's captivity in the city of Babylon, Cyrus, king of Persia, issued a proclamation which is thus recorded: –

"Now in the first year of Cyrus, king of Persia, that the word of the Lord by the mouth of Jeremiah might be fulfilled, the Lord stirred up the spirit of Cyrus king of Persia, that he made a proclamation throughout all his kingdom, and put it also in writing, saying, Thus saith Cyrus king of Persia, The Lord God of heaven hath given me all the kingdoms of the earth; and He hath charged me to build Him an house at Jerusalem, which is in Judah. Who is there among you of all His people? His God be with him, and let him go up to Jerusalem which is in Judah, and build the house of the Lord God of Israel (He is God), which is in Jerusalem. And whosoever remaineth in any place where he sojourneth, let the men of his place help him with silver and with gold, and with goods, and with beasts, beside the freewill offering for the house of God that is in Jerusalem." Ezra 1:1-4.

The number of those who went back to Jerusalem as the result of this proclamation is set down as "forty and two thousand three hundred and threescore, beside their servants and their maids, whom there were seven thousand three hundred thirty and seven; and there were among them two hundred singing men and singing women." "So the priests and the Levites, and some of the people, and the singers, and the porters, and the Nethinims, dwelt in their cities, and all Israel in their cities." Ezra 2:64, 65, 70.

The Lesson Still Unlearned

Not all the people went back to Jerusalem, but all might have gone. If all Israel had learned the lesson designed by the captivity, the long-deferred fulfillment of the promise might speedily have taken place; for up to the time of the beginning of the captivity the only definite line of prophecy was the period of seventy years. But just as the people were really in Babylonian captivity, that is, the bondage of pride and self-confidence before the carrying away by Nebuchadnezzar, even so they remained in the same captivity after the close of the seventy years. God foresaw that this would be the case, and so toward the close of that period He gave Daniel a vision, in which another time was fixed.

Of this great prophetic period and the events to which it brings us – the final call to come out of Babylon – we shall study next week.

Chapter 45

The Promises to Israel - The Time of the Promise at Hand

The Present Truth, March 11, 1897

In closing our study of the Babylonian captivity last week we saw that if Israel had learned the lesson of trust in God and had not continued still in the bondage of pride and self-confidence, the seventy years of Babylonian captivity would have brought them to a point where the long-deferred promise of an everlasting inheritance might speedily have been fulfilled; for, as already stated, up to the time of the beginning of the captivity in Babylon the only definite time of prophecy was the period of seventy years. But God foresaw before this time ended that the lesson had not been learned; and so, toward the close of that period He gave the prophet Daniel a vision in which another and longer time was fixed. The prophecy is briefly this: –

The Vision of Daniel 8

Daniel saw in vision a ram with the peculiarity that one horn was higher than the other, and the higher came up last. He "saw the ram pushing westward, and northward, and southward; so that no beasts might stand before him, neither was there any that could deliver out of his hand; but he did according to his will, and became great." Daniel 8:3, 4.

Next he saw a goat coming furiously from the west, having one notable horn between his eyes.

"And he came to the ram that had two horns, which I had seen standing before the river, and ran unto him in the fury of his power. And I saw him come close unto the ram, and he was moved with choler against him, and smote the ram, and brake his two horns; and there was no power in the ram to stand before him, but he cast him down to the ground, and stamped upon him; and there was none that could deliver the ram out of his hand. Therefore the he goat waxed very great; and when he was strong, the great horn was broken; and for it came up four notable ones toward the four winds of heaven. And out of one of them came forth a little horn, which waxed exceeding great, toward the south, and toward the east, and toward the pleasant land. And it waxed great, even to the host of heaven; and it cast down some of the host and of the stars to the ground, and stamped upon them. Yea, he magnified himself even to the Prince of the host," etc. Daniel 8:5-11.

After giving some further details concerning this wonderful little horn, the prophet thus concludes the account of the vision: –

"Then I heard one saint speaking, and another saint said unto that certain saint which spoke, 'How long shall be the vision concerning the daily sacrifice, and the transgression of desolation, to give both the sanctuary and the host to be trodden under foot?' And he said unto me, 'Unto two thousand and three hundred days; then shall the sanctuary be cleansed.'" Verses 13, 14.

The Angel's Interpretation

It is not the design to enter into the details of the prophecy, but simply to give the barest outline, so that we may be able to trace the history of the promise. An angel was commissioned to explain the vision to Daniel, which he proceeded to do as follows: –

"The ram which thou sawest having two horns are the kings of Media and Persia. And the rough goat is the king of Grecia; and the great horn between his eyes is the first king. Now that being broken, whereas four stood up for it, four kingdoms shall stand up out of the nation, but not in his power. And in the latter time of their kingdom, when the transgressors are come to the full, a king of fierce countenance, and understanding dark sentences, shall stand up. And his power shall be mighty, but not by his own power; and he shall destroy wonderfully, and shall prosper, and practice, and shall destroy the mighty and the holy people. And through his policy also he shall cause craft to prosper in his hand; and he shall magnify himself in his heart, and by peace shall destroy many; he shall also stand up against the Prince of princes; but he shall be broken without hand. And the vision of the evening and the morning is true." Daniel 8:20-26.

Two universal kingdoms that were to follow Babylon are named, and the other one is so clearly indicated, that we can readily name it. The power that acquired the lordship of the world as the result of the third revolution spoken of by Ezekiel was Rome, here plainly indicated by its work of standing up against the Prince of princes.

After the death of Alexander, king of Greece, his kingdom was divided into four parts, and it was by the conquest of Macedonia, one of these four divisions, in B.C. 68, that Rome acquired such strength that it could dictate to the world. Hence it is said to come forth from one of them.

A Long Prophetic Period

But there was a period of time connected with this vision, which the angel did not explain with the rest of the vision. It was the twenty-three hundred days, or, literally, twenty-three hundred evenings and mornings. That these are not literal days may be known from this: This is a prophecy of symbols, in which short-lived animals are used to represent kingdoms that existed during hundreds of years; it is perfectly in keeping with the method of symbolic prophecy to use days in connection with the symbols, but it is evident that they must represent a longer period, in the interpretation, since two thousand three hundred days – a little more than six years – would scarcely be the beginning of the first kingdom. So we are warranted in concluding that each day stands for a year, as in Ezekiel 4:6, where the Lord uses days in symbolizing years.

Later on the same angel came back, as the result of Daniel's prayer, to make known the remainder of the vision, namely, about the days. See Daniel 9:20-23. Beginning where he left off, as though not a moment had intervened, the angel said, "Seventy weeks are determined upon thy people," etc. Verse 24.

Seventy weeks, four hundred and ninety years, were determined or cut off from the two thousand three hundred years, upon the Jewish people. They were to begin from the going forth of the commandment to restore and to build Jerusalem. This commandment full and complete we find in Ezra 7:11-26, and it was given in the seventh year of Artaxerxes, king of Persia, which was B.C. 457. Beginning in the year 457 B.C., four hundred and ninety years would end in the year 34 A.D.

But the last one of these prophetic weeks was divided. Sixty-nine of them – 483 years – reaching to the year 27 A.D., marked the time of the revelation of the Messiah, or the Anointed One, the time when Jesus was anointed with the Holy Ghost at His baptism.

In the middle of the last week of years, namely three and one-half years after the baptism of Jesus, Messiah was "cut off, but not for Himself." During the entire week, or seven years, the covenant was confirmed.

The whole period of two thousand three hundred years, which can readily be calculated, reaches to the year 1844 A.D., which is in the past. Thus the longest prophetic period given in the Bible has expired, so that now indeed "the time of the promise" must be very near. When the Lord will come to restore all things, no one can tell, for "of that day and hour knoweth no man."

The Kingdom of God Taken from the Jewish People

But let us note further for a moment that period of four hundred and ninety years devoted to the Jewish people. Was it a time in which God would be partial, in that he would not regard the salvation of any other people? Impossible; for God is no respecter of persons. It was simply an evidence of the long-suffering of God, in that He would wait yet so many years on the people of Israel, to give them an opportunity to accept their high calling as priests of God, to make the promise known to the world. But they would not. On the contrary, they themselves so far forgot it that when the Messiah came they rejected Him.

So from being the ones around whom the kingdom of Israel, the fifth and last universal kingdom, should centre, they ceased to have any distinctive place in the promise. Believing the Gospel, just the same as others saved them. The desolate temple, with the rent veil revealing the fact that the glory of God no more dwelt in its most holy place, was a symbol of that people's standing in connection with the covenant. As individuals they may be grafted into the good olive tree, the same as any Gentiles, thus becoming Israel; but their position as leaders, as the religious teachers of the world, is forever gone, because they did not appreciate it. They knew not the time of their visitation.

The Final Call From Babylon

And now what remains? – Only this, that God's people hear and obey the call to come out of Babylon, lest by remaining they receive of her plagues. For although the city on the Euphrates was destroyed many hundred years ago, even several hundred years before Christ, yet nearly one hundred years after Christ the prophet John was by the Spirit moved to repeat the very threats uttered by Isaiah against Babylon, and in almost the identical words: –

"How much she hath glorified herself, and lived deliciously, so much torment and sorrow give her; for she saith in her heart, I sit a queen, and am no widow, and shall see no sorrow. Therefore shall her plagues come in one day, death, and mourning, and famine." Revelation 18:7, 8. Compare Isaiah 47:7-10.

Babylon was a heathen city, exalting itself above God. As shown in Belshazzar's feast (Daniel 5), it represented a religion that defied God. The same spirit exists to day, not simply in a certain society, but wherever men choose their own way in religion, rather than submit to every word that proceedeth out of the mouth of God. God in His longsuffering and tender mercy is but waiting until His people, coming out of Babylon, and humbling themselves to walk with Him, shall preach this Gospel of the kingdom, with all the power of the kingdom, even the power of the world to come, "in all the world for a witness unto all nations, and then shall the end come."

That "end" will be the destruction of Babylon, just as spoken through Jeremiah; but as Babylon of old was a universal kingdom, and its real king, as shown in Isaiah 14, was Satan, the god of this world, so the destruction of Babylon is nothing less than the judgment of God on the whole earth, when He delivers His people. For now read the words, which "Jeremiah prophesied against all the nations," when he prophesied about the end of the Babylonian captivity: –

God's Controversy With the Nations

"For thus saith the Lord God of Israel unto me; Take the wine cup of this fury at My hand, and cause all the nations, to whom I send thee, to drink it. And they shall drink, and be moved, and be mad, because of the sword that I will send among them.

"Then took I the cup at the Lord's hand, and made all the nations to drink, unto whom the Lord had sent me: to wit, Jerusalem, and the cities of Judah, and the kings thereof, and the princes thereof, to make them a desolation, an astonishment, an hissing, and a curse, as it is this day; Pharaoh king of Egypt, and his servants, and his princes, and all his people; and all the mingled people, and all the kings of the land of Uz, and all the kings of the land of the Philistines, and Askelon, and Azzah, and Ekron, and the remnant of Ashdod, Edom, and Moab, and the children of Ammon, and all the kings of Tyrus, and all the kings of Zidon, and the kings of the isles which are beyond the sea, Dedan, and Tema, and Buz, and all that are in the utmost corners, and all the kings of Arabia, and all the kings of the mingled people that dwell in the desert, and all the kings of Zimri, and all the kings of Elam, and all the kings of the Medes, and all the kings of the north, far and near, one with another, and all the kingdoms of the world, which are upon the face of the earth; and the king of Sheshach shall drink after them.

"Therefore thou shalt say unto them, Thus saith the Lord of hosts, the God of Israel; Drink ye, and be drunken, and spue, and fall, and rise no more, because of the sword which I will send among you. And it shall be, if they refuse to take the cup at thine hand to drink, then shalt thou say unto them, Thus saith the Lord of hosts; Ye shall certainly drink. For, lo, I begin to bring evil on the city, which is called by My name, and should ye be utterly unpunished? Ye shall not be unpunished: for I will call for a sword upon all the inhabitants of the earth, saith the Lord of hosts.

"Therefore prophesy thou against them all these words, and say unto them, The Lord shall roar from on high, and utter His voice from His holy habitation; He shall mightily roar upon His habitation; He shall give a shout, as they that tread the grapes, against all the inhabitants of the earth. A noise shall come even to the ends of the earth; for the Lord hath a controversy with the nations, He will plead with all flesh; He will give them that are wicked to the sword, saith the Lord. Thus saith the Lord of hosts, Behold, evil shall go forth from nation to nation, and a great whirlwind shall be raised up from the coasts of the earth. And the slain of the Lord shall be at that day from one end of the earth even unto the other end of the earth: they shall not be lamented, neither gathered, nor buried; they shall be dung upon the ground." Jeremiah 25:15-33.

This is the fearful doom to which all the nations of the earth are rushing. For that great battle they are all arming. Many of them are dreaming of federation and of universal dominion; but God has said of universal dominion on this earth, "It shall be no more, till He come whose right it is, and I will give it Him." Ezekiel 21:27.

The last general revolution will be at the coming of "the Seed to whom the promise was made" (Galatians 3:19), who will then take the kingdom to Himself. Yet a little while are these terrible judgments delayed, that all may have opportunity to exchange the weapons of the flesh for the sword of the Spirit, the Word of God, which is "mighty through God to the pulling down of strongholds, casting down imaginations, and every high thing that exalteth itself against the knowledge of God, and bringing into captivity every thought to the obedience of Christ." 2 Corinthians 10:4, 5.

This captivity is freedom. By God's Word we come from the Babylonian bondage of pride and self-confidence to the freedom of God's gentleness. Who will heed the call to come out, and exchange the bondage of human tradition and speculation for the freedom, which God's eternal Word of truth gives?

Chapter 46

The Promises to Israel - The Lost Tribes of Israel

The Present Truth, May 13, 1897

THERE is a popular, almost universal, idea that at the time of the Babylonish captivity, ten of the twelve tribes were wholly lost, and that only two tribes could be mustered to return to the land of Palestine at the close of the seventy years. So deeply rooted is this notion, that almost everybody knows at once what is referred to whenever the expression, "The ten lost tribes," is used. How this idea came to prevail, we shall not now stop to enquire, but shall content ourselves with ascertaining what the Bible has to say upon the subject of the lost Israelites.

Judah and Israel

First, however, it may be well to note a common misconception concerning the terms "Judah" and "Israel."

When the kingdom was divided, after the death of Solomon, the southern portion, consisting of the tribes of Judah and Benjamin, was known as the kingdom of Judah, with Jerusalem as its capital; while the northern portion, consisting of the remaining tribes, was known as the kingdom of Israel, with headquarters at Samaria. This northern kingdom it was that was first carried captive, and the tribes that composed it are the ones supposed to be lost.

The misconception is that the term "Jews" is limited to the people of the southern kingdom, namely, to the tribes of Judah and Benjamin, and that the term "Israelites" signifies only those tribes composing the northern kingdom, supposed to be lost.

Going on in the line of this supposition, "the warm, ungoverned imagination" of some speculative theologians has fancied that the people generally known as Jews are from the tribes of Judah and Benjamin alone, and that the Anglo-Saxon race, or more specifically, the people of Great Britain and America, are the Israelites, or, in other words, "ten lost tribes" discovered.

Character, not Nationality

It is easy to see how this theory originated. It originated in an utter failure to comprehend the promises of the Gospel. It was invented in order to bring in the Anglo-Saxon race as inheritors of the promises to Abraham, the fact having been lost sight of that those promises embraced the whole world, without respect to nationality, and that "God is no respecter of persons, but in every nation he that feareth Him and worketh righteousness, is accepted with Him." Acts 10:34, 35. If men had believed that "an Israelite indeed," is one "in whom is no guile" (John 1:47), they would have seen the folly of the idea that no matter how wicked and unbelieving people may be, they must be Israelites simply because they are a part of a certain nation. But the idea of a national church and of a national religion is wonderfully fascinating, because it is so much more pleasant for people to suppose that they are to be saved in bulk, regardless of character, instead of through individual faith and righteousness.

Bible Terms that Overthrow Unfounded Distinctions

A few texts of Scripture are sufficient to show that the terms "Jew" and "Israelite" are used interchangeably, each being applicable to the same person. For instance, in Esther 2:5 we read, "in Shushan the palace there was a certain Jew, whose name was Mordecai, the son of Jair, the son of Kish, a Benjamite." But in Romans 11:1 we have the Apostle Paul's statement, "I also am an Israelite, of the seed of Abraham, of the tribe of Benjamin;" and the same Apostle said, "I am a man which am a Jew of Tarsus." Acts 21:39. Here we have one man of the tribe of Benjamin, a Jew, and another man of the same tribe, an Israelite, and at the same time a Jew.

Again, Ahaz was one of the kings of Judah, and reigned in Jerusalem. See 2 Kings 16:1, 2; Isaiah 1:1. He was a descendant of David, and one of the ancestors of Jesus according to the flesh. 2 Kings 16:2; Matthew 1:9. Yet in 2 Chronicles 28:19, in an account of the invasion of "the south of Judah" by the Philistines, we are told that "the Lord brought Judah low because of Ahaz king of Israel; for he made Judah naked, and transgressed sore against the Lord."

When the Apostle Paul had returned to Jerusalem from one of his missionary tours, "the Jews which were of Asia, when they saw him in the temple, stirred up all the people, and laid hands on him, crying out, Men of Israel, help!" Acts 21:27, 28.

The reader can readily see the naturalness of this, when he remembers that all the twelve tribes were descended from one man, Jacob, or Israel. The term "Israel" is therefore applicable to any or all the tribes; while, because of the prominence of Judah, the term "Jew" came to be applied to any of the children of Israel, regardless of their tribe. In speaking of the covenants God says that He will "make a new covenant with the house of Israel and with the house of Judah" (Hebrews 8:8), in order to make it unmistakable that the new covenant is to be made with the entire, undivided people, just as the old covenant was.

Thus we see that the term "Jews" is rightly applied to the same people as is the term "Israelites;" but we must not forget that, strictly speaking, "he is not a Jew, which is one outwardly; neither is that circumcision, which is outward in the flesh; but he is a Jew, which is one inwardly; and circumcision is that of the heart, in the spirit, and not in the letter; whose praise is not of men, but of God." Romans 2:28, 29. The reckoning of the tribes has been lost among the people called Jews, but that makes no difference; they may be called Israelites just as properly as Jews; but neither term is in strict propriety applicable to any of them except to those who have real faith in Jesus Christ; and both terms are, in the strictly Scriptural sense, applicable to any who have such faith, though they be English, French, Greek, Turk, or Chinese.

None of the Tribes "Lost"

Now as to the "lost tribes." That the ten tribes were no more lost after the close of the Babylonian captivity than they were before, is as plain from the Scriptures as that the tribes of Judah and Benjamin were not lost. How does anybody know that these two tribes were not lost, that is, lost to sight? – By the simple fact that we find reference to them after the captivity; individuals belonging to those tribes are mentioned by name. In the same way we know that the other tribes existed as distinct after the captivity as before.

Not all the people of Israel were carried away to Babylon; the poorest and least prominent were left in their own land. But the majority of all the tribes were taken away, and so in the royal proclamation at the close of the seventy years, the permission to return was universal, as follows: –

"In the first year of Cyrus king of Persia, that the word of the Lord by the mouth of Jeremiah might be fulfilled, the Lord stirred up the heart of Cyrus king of Persia, that he made a royal proclamation throughout all his kingdom, and put it also in writing, saying, Thus saith Cyrus king of Persia, the Lord God of heaven hath given me all the kingdoms of the earth; and He hath charged me to build Him an house at Jerusalem, which is in Judah. Who is there among you of all His people? his God be with him, and let him go up to Jerusalem, which is in Judah, and build the house of the Lord God of Israel (He is the God), which is in Jerusalem." Ezra 1:1-3.

The permission to return was unlimited, but not all of any tribe took advantage of it. All the tribes, however, were represented; but those that remained were not thereby necessarily lost. A family cannot be said to be "lost" because they live in a foreign country. Later on Artaxerxes in his commission to Exra wrote: "I make a decree, that all they of the people of Israel, and of His priests and Levites in my realm, which are minded of their own free will to go up to Jerusalem, go with thee." Ezra 7:13.

"All Israel" Represented

Immediately following the proclamation of Cyrus we read, "Then rose up the chief of the fathers of Judah and Benjamin, and the priests and the Levites, with all them whose spirit God had raised, to go up to build the house of the Lord which is in Jerusalem." Ezra 1:5.

We know that the services of the sanctuary were re-established, and none but Levites could be employed in them; and in Ezra 3:10-12 we read that when the foundation of the temple was laid, "they set the priests in their apparel with trumpets, and the Levites the sons of Asaph with symbols to praise the Lord." Even after the resurrection and ascension of Christ we read of Barnabas, "a Levite, and of the country of Cyprus." Acts 4:36.

In Luke 2:36-38 we read of "Anna, a prophetess, the daughter of Phanuel, of the tribe of Asher," who recognized the infant Jesus as the Lord, "and spake of Him to all them that looked for redemption in Jerusalem."

Here we see representatives of two of the ten tribes that are supposed to have mysteriously disappeared, expressly mentioned by name as dwelling in Jerusalem. It is most certain that a thing cannot be lost when you know exactly where it is.

The other tribes are not specified, but in Ezra 2:70 we read, "So the priests, and the Levites, and some of the people, and the singers, and the porters, and the Nethinims, dwelt in their cities, and all Israel in their cities."

When the Apostle Paul was on trial for his life, before King Agrippa, he said, "Now I stand and am judged for the hope of the promise made of God unto our fathers; unto which promise our twelve tribes, instantly serving God day and night, hope to come." Acts 26:6, 7. Here we find that the twelve tribes were in existence in the days of the Apostle Paul, and were looking forward in hope to the fulfillment of the promise, which God made to the fathers.

Again, the Apostle James addressed his Epistle "to the twelve tribes which are scattered abroad." James 1:1.

We have here sufficient evidence that no one tribe of Israel was ever lost more than another. All tribal distinctions are now lost, and no Jew can tell to which of the twelve tribes he belongs; and so in that sense, not merely ten, but all of the tribes are now lost, although all the twelve tribes are represented in the Jewish people scattered over the earth. God, however, keeps the list, and in the world to come will put every person in his proper place, for the city for which Abraham looked, the capital of the inheritance promised to him and his seed, the New Jerusalem, has twelve gates, and on the gates are "the names of the twelve tribes of the children of Israel." Revelation 21:12.

Whom the Lord Counts an Israelite

The last two texts suggest another fact, namely, that God's reckoning of the tribes is not after man's reckoning. "Man looketh on the outward appearance, but the Lord looketh upon the heart" (1 Samuel 16:7), and "he is not a Jew, which is one outwardly; . . . but he is a Jew which is one inwardly; and circumcision is that of the heart." Romans 2:28, 29. All those who are saved will "enter in through the gates into the city" (Revelation 22:14), but each of those gates has the name on it of one of the twelve tribes, showing that the saved compose the twelve tribes of Israel. This is evident also from the fact that "Israel" means an Overcomer. The Epistle of James is addressed to the twelve tribes, yet there is not a Christian who does not know that its instruction and promises are for him.

And this brings us to the fact that in reality all the tribes are lost, "for all have sinned, and come short of the glory of God." Romans 3:23. "All we like sheep have gone astray; we have turned every one to his own way; and the Lord hath laid on Him the iniquity of us all" (Isaiah 53:6); therefore when the Lord Jesus came, He said, "The Son of man is come to seek and to save that which was lost." Luke 19:10. He declared, "I am not sent but to the lost sheep of the house of Israel" (Matthew 15:24), at the very moment when he was about to confer a blessing on a poor, despised Canaanitish woman, a descendant of those heathen who inhabited the land before the days of Joshua.

Here at last we have located the lost tribes of Israel. Not ten only, but all of the tribes are lost, so completely lost that the only hope of their salvation is in the death and resurrection of Christ. In this condition we find ourselves, and therefore we can read with delight, as pertaining to us, the promises concerning the gathering of Israel, which we shall next consider.

CHAPTER 47

The Promises to Israel - The Everlasting Covenant Complete

The Present Truth : May 13, 1897

"KNOWN unto God are all His works from the beginning of the world." Acts 15:18.

"And He shall send Jesus Christ, which before was preached unto you; whom the heaven must receive until the times of restitution of all things, which God hath spoken by the mouth of all His holy prophets since the world began." Acts 3:20, 21.

"To Him give all the prophets witness." Acts 10:43.

The final gathering of God's people, and their establishment in the earth restored, has been the theme of the prophets ever since the fall; and as a necessary consequence they have all borne witness that all who believe in Christ shall receive remission of sins, since it is only through the remission of sins that the gathering and restoration takes place. Let us then look at a few of these prophecies that tell of these things, and they will serve as representatives of all the others. We take first the eleventh of Isaiah.

"And there shall come forth a rod (shoot, R.V) out of the stem (stock) of Jesse, and a Branch shall grow out of his roots; and the Spirit of the Lord shall rest upon Him, the Spirit of wisdom and understanding, the Spirit of counsel and might, the Spirit of knowledge and of the fear of the Lord; and shall make Him of quick understanding in the fear of the Lord; and He shall not judge after the sight of His eyes, neither reprove after the hearing of His ears; but with righteousness shall He judge the poor, and reprove with equity for the meek of the earth; and He shall smite the earth with the rod of His mouth, and with the breath of His lips shall he slay the wicked. (Compare 2 Thessalonians 2:8)

"And righteousness shall be the girdle of His loins, and faithfulness the girdle of His reins. The wolf also shall dwell with the lamb, and the leopard shall lie down with the kid; and the calf and the young lion and the fatling together; and a little child shall lead them. And the cow and the bear shall feed; their young ones shall lie down together;

and the lion shall eat straw like the ox. And the sucking child shall play on the hole of the asp, and the weaned child shall put his hand on the cockatrice' den. They shall not hurt nor destroy in all My holy mountain; for the earth shall be full of the knowledge of the Lord, as the waters cover the sea." Verses 1-9.

The Gospel History in Outline

Here we have an outline of the entire Gospel history, including the blotting out of sin and sinners, and the establishing of the righteous in the earth made new, when "the meek shall inherit the earth, and shall delight themselves in the abundance of peace." Psalm 37:1, together with verses 9, 10.

Having given the whole story as already read, the prophet goes a little more into detail. Going back to the point where he began, he proceeds: –

"And in that day there shall be a Root of Jesse, which shall stand for an ensign of the people, to it shall the Gentiles seek, and His rest shall be glorious. And it shall come to pass in that day; that the Lord shall set His hand again the second time to recover the remnant of His people, which shall be left, from Assyria and from Egypt, and from Pathros, and from Cush, and from Elam, and from Shinar, and from Hamath, and from the islands of the sea. And He shall set up an ensign for the nations, and shall assemble the outcasts of Israel, and gather together the dispersed of Judah from the four comers of the earth." Verses 10-12.

Of this gathering of the elect from the four corners of the earth, we read also in Matthew 24:31. The power by which this gathering is to be accomplished will be no less than that which was manifested when the Lord set His hand the first time to gather His people; for we read:

"There shall be an highway for the remnant of His people, which shall be left, from Assyria, like as it was to Israel in the day that he came up out of the land of Egypt." Isaiah 11:16.

"Behold Your God!"

Of this gathering, first and last, we read also in the fortieth of Isaiah. The preaching of the Gospel, including the forgiveness of sins, the giving of the Comforter, the Holy Ghost, the setting forth of God as the only Power in the universe, the Creator and Preserver, and the announcement of the coming of the Lord in glory, is all found there. Then in the message, "Behold your God," we read: –

"Behold, the Lord God will come with strong hand, and His arm shall rule for Him; behold, His reward is with Him (compare Revelation 22:12), and His work before Him. He shall feed His flock like a shepherd; He shall gather the lambs with His arm; and carry them in His bosom, and shall gently lead those that are with young." Verses 10, 11.

We have before read about the gathering of the lost sheep of the house of Israel into one fold, so that there shall be "one fold and one Shepherd;" here we see that that gathering is begun by the preaching of the Gospel, and is completed only by the coming of the Lord in glory, with His angels; and further, that the power and glory of the coming of the Lord are identical with the power that must accompany the preaching of the Gospel.

The Lost Sheep Under the Apostasy

In the following verses we read the condition of the lost sheep of the house of Israel, and how the unfaithful shepherds scatter the sheep instead of gathering them: –

"Son of man, prophesy against the shepherds of Israel, prophesy and say unto them, Thus saith the Lord God unto the shepherds, Woe be to the shepherds of Israel that do feed themselves! should not the shepherds feed the flocks? Ye eat the fat, and ye clothe you: with the wool, ye kill them that are fed; but ye feed not the flock. The diseased have ye not strengthened, neither have ye healed that which was sick, neither have ye bound up that which was broken, neither have ye brought again that which was driven away, neither have we sought that which was lost; but with force and with cruelty have ye ruled them. And they were scattered, because there was no shepherd and they became meat to all the beasts of the field, when they were scattered. My sheep wandered through all the mountains, and upon every high hill; yea, My flock was scattered upon all the face of the earth, and none did search or seek after them.

"Therefore, ye shepherds, hear the word of the Lord; As I live saith the Lord God, surely, because My flock became a prey, and My flock became meat to every beast of the field, because there was no shepherd, neither did My shepherds search for My flock, but the shepherds fed themselves, and fed not My flock; therefore, O ye shepherds, hear the word of the Lord: Thus saith the Lord God, Behold I am against the shepherds; and I will require My flock at their hand and cause them to cease from feeding the flock; neither shall the shepherds feed themselves any more; for I will deliver My flock from their mouth, that they may not be meat for them. For thus saith the Lord God; Behold, I, even I, will both search My sheep and seek them out. As a shepherd seeketh out his flock in the day that he is among his sheep that are scattered, so will I seek out My sheep, and deliver them out of all places where they have been scattered in the cloudy and dark day. And I will bring them out from the people and gather them from the countries, and will bring them to their own land and feed them upon the mountains of Israel by the rivers, and in all the inhabited places in the country." (Compare Romans 4:18)

"And I will set up one Shepherd over them, and He shall feed them, even My servant David; He shall feed them, and He shall be their Shepherd. And I the Lord will be their God, and My servant David a Prince among them; I the Lord have spoken it. And I will make with them a covenant of peace, and will cause the evil beasts to cease out of the land (compare Isaiah 11:6-9); and they shall dwell safely in the wilderness, and sleep in the woods. And I will make them and the places round about My hill a blessing; and I will cause the shower to come down in his season; there shall be showers of blessing. And the tree of the field shall yield her fruit, and the earth shall yield her increase, and they shall be safe in their land, and shall know that I am the Lord, when I have broken the bands of their yoke, and delivered them out of the hand of those that served themselves of them. And they shall no more be a prey to the heathen, neither shall the beast of the land devour them; but they shall dwell safely, and none shall make them afraid." Ezekiel 34:1-13, 23-28.

Gathered by the Resurrection

Exactly how this final gathering is to be accomplished, we are told in chapter 37: –

"The hand of the Lord was upon me, and carried me out in the Spirit of the Lord, and set me down in the midst of the valley which was full of bones, and caused me to pass by them round about; and behold, there were very many in the open valley; and, lo, they were very dry. And He said unto me, Son of man can these bones live? And I answered, O Lord God, Thou knowest.

"Again He said unto me, Prophesy upon these bones, and say unto them, O ye dry bones, hear the word of the Lord. (Compare John 5:25-29.) Thus saith the Lord God unto these bones; behold, I will cause breath to enter into you, and ye shall live; and I will lay sinews upon you, and will bring up flesh upon you, and cover you with skin; and ye shall know that I am the Lord.

"So I prophesied as I was commanded; and as I prophesied, there was a noise, and behold a shaking, and the bones came together, bone to his bone. And when I beheld, lo, the sinews and the flesh came up upon them, and the skin covered them above; but there was no breath in them. Then said He unto me, Prophesy unto the wind prophesy Son of man, and say to the wind, Thus saith the Lord God Come from the four winds, O breath, and breathe upon these slain that they may live. So I prophesied as He commanded me, and the breath came into them, and they lived, and stood up upon their feet, an exceeding great army.

"Then He said unto me, Son of man, these bones are the whole house of Israel; behold, they say Our bones are dried, and our hope, is lost; we are cut off for our parts ("clean cut off," R.V.). Therefore, prophesy and say unto them, Thus saith the Lord God, Behold, O My people, I will open your graves, and cause you to come up out of your graves, and bring you into the land of Israel. And ye shall know, that I am the Lord, when I have opened your graves, O my people and brought you up out of your graves, and shall put My Spirit in you, and ye shall live, and I shall place you in your land; then shall ye know that I the Lord have spoken it, and performed it, saith the Lord." Verses 1-14.

"The Whole House of Israel"

Thus we see that the promise of the Lord to David, that He would appoint a place for His people Israel, and plant them, that they may dwell in a place of their own, and move no more, and no more be afflicted (2 Samuel 7:10), is to be fulfilled by the resurrection from the dead. And this gathering of Israel, the only one that has ever been promised, and it is enough, embraces all the faithful ones of all ages; for when the Lord speaks, "all that are in the graves shall hear His voice, and shall come forth."

We have seen that this gathering is to be of "the whole house of Israel;" the verses following show that at that time there will be no division of the kingdom, but only "one fold and one shepherd:" –

"The word of the Lord came again unto me, saying, Moreover, thou son of man, take thee one stick, and write upon it, For Judah, and for the children of Israel and his companions; and join them one to another into one stick; and they shall become one in thine hand. And when the children of thy people shall speak unto thee, saying, Wilt thou not show us what thou meanest by these? Say unto them, Thus saith the Lord God, Behold, I will take the stick of Joseph, which is in the hand of Ephraim, and the tribes of Israel his fellows, and will put them with him, even with the stick of Judah, and make them one stick, and they shall be one in Mine hand. And the sticks whereon thou writest shall be in thine hand before their eyes. And say unto them, Thus saith the Lord God: Behold, I will take the children of Israel from among the heathen, whither they be gone, and will gather them on every side and bring them into their own land; and I will make them one nation in the land upon the mountains of Israel; and one King shall be king to them all; and they shall be no more two nations, neither shall they be divided into kingdoms any more at all; neither shall they defile themselves any more with their idols, nor with their detestable things, nor with any of their transgressions; but I will save them out of all their dwelling places, wherein they have sinned, and will cleanse them; so shall they be My people, and I will be their God. And David My servant shall be king over them; and they all shall have one Shepherd; they shall also walk in My judgments, and observe My statutes, and do them. And they shall dwell in the land that I have given unto Jacob My servant, wherein your fathers have dwelt; and they shall dwell therein, even they, and their children, and their children's children for ever; and My servant David shall be their prince for ever." Ezekiel 37:5-25.

Now note particularly what follows: –

"Moreover I will make a covenant of peace with them; it shall be an everlasting covenant with them; and I will place them, and multiply them, and will set My sanctuary in the midst of them for evermore. My tabernacle shall be with them; yea, I will be their God, and they shall be My people. (Compare Revelation 21:1-3.) And the heathen shall know that I the Lord do sanctify Israel, when My sanctuary shall be in the midst of them for evermore." Verses 26-28.

God's Judgment Upon All Nations

That the deliverance of Israel is not a mere local affair, is plainly shown in the punishment threatened upon Babylon, in the twenty-fifth chapter of Jeremiah. It was at the close of the seventy years captivity that God purposed to bring this punishment; but, as we have already seen, Israel was not fully ready to be gathered at that time. From that day to this, many of God's people have been in Babylon, so that the word comes in these latter days, as well as then, "Come out of her My people." Jeremiah 51:45; Revelation 18:4. Nevertheless, God began the punishment of Babylon at that time, and the following verses will show that the promises to Israel, and the threats of punishment upon their oppressors, concern the whole earth: –

"Thus saith the Lord God of Israel unto me: Take the wine cup of this fury at My hand, and cause all the nations to whom I send thee to drink it. (Compare Psalm 75:8; Revelation 14:9, 10.) And they shall drink, and be moved, and be mad, because of the sword that I will send among them. Then took I the cup at the Lord's hand, and made all the nations to drink, unto whom the Lord had sent me; to wit, Jerusalem, and the cities of Judah, and the kings thereof, and the princes thereof, to make them a desolation, an astonishment, an hissing, and a curse; as it is this day; Pharaoh, king of Egypt, and his servants, and all his people; and all the kings of the north, far and near, one with another, and all the kingdoms of the world which are upon the face of the earth: and the king of Sheshach shall drink after them.

"Therefore thou shalt say unto them, Thus saith the Lord of hosts, the God of Israel; Drink ye, and be drunken, and spue, and fall, and rise no more, because of the sword which I will send among you. And it shall be, if they refuse to take the cup at thine hand to drink, then shalt thou say unto them, Thus saith the Lord of hosts, Ye shall certainly drink. For lo, I begin to bring evil upon the city that is called by My name, and should ye be utterly unpunished? Ye shall not be unpunished; for I will call for a sword upon all the inhabitants of the earth, saith the Lord of hosts. Therefore prophesy against them these words, and say unto them, The Lord shall roar from on high, and utter His voice from His holy habitation; He shall give a shout, as they that tread the grapes, against all the inhabitants of the earth. A noise shall come even to the ends of the earth, for the Lord hath a controversy with the nations, He will plead with ill flesh; He will give them that are wicked to the sword, saith the Lord. Thus saith the Lord of hosts, Behold, evil shall go forth from nation to nation, and a great whirlwind shall be raised up from the coasts of the earth. And the slain of the Lord shall be at that day from one end of the earth even unto the other end of the earth; they shall not be lamented, neither gathered, nor buried; they shall be dung upon the ground. Howl, ye shepherds, and cry; and wallow yourselves in the ashes, ye principal of the flock: for the days of your slaughter, and of your dispersions are accomplished; and ye shall fall like a pleasant vessel. And the shepherds shall have no way to flee, nor the principal of the flock to escape.

A voice of the cry of the shepherds, and an howling of the principal of the flock shall be heard; for the Lord bath spoiled their pasture." Jeremiah 25:15-84.

The Time of Deliverance

Notice that this is at the time of the punishment of the false shepherds, as prophesied in Ezekiel 34, when Israel shall be gathered, and a covenant of peace made with them. Of the nature of this covenant and the time of the making of it, we have the clearest information in the book of Jeremiah, especially when read in connection with the scriptures already quoted. A brief sketch of two chapters will suffice to make the story complete, so far as our present study is concerned.

We begin with chapter 30: –

"The word that came to Jeremiah from the Lord, saying. Thus speaketh the Lord God of Israel, saying, Write thee all the words that I have spoken unto thee in a book. For, lo, the days come, saith the Lord, that I will bring again the captivity of My people Israel and Judah, saith the Lord; and I will cause them to return to the land that I gave to their fathers, and they shall possess it." Verses 1-3.

Here we are on familiar ground. These verses mark the time when the things later spoken of shall take place when God brings His people back to their own land. So we proceed: –

"And these are the words that the Lord spake concerning Israel and concerning Judah. For thus saith the Lord: We have heard a voice of trembling, of fear, and not of peace. Ask ye now, and see whether a man doth travail with child? Wherefore do I see every man with his hands on his loins, as a woman in travail, and all faces are turned into paleness? Alas! For that day is great, so that none is like it; it is even the time of Jacob's trouble; but he shall be saved out of it. For it shall come to pass in that day, saith the Lord of hosts, that I will break his yoke from off thy neck, and will burst thy bonds, and strangers shall no more serve themselves of him; but they shall serve the Lord their God, and David My servant, whom I will raise up unto them." Verses 4-9.

Compare with this Daniel 12:1: "And at that time shall Michael stand up, the great Prince which standeth for the children of thy people, and there shall be a time of trouble, such as never was since there was a nation, even to that same time; and at that time thy people shall he delivered, every one that shall be found a written in the book." Although God's people are to be delivered in the time of trouble that immediately precedes the coming of the Lord, so that no evil shall befall them, nor any plague come nigh their dwelling (Psalm 91), yet it is impossible that they should behold and see the reward of the wicked without themselves being filled with fear and trembling; for it is no small thing when God arises.

Therefore He says: –

"Fear thou not, O My servant Jacob, saith the Lord: neither be dismayed, O Israel; for, lo, I will save thee from afar, and thy seed from the land of their captivity; and Jacob shall return, and shall be in rest, and be quiet, and none shall make him afraid. For I am with thee, saith the Lord, to save thee; though I make a full end of all nations whither I have scattered thee, but will I not make a full end of thee; but I will correct thee in measure, and will not leave thee altogether unpunished." Jeremiah 30:10, 11.

"Thus saith the Lord God: Behold, I will bring again the captivity of Jacob's tents, and have mercy on his dwelling-places; and the city shall be builded on her own heap, and the palace shall remain after the manner thereof. And out of them shall proceed thanksgiving, and the voice of them that make merry; and I will multiply them, and they shall not be few. Their children also shall be as aforetime, and their congregation shall be established before Me, and I will punish all that oppress them. And their nobles shall be of themselves, and their governors shall, proceed from the midst of them; and I will cause him to draw near, and he shall approach unto Me; for who is this that engaged his heart to approach unto Me? saith the Lord. And ye shall be My people, and I will be your God. Behold, the whirlwind of the Lord goeth forth with fury, a continuing whirlwind (a sweeping tempest, R.V.); it shall fall with pain upon the head of the wicked. The fierce anger of the Lord shall not return until He have done it, and until He have performed the intents of His heart: in the latter days ye shall consider it." Verses 18-24.

Ransomed from the Grave

"At, the same time, saith the Lord, will I be the God of all the families of Israel, and they shall be My people. Thus saith the Lord, the people which were left of the sword found grace in the wilderness; even Israel, when I went to cause him to eat. The Lord hath appeared of old unto Me, saying, Yea, I have loved thee with an everlasting love; therefore with lovingkindness have I drawn thee." Jeremiah 31:1-3.

"Hear the word of the Lord, O ye nations, and declare it in the isles, afar off, and say; He that scattered Israel shall gather him, and keep him, as a shepherd doth his flock. For the Lord hath ransomed Jacob, and ransomed him from the hand of him that was stronger than he. Therefore they shall come and sing in the height of Zion, and shall flow together to the goodness of the Lord, for wheat; and for wine, and for oil, and for the young of the flock and of the herd, and their soul shall be as a watered garden; and they shall not sorrow any more at all." Verses 10-13.

"Thus saith the Lord; A voice was heard in Ramah, lamentation, and bitter weeping; Rachel weeping for her children refused to be comforted for her children, because they were not. Thus saith the Lord: Refrain thy voice from weeping and thine eyes from tears; for thy work shall be rewarded, saith the Lord; and they shall come again from the land of the enemy. And there is hope in thine end, saith the Lord, that thy children shall come again to their own border." Verses 15-17.

Here we have another sure guide as to where we are, or rather, as to the time with which the prophecy deals. We know that this prophecy was partly fulfilled when Herod slew the babes of Bethlehem. Matthew 2:16-18. But the Lord says to the mourners, that the last ones shall come from the land of the enemy (See 1 Corinthians 15:36) to their own border. Thus we see again that it is only by the resurrection of the dead that Israel's captivity is to be turned, and they be gathered to their own land; and we note that, the time of which we are now reading in Jeremiah is the time when God turns the captivity of His people. So, speaking of this same period, the prophet continues: –

"Behold, the days come, saith the Lord, that I will sow the house of Israel and the house of Judah with the seed of man, and with the seed of beast. And it shall come to pass, that like as I have watched over them, to pluck up, and to break down, and to destroy, and to afflict: so will I watch over them to build and to plant, saith the Lord. In these days they shall say no more, The fathers have eaten a sour grape, and the children's teeth are set on edge. But every one shall die for his own iniquity; every man that eateth the sour grape, his teeth shall. be set, on edge." Verses 27-30.

The New Covenant

From the connection, there cannot be the slightest doubt as to what time is here referred to; it is the time of the punishment of the wicked, and the reward of the righteous; the time when God's people are to be for ever delivered from all wickedness and oppression, and to be established in the land, to possess it to all eternity in peace and righteousness. So, still speaking of that same time, the prophet proceeds: –

"Behold, the days come, saith the Lord, that I will make a new covenant with the house of Israel, and with the house of Judah; not according to the covenant that I made with their fathers in the day that I took them by the hand, to bring them out of the land of Egypt; which My covenant they brake, although I was an husband unto them, saith the Lord. But this shall be the covenant that I will make with the house of Israel; After those days, saith the Lord, I will put My law in their inward parts, and write it in their hearts; and will be their God, and they shall be My people. And they shall teach no more every man his neighbour, and every man his brother, saying, Know the Lord; for they shall all know Me, from the least of them unto the greatest of them, saith the Lord; for I will forgive their iniquity, and I will remember their sin no more. Thus saith the Lord, which giveth the sun for a light by day, and the ordinances of the moon and of the stars for a light by night, which divideth the sea when the waves thereof roar; the Lord of hosts is His name: If those ordinances depart from before Me, saith the Lord, then the seed of Israel also shall cease from being a nation before Me for ever. Thus saith the Lord: If heaven above can be measured, and the foundations of the earth searched out beneath, I will also cast off all the seed or Israel for all that they have done, saith the Lord." Jeremiah 31:31-37.

Here we have the conclusion of the whole matter. With the making of the new covenant, the days of exile and captivity are ended, and God's people dwell in His unveiled presence for evermore. That covenant remains yet to be made; yet by living faith all its blessings may now be enjoyed, even as the power of the resurrection, by which God's people are finally established in their own land, is the power by which they are prepared for that glorious day.

The Old and the New Covenants

We have long since in this study of the Promises to Israel seen why, and under what circumstances, the old covenant was made, when Israel stood at the base of Sinai. That is called the first or, old covenant, not because there was no covenant that preceded it, but because it was, the first that was made "with the house of Israel and with the house of Judah" – with the whole house of Israel as such. The covenant with Abraham was more than four hundred years earlier, and it embraced everything that God can possibly bestow upon any people. It is by virtue of that covenant with Abraham, confirmed by God's oath, that we now come with boldness to the throne of grace, and find strong consolation in all our trials. Hebrews 6:18-20. All the faithful are children of Abraham.

But Israel of old proved unfaithful, and forgot or despised the everlasting covenant made with Abraham. They wished to walk by sight, and not by faith. They trusted in themselves, rather than in God. In the test, when God reminded them of His covenant with Abraham, and as a help to their faith in the power of His promise, reminded them of what He had already done for them, they presumptuously took upon themselves the responsibility of their own salvation and entered into a covenant from which nothing but bondage and death could come. God, however, who abides faithful, even though men believe not, used even this as an object lesson. From the shadow they could learn of the reality; even their bondage should contain a prophecy and promise of freedom.

When the New Covenant Will Be Entered Into

God does not leave His people in the place where their own folly has placed them. So He promised a new covenant. Not that anything was lacking in the covenant made with Abraham, but He would make the same covenant with the whole people of Israel, as a nation. This promise of the new covenant still holds good, for by the oath of God, and by His own sacrifice has Jesus been made "surety of a better covenant." Hebrews 7:22. So surely as Jesus died and rose again, and by the power of that death and resurrection, will all Israel be gathered, and the new, the everlasting covenant be established with them, the righteous nation that keepeth the truth. The covenant will be made with none but Israel, yet none need be left out, for whoever will, may come.

When the first covenant was made with all Israel, God came with all the angels; the trumpet of God sounded, and His voice shook the earth as the law was spoken. So when the new covenant shall be made, all Israel will be present, there will be none who are not gathered, – "Our God shall come, and shall not keep silence" (Psalm 50:3); "the Lord Himself shall descend from heaven with a shout, with the voice of the Archangel, and with the trump of God" (1 Thessalonians 4:16), "in the glory of His Father, and all the holy angels with Him." Matthew 16:2; 25:31. His voice shook the earth, but this time it will shake not only this earth, but heaven also. Thus will the whole universe be a partaker in this grand consummation, and the Israel of God all thus be joined to "the whole family in heaven." By the cross of Christ, "the blood of the everlasting covenant," is God's throne established; and that which saves the lost of earth is the pledge of the eternal safety of the unfallen beings.

The First Dominion Restored

One lesson that must be pointed out in closing is that the new covenant brings in nothing new, except the new earth, and that is that which was from the beginning. The men with whom it is made will have already been made new in Christ. The first dominion will be restored. Let no one therefore think to excuse himself from keeping the commandments of God, by saying that he is under the new covenant. No, if he is in Christ, then is he in (not under) the covenant with Abraham, and as a child of Abraham, an heir with Christ, he has hope in the new covenant, of which Christ is surety. Whoever does not acknowledge himself to be of the generation of Abraham, Isaac, and Jacob, in fellowship with Moses, David, and the prophets, has no ground for hope in the new covenant. And whoever rejoices in the promises of the new covenant, the blessings of which the Holy Spirit even now makes real, must remember that it is the virtue of the new covenant that the law of God is put into our hearts. The old covenant brought nobody to the obedience of that law, but the new covenant makes it universal, so that the earth shall be full of the knowledge of the Lord, as the waters cover the sea. Therefore,

"Thanks be unto God for His unspeakable gift!"

"For of Him and through Him, and, to Him are all things; to whom be glory for ever. Amen."

www.ingramcontent.com/pod-product-compliance
Lightning Source LLC
Chambersburg PA
CBHW060458010526
44118CB00018B/2457